INDONESIA: AN ANTHROPOLOGICAL PERSPECTIVE

INDIA

CHINA

Mandalay

BURMA

Canton

Hong Kong

BAY OF BENGAL

Hanoi

LAOS

HAINAN

Rangoon

GULF OF TONGKING

NORTH VIETNAM

THAILAND

Bangkok

ANDAMAN SEA

SOUTH CHINA SEA

CAMBODIA

SOUTH
VIETNAM

Manila

ISTHMUS OF
KRA

Phnom Penh

Saigon

STRAITS OF
MALACCA

GULF OF SIAM

PALAWAN

Kutaradja

SULU
SEA

Medan

MALAYA

SABAH

Kuala Lumpur

Malacca

SARAWAK

Bukittinggi

Singapore

Padangpandjang

Kepulauan Riau

BORNEO
(KALIMANTAN)

Padang

LINGGA

Pontianak

SUMATRA
(SUMATERA)

BANGKA

Bengkulu

Palembang

Bandjarmasin

INDIAN OCEAN

Banten

Djakarta (Batavia)

Tuban

Makassar

KRAKATAU

Tjirebon

Semarang

Bogor

Demak

Surabaja

Bandung

MADURA

Pekalongan

Borobudur

LOMBOK

Bima

Jogjakarta

Gresik

(Solo) Surakarta

Madiun

BALI

SUMBAWA

JAVA
(DJAWA)

SUMBA

INDONESIA

TAIWAN

PHILIPPINE ISLANDS

PACIFIC OCEAN

SULU ARCH.

Ternate
Manado
HALMAHERA
Minahasa
MOLUCCAS
NEW GUINEA
CELEBES
WEST IRIAN
(IRIAN BARAT)
BURU   Ambon   CERAM
ARU
WETAR
FLORES
TIMOR

GOODYEAR REGIONAL ANTHROPOLOGY SERIES

Edward Norbeck, Editor

ANTHROPOLOGICAL PERSPECTIVES OF:

MODERN EUROPE
Robert T. Anderson

INDIA
Stephen A. Tyler

INDONESIA
James L. Peacock

CIRCUMPOLAR PEOPLES
Nelson H. Graburn and Barry S. Strong

ABORIGINAL NORTH AMERICA
William W. Newcomb, Jr.

Additional Volumes Forthcoming:

Southeast Asia

China

Africa

Philippines

Polynesia and Micronesia

Middle East

Latin America

INDONESIA: AN ANTHROPOLOGICAL PERSPECTIVE

JAMES L. PEACOCK

UNIVERSITY OF NORTH CAROLINA

GOODYEAR PUBLISHING COMPANY, INC.
Pacific Palisades, California

Library of Congress
Catalog Card Number:
72-82233
(Paper) Y-0722-2
(Cloth) Y-0730-5
ISBN: 0-87620-072-2
        (Paper)
        0-87620-073-0
        (Cloth)

Current printing (last
digit)

10 9 8 7 6 5 4 3 2 1

Printed in the
United States of America

TO MY MOTHER
AND FATHER

CONTENTS

PREFACE

This introductory survey of Indonesia differs from others in its mixture of history, anthropology, and travelogue. More attention is paid to Indonesian prehistory, tribal or ethnic diversity, and sociocultural patterning than in the typical historical survey. More attention is given history and national life than in the typical anthropological survey. Several chapters, especially the last, include firsthand impressions based on recent travel and research in the archipelago.

The spelling of Indonesian words poses a problem owing to the variety of systems in use. In this book, islands and island groups are referred to by their familiar English names rather than their Indonesian ones: Sumatra (rather than Sumatera), Java (rather than Djawa), Borneo (Kalimantan), Celebes (Sulawesi), the Moluccas (Maluku), the lesser Sunda Islands (Nusa Tenggara), and West New Guinea (Irian Barat). Other Indonesian place names, proper names, and other terms occur in the Indonesian spelling used in a standard Indonesian dictionary.* Indonesian pronunciation resembles Latin in its pronunciation of vowels, but resembles the Germanic languages, including Dutch, in that "j" is pronounced like the "y" of "yellow," "dj" is equivalent to the "j" in "just," "sj" to the "sh" in "show," and "tj" to the "ch" in "chair."** Most sources in the Malay language and many in the English language follow English rather than Dutch conventions, spelling Indonesian words with the "y" insetad of "j," "j" instead of "dj," "sh" instead of "sj," and "ch" instead of "tj."

Grateful acknowledgment is made to Professor James Fox for critically reading a draft of the entire manuscript, to Professors Donald

Brockington and Wilhelm Solheim II for reading
the chapter on prehistory, to Anthony Milner
and William O'Malley for reading the chapters
on history, and to Linda Lester and Mildred
Stockwell for indispensable research assistance.
Without the aid of the National Institute of
Mental Health, the National Science Foundation,
the American Council for Learned Societies, the
University of North Carolina, and the Lembaga
Ilmu Pengetahuan Indonesia, the information
and impressions drawn from two anthropological
field trips to Indonesia would not have been
available. To the many Indonesians who were
such gracious hosts during those visits,
particularly the inhabitants of Surabaja and the
members of the Muhammadijah, I can only
express my deepest gratitude and my sincere
hope that this book accurately depicts at least
the major contours of their complex and
enthralling history and culture.

*For example, see W. J. W. Poerwadarminta,
Kamus Umum Bahasa Indonesia (Djakarta: Balai
Pustaka, 1961); or John M. Echols and Hassan
Shadily, An Indonesian English Dictionary, 2nd ed.
(Ithaca, N.Y.: Cornell Univ. Press, 1963).
**In accord with Javanese practice, the spelling of "Jog-
jakarta" in this manuscript differs from these rules of mod-
ern Indonesian.

ONE:

LAND AND PEOPLE

*By comparison with Java, Surrey seems
underpopulated.*
Aldous Huxley, Jesting Pilate[1]

Indonesia, known before World War II as the Netherlands Indies, comprises more than 3,000 islands stretching from northern Sumatra to western New Guinea for a distance of some 3,400 miles. In Europe the island chain would reach from west of Ireland to east of the Caspian Sea; in the United States, from the Atlantic coast to the Pacific. Accounting for half of the territory of Southeast Asia, Indonesia's land area is by far the largest of any nation in that region. Indeed, the land area of Indonesia is exceeded in all of Asia only by India and Communist China. Indonesia is thus a big nation, and in its natural features a rich and beautiful one, bordering the equator with a fertile and varied tropical topography.

Indonesian history encompasses a succession of invasions from sea travelers. Chinese and Indian merchants and priests were followed by the Arabs, who were succeeded by the Portuguese, each bearing a distinctive culture. Most recently occupied by the Japanese, Indonesia has been more heavily influenced by Holland, which sent not only colonizers but adventurers and romantics, the Almayers and Willems depicted in the novels of Joseph Conrad.[2] Spices, coffee, sugar, tobacco, and rubber flourish in Indonesian soils, filling the treasuries of the prewar Netherlands and stimulating a vigorous export trade in the Indies. Possessing important reserves of petroleum, tin, bauxite, manganese, coal, iron, and other metals, Indonesia's known resource base is capable of supporting some degree of industrialization.

Ridging the center of the chain of islands, mountains rise over 10,000 feet to snow-capped peaks. Covered at the higher levels by teak, oak, and pine, they are surrounded by tropical forest laced with ferns and orchids and inhabited by tigers, orang-utans, rhinoceroses, and exotic birds. In the western islands, the flat, cleared lowlands form a green and shimmering surface of rice paddies and *alang-alang* grass, cut by wide rivers which catch the rushing mountain streams before flowing toward mangrove swamps and palmy beaches. In the eastern islands, beyond idyllic Bali, the landscape becomes more barren and brown, displaying such Australian-style flora and fauna as eucalyptus trees and marsupials. Framing all the islands is the blue, calm, and generally shallow sea on which glide the graceful outrigger vessels that have been manned by the Indonesians since prehistoric times.

From northwest Sumatra through Java, Bali, the Lesser Sundas, and then north and east through the Moluccas toward the Philippines, volcanoes succeed each other in continuous lines. Occasionally they erupt. Most disastrous was the 1883 eruption of Krakatau, which before that date was a volcanic island 2,000 feet high. Destroyed by an explosion so terrific that 30,000 persons were killed, Krakatau's ash is said to have circled the globe two or three times before settling. The most recent major eruption, in 1963, was that of Gunung Agung in Bali. Lives and crops were destroyed, noon was rendered dark as night, and a layer of dust many inches thick covered fields, streets, and houses for a radius of more than a hundred miles. On Bali the failure of crops and dislocation of villagers doubtless contributed to the communal conflict that resulted in the massacre of thousands of Balinese during the purge of Indonesian Communists in 1965. Yet the terrors of eruption are compensated by the fecundity of soil fertilized by volcanic ash. Peasants on Java brave the danger of fields scorched by lava to farm virtually on the brink of the craters.

Abundant rain falls on most of Indonesia. On none of the islands is rainfall less than 40 inches per year, and in the equatorial rain belt that covers most of Sumatra, Borneo, and Celebes, 90 to 100 inches per year are regularly recorded. Bogor, near Djakarta, boasts the world's maximum number of rainstorms per year, 322. In eastern Indonesia, the climate is much drier. Though dry and wet seasons are distinguishable throughout Indonesia, no winter or summer exists there. Coastal temperatures range between 68 and 86 degrees fahrenheit throughout the year, with only two degrees variation between the warmest and coldest months. Temperatures do vary with height, dropping approximately one degree for each 300 feet of ascent, so that mountain

weather is cool and invigorating. Beautiful mountain resorts were built
by the Dutch, who also delighted in the cool climate of such highland
cities as Bandung. Even coastal climates are no more enervating than
summer in the southeastern United States; hot coastal forenoons are
followed by golden afternoons and breezy nights.

POPULATION DENSITY

Of the 3,000 islands, five account for nine-tenths of the nation's land
area: Sumatra, Celebes, Indonesian Borneo (the southern and central
portions of that island), west New Guinea, and Java. Java, extending
750 miles from west to east and roughly equal in size to New York
State, comprises only 6 percent of the total land area of Indonesia, yet
it supports well over half of its people. Virtually every usable patch
of Java's land is under cultivation, its forest reserves are dangerously
reduced, and its rural areas average 477 persons per square kilometer,
one of the highest rural densities in the world. As the quotation from
Aldous Huxley suggests, the traveler in colonial Java was likely to note
its crowdedness, and today one will observe the closely packed villages,
the crowds of peasants streaming along the rural roads, and the towns
and cities which look so small by comparison with American ones
of comparable population.

In population density, Indonesian Borneo lies at the other extreme
from Java. Nine-tenths of it is covered with jungle and it averages only
seven persons per square kilometer. Associated with the difference in
population density is a contrast in mode of agriculture. Farming on
Java consists largely of the irrigated rice paddy (*sawah*) that can be
cultivated year after year by the peasants who live near it. Farming
in interior Borneo is the slash-and-burn or swidden (*ladang*) type practiced by seminomadic tribesmen. The swidden farmer slashes and burns
the undergrowth to create a dry, unirrigated field, then he plants his
crop and reaps his harvest. After farming for several seasons, he moves
on to clear a new field, leaving the old one to lie fallow for 15 to
25 years before he clears and cultivates it again. Because an irrigated
field can be cultivated repeatedly for an indefinite period, the irrigated
type of agriculture can support a denser concentration of people than
can swidden agriculture, and throughout Indonesia dense population
is found associated with irrigated agriculture, sparse population with
swidden.

Boasting a 1970 population of 120 million, Indonesia represents the
world's fifth most populous nation, exceeded only by India, Russia,
China, and the United States. Indonesia's rate of population increase

is one of the highest in the world. Between 1930 and 1961 its population increased by about 60 percent. By 1969 it had increased approximately 22 percent over the 1961 figures.[3] It is estimated that at the present rate of growth, Indonesia will have a population of 250 million by A.D. 2000, which is to say that its present population will double during the next 30 years. A disproportionate amount of that growth has been on Java, where the population increased at a very rapid rate during the nineteenth century and is expected to reach 150 million by A.D. 2000. Efforts by the government and others to encourage Javanese to migrate to less-crowded islands have not significantly reduced the growth rate of Java, nor can they be expected to do so. Many more people are born yearly on Java than could be carried away by Indonesian government ships. Nor have birth control or family-planning programs yet significantly curbed population growth on Java, partly because rural Javanese who tend to identify fertility with virility and prosperity resist the introduction of contraceptives.

Population pressure in rural areas prompts migration to urban areas. As a result, the populations of major cities—Djakarta, Surabaja, Bandung, Semarang, Medan, and Palembang—have tripled or quadrupled during the past 30 years. Djakarta now has a population of some three million; Surabaja, over one million; and the others not many less. All but two of these major cities are on Java. None of them is highly industrialized and none offers enough jobs for their inhabitants. Nor can they muster anything like adequate housing and sanitary, health, or welfare facilities for the masses who flock to their bright lights. The consequence is poverty concentrated in shanty towns exhibiting an excess of those qualities that Lévi-Strauss considers the "natural setting" for urbanization: "filth, promiscuity, disorder, physical contact; ruins, shacks, excrement, mud . . . ."[4] Disease and crime are rife, and death rates in Indonesia are higher in urban than in rural areas.

RACIAL TRAITS

Most of the Indonesian peoples display the so-called Malay racial traits. Their skin varies in color from light tan to dark brown and their facial features are of a Mongoloid cast but without the Mongoloid nasal flatness or eye fold. The hair of their heads is black and straight or wavy, and that of their faces and bodies is sparse. They are generally short in stature, averaging five feet, two or three inches for men. In the Lesser Sunda islands and in the Moluccas, Australoid, Negrito, and Oceanic Negroid traits occur, suggesting connections with the dark, frizzy-haired peoples of New Guinea and Melanesia, and, more remotely, with the hirsute, brown-skinned, heavy-browed aborigines of Australia.[5]

Most numerous of the recent immigrants to Indonesia are the three million Chinese. They are usually distinguishable from the Malay by their lighter skin and more strongly Mongoloid appearance, but it should be said that certain Indonesian groups, such as the Minahasans of north Celebes, look quite Mongoloid, and that certain Chinese, many of whom are descended from Indonesian mothers, look quite Malay. Arabs represent the second most prominent group of recent migrants, tens of thousands of whom have followed the spread of Islam from such regions as southern Arabia to Indonesia. Since many Arabs have intermarried with Indonesian women, Indonesians in the strongly Islamic coastal area are sometimes quite Arab in appearance.

On the eve of World War II there lived in Indonesia some 60,000 Netherlands-born Dutchmen and approximately 200,000 "Indo-Europeans" born of unions between Europeans and Indonesians. After Indonesia won its independence from the Netherlands in 1949, the majority of the Dutch and Indos left for Holland, but some of the latter remained in Indonesia and were assimilated into native populations. Even today in remote slums of coastal melting pots, one may see "Indonesians" with the appearance of blond-haired, fair-skinned Dutchmen.

Peoples bearing "Indonesian" racial and cultural traits are not confined within the boundaries of the Indonesian nation. Beginning around 4000 B.C., the peoples who have come to populate much of Indonesia were sailing to other regions as well. Some of them may have been driven north by storms to the southern islands of Japan while others filtered east to the islands of the Pacific and west to the east coast of India. Other Indonesians sailed as far as the east coast of Africa, where they settled Madagascar around the time of Christ. In recent centuries Indonesians have migrated northward to found kingdoms and states in Malaya, and tribesmen from Indonesian Borneo in recent years have moved in large numbers across the border into Sarawak, which is part of the nation of Malaysia. Though under the control of Portugal, the Indonesians who live in the Portuguese section of Timor are in certain respects as much "Indonesian" as their neighbors in Indonesian Timor. Political boundaries never correspond perfectly with those of race and culture, but it remains true that certain unified patterns of behavior and certain styles of life have come to be concentrated within the boundaries of that nation called Indonesia and to characterize at least the majority of its peoples, particularly those of the Malay type. From these unities have emerged the beginnings of a national culture which to some extent is being spread among the diverse peoples of the archipelago.

REFERENCES

[1] Aldous Huxley, *Jesting Pilate: An Intellectual Holiday* (New York: Doran, 1926), p. 232.

[2] See Joseph Conrad's *Almayer's Folly* (Garden City, N.Y.: Doubleday, Page, 1921); *Lord Jim* (New York: Doubleday, 1900); and *Outcaste of the Islands* (Garden City, N.Y.: Doubleday, Page, 1925).

[3] John W. Henderson *et al. Area Handbook for Indonesia* (Washington, D.C.: U.S. Govt. Printing Office, 1970), Chap. 4. Detail is given in Widjojo Nitsastro, *Population Trends in Indonesia* (Ithaca, N.Y.: Cornell Univ. Press, 1970), p. 206.

[4] Claude Lévi-Strauss, "Crowds," *New Left Review*, No. 15 (1962), p. 3, quoted in T. G. McGee, *The Southeast Asian City: A Study of the Primate Cities of Southeast Asia* (New York: Praeger, 1967), p. 20.

[5] Carlton Coon, *The Living Races of Man* (New York: Knopf, 1965), p. 182.

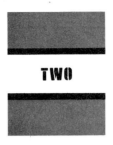

TWO

PREHISTORIC ORIGINS

The first men appeared in Indonesia as early as 1,900,000 years ago. These early creatures were Australopithecinae, possessing bodies and brains hardly larger than those of the chimpanzee but manlike in appearance. By 400,000 to 600,000 years ago, during the early Pleistocene period, a more advanced man known as *Homo erectus* could be found in Java as well as in Choukoutien (near Peking) and throughout the Old World. The Indonesian *Homo erectus* fossils, all found in central Java, were originally called Pithecanthropus or simply Java Man to distinguish them from the Chinese fossils referred to as Sinanthropus or Peking Man.

JAVA MAN

Given the paucity of postcranial remains for Java Man, little concerning his appearance can be stated with certainty, but probably he was much like modern man below the neck though possessing a smaller skull (approximately 1,000 cubic centimeters as opposed to 1,450 for modern man). His facial structure was more rugged with heavy brow ridges, a low forehead, a low-bridged nose, and a chin that was extremely receding. He was probably less bright than modern man but capable of making tools. No tools have been found at the Javanese *Homo erectus* sites, but stone tools, bone tools, and shell objects as well as evidence of knowledge of fire have been discovered at the related Chinese sites, and heavy scrapers and chopping tools found in layers of earth in Java (Trinil) probably derived from the era of Java Man. During the early phase of Java Man's existence, the archipelago and the Asian mainland were a single land mass inhabited by physically and culturally related groups, and Java Man probably used tools like those found throughout South and Southeast Asia. He probably got his food by gathering it and hunting small and middle-sized animals, and he lived in small family groups.[1]

AUSTRALOID PEOPLES

Pithecanthropus evolved through a series of stages until, around 38,000 B.C. or perhaps earlier, Wadjak Man emerged and the threshold from *Homo erectus* to *Homo sapiens* was crossed.[2] Indonesia now was probably inhabited by men physically resembling the contemporary Negroid-featured inhabitants of New Guinea and aboriginal Australia. Hunters of small game and gatherers of mollusks, these peoples produced crudely chipped tools of the Hoabinhian type. By as early as 15,000 B.C. they may have developed a kind of jungle gardening, cultivating starchy root and fruit crops such as taro, yam, banana, and breadfruit in the sunless tropical forests. By around 8000 B.C. the Australoid peoples had ceased to be dominant on the islands, even though they survive today as a recognizable physical and cultural type in the eastern parts of Indonesia and in New Guinea and Australia.

MONGOLOID PEOPLES

The Australoids were gradually replaced by Mongoloids migrating from the south Chinese and Indochinese mainland. The Mongoloids may have gained an adaptive advantage from their mode of agriculture. Bringing their techniques of cereal crop cultivation from mainland Southeast Asia, the Mongoloid settlers of Indonesia grew millets and rice. Initially, like the Australoids, they were swidden farmers, utilizing stone axes and fire to clear the virgin forest, after which they would sow, reap, and move on to clear new fields. Bronze may have been in use in mainland Southeast Asia by 4000 B.C. and iron by 700 B.C. The introduction of bronze and then iron into Indonesia for hoes and axes must have made possible larger clearings. Eventually a system would have become necessary to prevent the plots of one family from running into those of another. Such a system could have been that used by swidden farmers in contemporary Indonesia, where each family carries through its swidden cycle only within a particular territory to which it has rights of use.

Irrigated agriculture was probably introduced during the thousand-year period before the birth of Christ. Though one cannot be certain that irrigated agriculture followed swidden, rather than the reverse, several facts suggest the swidden-to-irrigation sequence. One is that evolution tends to go from simplicity to complexity, and swidden farming is simpler in that it requires only the one step of planting seeds in the cleared ground, whereas irrigated agriculture involves first the nurturing of seedlings in a bed and then the transplanting of seedlings to the paddy. A second fact is that archeological finds in China and Indochina do document convincingly a shift from swidden to irrigated agriculture.[3] In the absence of conflicting evidence, we may assume that a similar sequence occurred in Indonesia.

MALAYO-POLYNESIANS

Around 500 B.C., possibly under pressure from Chinese to the north, Malayo-Polynesian-speaking peoples of southeastern China began moving out of China and south along the west coasts of islands in the Philippines until they reached the western tip of Borneo. Some then moved east, spreading into eastern Indonesia; others moved west into Sumatra and from there, about a thousand years ago, into southern Malaya. These people (in varying combination with peoples already inhabiting the islands) were the ancestors of the present-day Malay groups of Indonesia.[4]

Speculating daringly by examining patterns in the contemporary and historical Melanesian and Malayo-Polynesian culture, one may suggest certain changes in religious and social life that accompanied the shift from dry-rice to wet-rice farming.[5] Religion for the food-gatherers and root-crop growers was probably an aggregate of rites which placated spirits and rectified the violation of taboos. Neither the rites, the spirits, nor the taboos were organized into a system of ethics and theology but were simply scattered responses to myriad locales and situations. A tree spirit, a mountain spirit, or an ancestral spirit would each call forth a rite of veneration or propitiation. The eating of a taboo fish, bird, or plant, or the trespassing of a female into an area restricted to males would each necessitate a special ritual to reestablish the proper state of order.

As the introduction of swidden agriculture spurred expansion into new areas, the resulting competition among tribes and families for land would seem to have encouraged warfare. As part of the warfare there emerged headhunting of the type practiced until recently by swidden groups throughout the islands. The competitive spirit found expression in a complex of feasts and megaliths like that found among swidden (as well as some wet-rice) groups of island and mainland Southeast Asia today.[6] To display its high productivity and resulting wealth, a family with a good crop would stage a feast during which it ostentatiously distributed food to guests. Gaining status through its generosity, the family would then erect a megalithic monument to commemorate its new prestige. In the more settled communities, a well-defined ladder of feasts emerged, the rungs of which a family must climb in order to achieve high rank.

IRRIGATION AND SETTLEMENT

Swidden families may have temporarily distinguished themselves by their productivity, but swidden ecology was not equipped to support a permanently stratified society. The Indonesian swidden system operates with a narrow balance between production and labor; it "tends to support just about as many workers as it needs and needs just about as many as it supports."[7] Swidden surpluses are not enough to support a permanently nonworking elite.

With the emergence of irrigated rice, however, this constriction is escaped. Irrigation increases the fertility of each field, so that surpluses are sufficient to support a leisure class. At the same time, irrigation systems and associated social organization become so complex as to require a specialized nonworking class of coordinators. Furthermore, irrigated fields preserve their fertility so that they can be used repeatedly. Hence the farmer need not move from field to field. He can meet his needs with a small acreage, and a number of farmers can live in a concentrated settlement. A densely populated settlement of tightly packed fields and sources of water requires a stable system of coordination to avoid conflict. Such leadership could come from an hereditary elite class which forms a ruling coalition and council. In archeological sequences documented for China and Indochina, the shift from swidden to irrigated agriculture was indeed accompanied by the emergence of an elite class and also by the development of bronze drums and ornaments to symbolize their high rank.[8]

Whether the bronze drums and ornaments found in Indonesia had this meaning, and whether evolution in Indonesia took this form, are both questions answerable only by speculation. What is certain, however, is that the development of irrigation agriculture allowed the settlement of communities of considerable size, density, and complexity, and the emergence of leaders to rule them. By conquest or diplomacy certain leaders extended their rule to villages other than their own. In extending their rule, the leaders would find it necessary to delegate work and authority. Thus would emerge a rudimentary bureaucracy of officials, soldiers, and clerks.

The early Indonesians were vigorous seamen as well as farmers. Their travels extended as far as east Africa, and they sailed to the ports of Ceylon and India just as the seamen of India came to the Archipelago. Certainly there was contact, and Indonesian rulers became acquainted with Hindu belief. Eventually Hindu priests—the Brahmins—were called to the courts of Indonesia where they first served in religious capacities but later may have been employed as chancellors, advisers in governmental affairs, supervisors of the construction of Hindu tombs, monuments, and temples, and dispensers of legitimacy.[9] These Brahmins must have helped propagate the belief that certain Javanese rulers were the incarnation of the Hindu gods, Vishnu or Shiva, and that they embodied the power of the Hindu cosmos. Such a belief could lend a mythical sanctity to the kings that would provide them authority not possible under the less elaborate and more egalitarian systems of indigenous religion. In this way Hinduism may have stimulated the florescence of kingdoms in Java, first in the center and later in the east, from the eighth to the thirteenth centuries A.D.

REFERENCES

[1] A concise summary of current opinion concerning Java Man is in *Anthropology Today* (Del Mar, Calif.: Communications Research Machines, 1971), Chap. 11. More detail is in G. H. R. Von Koeningswald, *Meeting Prehistoric Man*, trans. Michael Bullock (London and New York: Thames and Hudson, 1956).

[2] The remainder of this chapter is a speculative synthesis of sometimes conflicting interpretation based on skimpy evidence. The primary sources are Kwang-chih Chang, "Major Problems in the Culture History of Southeast Asia," *Bulletin of the Institute of Ethnology: Academica Sinica*, No. 13 (Spring 1962), pp. 1–23; and Wilhelm G. Solheim II, "The 'New Look' of Southeast Asian Prehistory," *Journal of the Siam Society*, Vol. 60, Pt. 1 (January 1972), pp. 1–20. Supplementary synthesizing sources include Carlton Coon, *The Origin of Races* (New York: Knopf, 1962), Chap. 9; and Clifford Geertz, *The Development of the Javanese Economy: A Socio-Cultural Approach* (Ann Arbor, Mich.: University Microfilms, 1956). For facts, see R. Van Heekeren, *The Stone Age of Indonesia* (The Hague: Nijhoff, 1957); and *The Bronze-Iron Age of Indonesia* (The Hague: Nijhoff, 1958). Potentially of great significance is the largely unpublished research of Wilhelm G. Solheim II, which suggests that the cultivation of rice and the casting of bronze may have originated not in China but in mainland Southeast Asia, after which these elements spread north to China and then to Indonesia. This particular hypothesis does not directly affect this chapter's interpretation of what happened within Indonesia, since it is mainly concerned with what happened on the mainland, but it does bear on the question of the origins of Indonesian culture.

An additional complication is suggested by detailed linguistic analyses which muster strong evidence that the Indonesian *languages* may have derived from the south (perhaps from Melanesia) rather than from the north. Languages could have migrated, of course, in a different direction from the Mongoloid peoples and associated facets of culture. See Isodore Dyen, *A Lexicostatistical Classification of Austronesian Languages* (Baltimore: Waverly, 1965).

[3] Chang, "Major Problems in the Culture History of Southeast Asia," p. 18.

[4] Solheim, "The 'New Look,'" pp. 17–18.

[5] Much of this speculation is suggested by Geertz, *Development of the Javanese Economy*, pp. 23–26, 38–41, and 78–81.

[6] Several ethnographic and archeological sources concerning the relation between Indonesian megaliths and feasts are listed in James L. Peacock, "Pasemah Megaliths: Historical, Functional, and Conceptual Interpretation," *Bulletin of the Institute of Ethnology: Academica Sinica*, No. 13 (Spring 1962), pp. 53–61.

[7] Geertz, *Development of the Javanese Economy*, p. 25.

[8] Chang, "Major Problems in the Culture History of Southeast Asia," pp. 13–20.

[9] J. C. van Leur, *Indonesian Trade and Society* (The Hague: Van Hoeve, 1955), p. 104; Theodore Pigeaud, *Java in the Fourteenth Century: A Study in Cultural History*, 5 vols. (The Hague: Nijhoff, 1960–1963), Vol. IV, p. 478.

THREE

INDIANIZED KINGDOMS

There in Sripala Tikta (Madjapahit) is He,
being obeyed, working out the welfare of
the world.
     Prapantja, "Nagarakertagama"[1]

The first of the Hindu-Javanese kingdoms was Mataram, under the rule of King Sandjaja. Flourishing in central Java at the beginning of the eighth century, Mataram was Shivaistic in religion, and it left behind on the cool and lofty Dieng Plateau some of the earliest of Java's Hindu monuments. Sandjaja's kingdom eventually declined, however, and was followed by a Buddhist Sjailendra dynasty based on Sumatra but acting with an overlord's power in central Java, exercising suzerainty over the local dynasties and driving the more conservative Hindu forces into the eastern part of that island.

The south Sumatran city of Palembang, strategically situated midway between the Straits of Malacca bordering Malaya and the Straits of Sunda bordering Java, controlled the two channels through which all traffic between China and India must pass. Based in Palembang, the Sjailendra empire of Srividjaja policed these channels and the Sumatran coast, exacting tax from passing ships. By the seventh century, the harbor capital of Srividjaja was a busy center of commerce and also of Mahayana Buddhism. The Chinese pilgrim I-tsing observed a thousand Buddhist monks there during his visit in A.D. 671.

In the eighth century, the Sjailendra dynasty, establishing itself firmly in central Java, produced the massive and still-standing Buddhist temple, Barabudur. In the ninth century, that Buddhist kingdom was replaced on Java by another Shivaite kingdom which claimed to restore the empire of Sandjaja and was called Mataram. Mataram produced one of Java's greatest Shivaistic monuments, Prambanan. The deposed

Buddhist prince returned to Sumatra to take over the rule of Srividjaja, and that empire endured until the thirteenth century, later transferring some of its power to the Malay port of Malacca.

Mataram fell, however, partly as a result of conflict with Srividjaja. Prince Airlangga, heir-designate to the throne of Mataram's East Java kingdom, was forced to take refuge in a hermitage in the face of a Srividjaja attack in A.D. 1006. After years of waiting, he came out of monastic seclusion to wage war and reunite his kingdom in 1019. He then returned to seclusion, conforming to a model of the life cycle followed by Hindu-Javanese kings preceding and succeeding him. (Airlangga and the others may have been influenced by the Hindu view that meditation is the proper life style for males at certain ages.) Relinquishing his political control, Airlangga divided his kingdom between his two sons, and these two kindoms were later reunited under Ken Angrok, who founded the empire of Singhosari. Singhosari, though rent by internal conflict, was expanding into an extensive empire under Kertanegara when his reign was ended in 1292 by invaders from the Mongol dynasty of China. Kertanegara's son-in-law, Widjaja, having exploited the invaders' aid in eliminating the former king, tricked them into supporting his own bid for the throne. Trapping the invaders, Widjaja forced them to retreat home. He seized control of domestic affairs and established the pinnacle of Hindu-Javanese civilization, the last and greatest Hindu-Javanese kingdom: Madjapahit. During the fourteenth century under the direction of King Hajam Wuruk's chief minister, Gadjah Mada, Madjapahit combined the agricultural strength of an island kingdom with the commercial power of a coastal empire to extend its might over most of present-day Indonesia. Gradually, however, Madjapahit disintegrated, weakened by the rise of Malacca as a commercial center and by the spread of Islam. By the early sixteenth century it had passed into legend.

HINDU-JAVANESE CONCEPTIONS
OF KINGSHIP AND SOCIETY

Represented in courtly literature and monumental architecture of the Hindu-Javanese kingdoms was a conception that the terrestrial order mirrored and embodied the celestial. The king, therefore, was a god: "Shiva-Buddha is He, material-immaterial by nature," sang the poet of Madjapahit of his king, "He is surely Ruler over the rulers of the world."[2] Of Airlangga it is said that he was an incarnation of Vishnu, and also incarnated as Shiva, an event celebrated by a volcanic eruption at his birth. Ken Angrok, incarnated as Vishnu, was also the adopted child of Shiva; to assure that Ken Angrok exuded the divine light and heat of royalty (*wahju*), he was married to a woman with a flaming womb.[3]

From the Hindu-Javanese viewpoint, what was to be avoided at all costs was disorder and change. Because the kingdom was incessantly in flux and chaos, it was frequently believed to be on the verge of collapse, to exist in the epoch of Kalijuga, the ominous fourth epoch in Hindu history after which occurs the world's destruction. When the reign was beset by war, crime, disease, and the placing of fools on pedestals, conditions were considered serious enough to call down Vishnu from on high and incarnate him in the person of the king. Only such a god-king could fulfill the function of calming and ordering the turbulent earthly society by meshing it with the cosmic harmony.[4]

Prapantja, poet of the fourteenth-century court of Madjapahit, relates in the poem "Nagarakertagama"[5] how the king toured the countryside to harmonize the world. Riding in the midst of his royal cortege of men, horses, elephants, and women of the harem, the king far outshone the rest through the blinding radiance of his jewels, gold, and metallic umbrella. Coming to a complex of floating ocean pavilions, he performed an important rite which required that he bathe with a company of women in the sea. Joining in a symbolic marriage the king (who represented Java's social order) and the goddess of the South Seas (who represented the natural order of sky and ocean), the rite was said to bestow a sense of peace on the onlookers who viewed the shimmering image created by king and consorts bathing in the moving waters. In the performance of such ceremonies, enthuses Prapantja, no one is so perfect as his king. A more explicitly erotic experience was the king's visit to a Brahminist convent in the forest. Reposing for several nights among the virgins, the king "practiced joy unremittingly,"[6] leaving the young girl anchorites languishing and enamored for this god of love come down from heaven. A final adventure during a hunting trip demonstrates that the king's magical charms worked even for animals. Ferociously repulsing attack for each less-than-royal stratum of society, ranging from dogs to courtiers, the wild animals of the jungle swooned in delight at the appearance of the king, and they died gladly at his hand.

The kingdom as well as the king was designed to replicate and order the cosmos. The capital was oriented to the four points on the compass, as was the cosmos conceived in Hindu-Buddhist philosophy. The temple or the palace symbolized the holy center of that cosmos, representing Mount Meru or some other holy pivot. Four queens or four goddesslike princesses, each representing a cardinal direction, further personified the cosmic design. In these arrangements, which joined kingdom and cosmos, the Javanese society expressed a magicomystical world view found throughout Hinduized Southeast Asia.

Caste was never so important in Indonesia as it was in India, a situation associated with the lack of Indonesian emphasis on pollution and purity. Indonesian priests were never able, in the manner of the Indian Brahmins, to outrank the kings sheerly through their ritual purity, and in Indonesia the god-king remained paramount. Nevertheless, the two highest castes in India, the priestly and the royal, were also the highest ranks in the Hindu-Javanese society, and the bureaucratic as well as the ecclesiastical orders were carefully graded into ranks descending in importance from these exalted ones. To order relations between high and lowly, complex and refined systems of etiquette were developed. Where one sat, where one marched, or when one danced at courtly celebrations, how many lines one merited in the poems of veneration—all meticulously reflected one's status.[7] Javanese during the time of Madjapahit, like Javanese today, may have entertained a view that by ordering the social hierarchy, other realms—from the inner depths of the soul to the outer expanse of the cosmos—are ordered as well.

Like the Egyptian pyramids, Hindu-Buddhist monuments of Java symbolized conceptions of society and cosmos as well as honoring dead kings and worshipping the divine forces. Barabadur of central Java, constructed to glorify the Lords of the Mountain, the dynasty of Sjailendra, replicates the Hindu-Buddhist hierarchical image of society and cosmos. Exhibiting 27,000 square feet of stone surface carved in high relief, Barabadur depicts the ten levels in the Buddhist ascent to salvation as six square and three round terraces rising to a bell-shaped stupa.[8] Though tragically near collapse today, the magnificent Barabadur still provides an experience of transcendence, as the climber proceeds from crowded images in the bottom layers to lofty and airy realms of formlessness at the top.

Javanese knowledge of Hindu mythology is revealed by the tense and dynamic imagery of the temple of Prambanan, the central Javanese monument completed as early as the middle ninth century in honor of Shiva, the creator and destroyer. Prambanan depicts the adventures of heroic figures of the Hindu epic, the *Ramayana*: Prince Rama, Princess Sita, and the white monkey Hanuman. The other great Javanized Hindu epic, the *Mahabharata*, was narrated in court literature that flourished during the east Javanese ascendency. Prose transcriptions were in the old Javanese language of *Kawi*, and certain episodes were set to poetry of the *kekawin* type. Among the important episodes was the battle between the five knightly brothers, the Pandawas, and the rival princes, the Kurawas.

Most expressive of Javanese perception of Hindu mythology is the shadow play, the *wajang kulit*. Performed by a sacred puppeteer (*dalang*) who moved leather figures in front of an oil lamp to cast flickering shadows on a white screen, the wajang kulit was enjoyed and revered by Javanese even before the founding of Madjapahit. Wajang kulit, a performance which lasted all night, was a rite as well as a drama. Wajang worshipped the gods, placated the spirits, purified the soul, and harmonized the community as well as portraying tales of the *Ramayana* and *Mahabharata*. Wajang may have originated in China or south India, but most likely in Indonesia itself.

Though certain aspects of Madjapahit-period wajang kulit have certainly changed (for example, the shape of the puppets), others, such as the basic stories and characters, remain essentially the same today. Through experiencing contemporary live wajang performances, one may imagine something of the ethos conveyed by the world of the shadow puppets during the era of Madjapahit.[9]

Wajang kulit characters are carefully ranked according to their status and their refinement of temperament and manner. The *halus* (refined) characters tend to appear on the puppeteer's right, the *kasar* (crude) ones on his left. The refined princes, epitomized by Ardjuna, have narrow, almond-shaped eyes, a down-turning nose, a slightly bowed head, no chin whiskers, and a delicate, almost effeminate physique. Crude monsters, typified by Burisrawa, are fat, with heavy, bristling eyebrows, round eyes, bulbous noses, and red faces. Key scenes represent battles between halus heroes and their kasar enemies. Conflicts like these carry psychological as well as political meanings, symbolizing the war between kasar desire of the flesh and halus aspirations of the spirit—a war waged, according to traditional philosophizing, in the psyche of every Javanese.

Unique in character is Semar, the short-legged, stout, hermaphroditic clown. Regarded by many Javanese as the most sacred figure of the wajang, Semar was of pre-Hindu Javanese origin (c. A.D. 600). Though he plays the role of clown and servant to the Hindu princes, he is a fallen Javanese god, brother of Shiva. When the gods descend, causing the princes to fall prostrate in worship, Semar stands erect and speaks to the gods directly, as an equal, in familiar Javanese language. Possessing immense wisdom and power, Semar is the character who appears on the screen at midnight, the time when the elements wage, to restore order. The poignant might of Semar is expressed in the story of his death. Semar's master, Prince Ardjuna, has been bewitched by Shiva into promising to murder Semar. Grieving over this obligation, for he loves Semar, Ardjuna still feels compelled to proceed with the slaughter. Semar suggests that he ease Ardjuna's dilemma by simply burning himself. Semar builds a bonfire and stands in it, but instead of dying he turns into his godly form and defeats Shiva.

If Semar represents, as some have suggested, the earthy Javanese substance underneath the courtly Hindu glaze, Ardjuna is the consummate Satriya, the cultured and noble knight. On the eve of the great battle with his Kurawa cousins, Ardjuna is saddened by the need to kill his boyhood playmates. He turns in his distress to his divine mentor, Krishna. But Krishna explains that Ardjuna is a Satriya. He must fulfill the code of his knightly caste and follow the predetermined path of his life; he must slay the enemy. He should perform that deed, however, while maintaining an inner detachment from it. Inner detachment from outer action, a dualism that permits spiritual tranquility in the midst of worldly conflict, is a core ideal of Hindu-Javanese theosophy. Expressed in mystical texts as well as in the wajang theater, such notions may have guided the Madjapahit courtiers just as they guide Javanese officials today.

THE VILLAGE[10]

Since virgin lands were abundant in Java at the time of Madjapahit, village houses were perhaps arranged in straggling lines rather than in the tight clusters of today's village, but certain communal values must have been important in village life then as now. By comparison with the hierarchical court, village society was egalitarian. Villagers were ranked into strata according to their rights to land, and the core villagers inherited their rights from an ancestor who had founded the village. But even these core villagers possessed only rights of use, since full ownership of the land was vested in a village council. Rites to purify the village and to placate its guardian spirit (*pundèn*) served to keep alive something of a communal ethos in the ancient Javanese village just as in the contemporary one.

The village was regarded as existing in a realm separate from the court, for the villagers were earthy and crude while king and courtiers were felt to partake of godliness if they were not actually divine. Yet the rice cultivated by the village was the material basis of the glittering life and culture of the palace. Officials and priests traveled through the countryside collecting taxes in kind as payment from the people to the king for the military protection and spiritual harmony which he so generously provided. Stored in royal warehouses in the palace, such tribute fed the officials, the army, and the royal household. Noteworthy is the conception that the king and lords had rights not to the villagers' lands but to their labor and its product. Javanese culture was not, therefore, based on a system of feudal fiefs, no strong landed gentry ever emerged in Java, and the class structure and world view of the Javanese were quite different from that of feudalism.

The village was as concerned to coordinate its rituals and agricultural cycles, to remain in harmony with the natural order, as was the court to mesh with the supernatural. Neither village nor court was

disposed to desire change and development, unless it permitted a return
to a former state of equilibrium and order. The good kingdom was
not a development agency which jarred and transformed village life,
but a protective covering, like the *banjan* tree which spread its branches
and shade over those who squatted beneath. So long as the village paid
its taxes it was left to run its own affairs. Crimes were judged and
punished by village elders or chiefs in accord with custom; only disturbance of the king's peace and the cosmic order by some sexual irregu-
larity or other crime provoked Royal Justice administered by Royal
Judges in accord with Hindu-Javanese books of law.

The villager's defense against a kingdom's excessive interference
with his affairs was simply to move. During the great epochs of monument building when kings demanded excessive labor from peasants,
whole villages migrated to new regions. The migration of villages transferred the material base for kingdoms and probably contributed to the
shift of royal power from central to east Java.

The hills and plains of the Javanese countryside sheltered, in addition to peasant villages, Shivaistic and Buddhist hermitages. The poem
by Prapantja describes the pastoral Shivaite hermitage, Sagara, where
a community of learned scholars and holy men lived in "huts" (*pondok*) like those later to form Muslim schools. The Madjapahit king's
visit to Sagara was probably prompted not merely by courtesy and curios-
ity but by a longing for spiritual guidance. Throughout Javanese history,
even to the present, Javanese rulers have cherished their spiritual mentors and advisers, their *gurus*.

THE PORT

The economic base of a coastal kingdom such as Srividjaja differed
from that of an inland kingdom such as Mataram. The prince of Srividjaja gained his revenue by taxing ships that passed through his waters
and exploiting merchants who lived in his ports. Inland peoples of
Sumatra were not sedentary peasants cultivating irrigated rice but seminomadic, swidden tribesmen. Their farming produced no significant
surpluses, and Srividjaja was forced to import rice. The Srividjaja king
could get little from the inland tribesmen except forest products which
he could sell to the foreign merchants. With no extensive bureaucracy
to exact tribute in work from the inland tribesmen, Srividjaja was un-
able to mobilize mass labor for the construction of public works. This
lack partly explains why no monument on Sumatra is remotely comparable to Barabadur or Prambanan on Java.[11]

The coastal emporia developed their own culture in opposition to
that of the inner lands. Light literature—narrative, romantic, anecdotal,
erotic—and light music such as the quatrain (*pantun*) songs may have

originated in the polyglot traders' quarters as entertainment to while away the time of waiting for the turn of the monsoon.[12] Less popular in the ports than in the inland courts were the shadow play, the refined dance, or the percussion orchestra (*gamelan*) which were adapted to the pomp and pageantry, the knightly ethic, of royalty and aristocracy. In religion too there were differences. Mahayana Buddhism flourished more strongly in the Sumatran ports than in the Javanese inland courts. The Mahayana type of Buddhism certainly possessed feudal characteristics—for example, the notion of the ruler as a god-king Boddhisatva. Nevertheless, Buddhism would seem to have been better suited than the communal and hierarchical Hinduism to the individualism of the commercial harbor.

Whatever the difference in culture, the opposition between inland and coastal kingdoms is a major theme throughout Indonesian history, and one that gains resonance with the coming of a new religion, the Islamic.

REFERENCES

[1] Theodore Pigeaud, *Java in the Fourteenth Century: A Study in Cultural History*, 5 vols. (The Hague: Nijhoff, 1960-1963), Vol. III, p. 20 (Canto 17, Stanza 1).

[2] *Ibid.*, Vol. II, p. 3 (Canto 1, Stanza 1).

[3] B. Schrieke, *Indonesian Sociological Studies, Part II: Ruler and Realm in Early Java* (The Hague: Van Hoeve, 1957), p. 12.

[4] *Ibid.*, pp. 77–86.

[5] Pigeaud, *Java in the Fourteenth Century*, Vol. III, pp. 20–42 (Canto 17–33).

[6] *Ibid.*, Vol. III (Canto 31, Stanza 4).

[7] *Ibid.*, Vol. IV, pp. 500–531.

[8] Claire Holt, *Art in Indonesia: Continuities and Change* (Ithaca, N.Y.: Cornell Univ. Press, 1967), pp. 42–51.

[9] On the contemporary wajang as expressive of the ethos of ancient Hindu Java, see Holt, *Art in Indonesia*, pp. 140–149. Suggestive general treatments of the wajang ethos include Benedict Anderson, *Mythology and the Tolerance of the Javanese* (Ithaca, N.Y.: Modern Indonesia Project, Cornell University, 1965); James Brandon, *On Thrones of Gold: Three Javanese Shadow Plays* (Cambridge, Mass.: Harvard Univ. Press, 1970); Clifford Geertz, *Religion of Java* (New York: Free Press of Glencoe, 1959), pp. 261–278; Mantle Hood, "The Enduring Tradition: Music and Theater in Java and Bali," in Ruth T. McVey (ed.), *Indonesia* (New Haven, Conn.: Southeast Asia Studies, Yale

University, 1963), pp. 438–474; K. G. P. A. A. Mangkunegara VII of Surakarta, *On the Wajang Kulit (Purwa) and Its Symbolic and Mystical Elements*, trans. Claire Holt (Ithaca, N.Y.: Modern Indonesia Project, Cornell University, 1957); J. Kats, *Het Javaansche tooneel*, Deel I, *Wajang Poerwa* (Weltevreden: Volks-lectuur, 1923).

[10] On the Javanese village and its relationship to the royal bureaucracy in Madjapahit times, see Pigeaud, *Java in the Fourteenth Century*, Vol. IV, pp. 467–525.

[11] On the general character of Srividjaja, see W. F. Wertheim, "Southeast Asia," *International Encyclopedia of the Social Sciences*, Vol. 1 (New York: Macmillan, 1968), pp. 423–438. For detail, see O. W. Wolters, *Early Indonesian Commerce: A Study of the Origins of Srivijaya* (Ithaca, N.Y.: Cornell Univ. Press, 1967); and *The Fall of Srivijaya in Malay History* (Ithaca, N.Y.: Cornell Univ. Press, 1970).

[12] Pigeaud, *Java in the Fourteenth Century*, Vol. IV, p. 501.

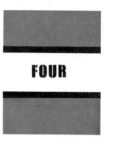

FOUR

THE RISE OF ISLAM

During the period of the Indianized kingdoms, trade was gradually expanding on the sea routes of the archipelago in connection with commercial networks stretching from Asia to Europe. By the time of the Crusades in the late eleventh century, the Far East, Southeast Asia, India, western Asia, and the Mediterranean were linked by trade and shipping carried on by Arabs, Persians, Indians, Chinese, and by Indonesians themselves (the latter were the most prominent long-distance traders in the Indian Ocean and China Sea from around 200 B.C. to the ninth or tenth century A.D., when the other groups became important). Such ports as Cambai on the Gulf of Cambai, Gujerat in northwestern India, and Calicut on the Malabar Coast had become major international emporia. Raw silk, textiles, gold, sandalwood, porcelain, camphor, pepper, nutmeg, and handicrafts were among the goods circulated along the routes in which Srividjaja and even the east Javanese kingdoms participated. By 1400, Madjapahit had extended its trade into Timor, the Moluccas, and the Philippines.

Madjapahit's commercial florescence was undermined, however, by the rise of the port of Malacca on Malaya's south coast. Under the shrewd Iskandar, a refugee prince of Srividjaja driven from his homeland by Madjapahit, Malacca had developed from a small fishing village to a great commercial port. The conversion of a Malaccan ruler from Buddhism to Islam encouraged Muslim traders to concentrate in his harbor, and by thrusting itself into the trade route between the Moluccas and India, Malacca "cut one of the sinews of the strength of Madjapahit itself."[1] The north-coast Java ports were in time drawn out of the orbit of the declining Madjapahit into that of Malacca. In 1511 Malacca was captured by the Portuguese, after which its royal family moved elsewhere in the Malay Peninsula, and the commercial might of Malacca declined. But other Muslim ports of similar character, such as Atjeh across the

Straits of Malacca and Bantam on the Sunda Straits, rose to take its place.

From the Muslim ports outward and through the islands spread religion as well as commerce. Muslim merchants had been active in Asian trade since the seventh century and these, whether Arab, Indian, or Persian, naturally bore their faith. Intermarrying with local women, they were the most mobile representatives of Islam in the islands, and they doubtless played an important part in its spread. The chronology of the Islamization of Indonesia is not precisely known. Marco Polo's report of a Muslim community in northern Sumatra in 1292 has been questioned, but other evidence indicates scattered enclaves of Islam in the islands by the end of the thirteenth century.[2] Not until the fourteenth and fifteenth centuries, however, did Islam inundate the islands. The conversion of Malacca was followed by that of the Javanese ports of Demak, Djepara, Tuban, and Surabaja. In the sixteenth and seventeenth centuries sultanates were created in the Moluccas, and Makasar in the Celebes was converted, followed by small coastal kingdoms in the Lesser Sundas. Characteristically, the ruler converted first, then his native subjects followed.

Why did the rulers convert? Their motives were partially economic and political. The Muslim merchants swarming about the islands were more easily attracted to the ruler's port if he were an Islamic sultan than if he were a Hindu king. Further, under the banner of the new and mighty Islam, the sultans could oppose rival faiths and powers, such as the encroaching Portuguese who strove to convert the natives to Christianity as well as to steal their trade. That the kings also converted for religious reasons is suggested by the intriguing theory that Islam was carried to them by mystical teachers—the Sufi—and that Islam began to grow vigorously only after the fourteenth century, which was when the Sufi arrived.[3]

Sufi orders did not flourish in the Middle East until after Baghdad fell to the Mongols in 1258. During the next years, Sufi orders became stable, disciplined foundations and they affiliated themselves with craft guilds and trade corporations of which the Muslim cities were composed. When the Muslim traders climbed on board their ships to the East in the fourteenth century, they were perhaps accompanied by Sufi teachers who came to minister to the spiritual needs of the traders and to serve the craft guilds to which they were affiliated, and which were probably being established in rising ports such as Malacca. As members of a missionary order, the Sufi came with a missionary purpose, to spread the word of Islam.

Espousing poverty, traveling light, Sufi missionaries ranged over all of greater Asia. Journeying by caravan over land to China and central Asia, they went by ship to the archipelago, Columbo, the Gujerat, and back to Mecca. Their teachings had quick appeal, for Sufism was a religion of the heart and the imagination. Sufis rejected the ossified, dry, and tortuously complex legal systems of the medieval Muslim scholastics. They were unfulfilled, too, by the bare-bones simplicity of the original Islam of the desert. Seeking emotional and philosophical meaning, the Sufis elaborated speculative theosophies illuminating the inner life of the divine creator and the bond between creator and creation. They taught chants that led to trance, and stages of mortification of the flesh that culminated in ecstatic and sensual union with the divine spirit. The simplicity of early Islam may have suited the tribal Arabs, but the Indonesians, like the Persians, the Chinese, and the Indians, partook of a civilization already possessing complex cosmologies and ecstatic mysticism. Especially since the Sufis proved willing to syncretize their own teachings with the native ones, and also because the Sufi teachers boasted personal charisma and the power to do magic and to heal, the Indonesians were receptive to their teachings.

Sufi holy men were graciously received and heard by kings throughout the archipelago. Some of them managed to marry princesses, thus gaining the added prestige of royal blood. Many won strong influence in the courts; one example is Sjamsuddin, who rose to the post of dignitary at the court of Atjeh and tutored the sultan Iskandar Muda himself before dying in 1630.

Moving inland, the Sufi teachers and dervishes converted the Hindu-Buddhist hermitages and monasteries to Islam, transforming them into the rural Muslim schools, the *pondok* and *pesantrèn*, which made their appearance in Java by 1600.[4]

THE SANTRI PATTERN

By the eighteenth century, an Islamic life style had been established in ports such as Atjeh, Bantam, Demak, Tuban, and Gresik, and in interior Muslim enclaves formed by the pesantrèn and the villages surrounding them. Notable was the absence of a centralized religious bureaucracy like that of the inland Hindu kingdoms. The princes who ruled the ports were responsible for protecting the faith, but they neither formed ecclesiastical hierarchies within their ports nor united the various ports to compose a mightly Muslim empire. The pesantrèn were not part of a bureaucracy either, but rather rural retreats standing apart from the governments which controlled the territories which they inhabited. What integrated the Indonesian Islamic world was a shared Muslim culture and the movement of individuals among its centers and outposts. A typical devout Muslim would drift from pesantrèn to pesantrèn, absorbing what he could from each teacher, then he would depart from a port such as Atjeh for the holy city of Mecca. Returning with the prestigious title of *hadji* (indicating that he had made the pilgrimage, the *hadj*), or even with a certificate from a Sufi order giving him authority to found a branch in Indonesia, he would reenter the countryside whence he had come and found his own pesantrèn.

The port kingdoms such as Atjeh ensured connection between the archipelago and points west. For a time Indonesia's chief emporium of trade with India and the Red Sea, Atjeh was the gate to the holy land. The stream of pilgrims to Mecca and back to Atjeh brought home the wisdom, fads, and mystical cults of the holy city, and the Atjehnese in turn kept gifts flowing to that sacred place; at one point Mecca even sent an ambassador to Atjeh to honor the kingdom and solicit its material support. Indian as well as Arabic customs penetrated Atjeh from the West; at a certain period the Atjehnese kingdom boasted elephants in the army, a harem, dancing girls, and the sultan's habit of giving audience from an upstairs window.⁵ During the sixteenth and seventeenth centuries, Atjeh and similar Indonesian kingdoms were hospitable asylums for Muslim scholars from the Middle East—the case of Sjamsuddin has already been mentioned—and through the patronage of the Atjehnese sultan a number of Malay and Arabic writings in Islam diffused through the archipelago.

In the countryside stood the pesantrèn, that institution which has been so significant in Indonesian history for spreading literacy and a certain independence of thought. Rising from his mat at dawn, cooking his own rice breakfast over a flame, laboring by day in the fields, and contemplating sacred texts by night, the adolescent student (called a *santri*) at the pesantrèn led an ascetic, individualistic, and disciplined life. Above all else he strove to absorb the knowledge that was embodied in the soul and books of his teacher, the *kiai*. The content of that knowledge, as the santri perceived it, is revealed in antique notebooks in which students recorded what they heard from the lips of the dictating kiai.⁶

Emphasized in these notes is the notion of *gusti-kawula* or Lord-servant. Of Hindu-Javanese origin, this image of the bond between Lord and servant is taken as a metaphor for the relationship between God and man. Even more fundamental, however, is the self, the "I," to which all existence, including God, reduces. Contemplation of the self through mystical meditation was all important. Showing influence of the Shattariyya orders of Sufism, the notebooks record spells and incantations of indigenous origin and coloration in addition to the customary Sufi litanies, prayers, and repetitive trance-inducing formulae. Along with music, dance, song, exercises, juggling, and fakir tricks, the chanting of these sayings brought trance among the pesantrèn youth. Doubtless the mystical experience of adolescence derived from a stay in the pesan-trèn was significant in forming the Indonesian's adult personality; exact-ly how has never been delineated, even though the mystical practices and the pesantrèn study continue among Indonesian Muslim adoles-cents to this day.

Religious life in the village centered around the mosque and the small prayer house. In the prayer houses, groups of men (but no women) met for the daily prayers and evening Sufi exercises and for special rituals during the month of the fast. Boys younger than pesantrèn age came to the prayer house to learn how to recite the Qur'an (Koran) and to know the basic tenets of the faith.

Services in the mosque united the religious community comprising the devout males of the entire village. Each Friday in the noon heat they would bathe themselves in the mosque waters, lower and raise their bodies while chanting obeisance to Allah, and sit on the floor to hear a sermon. The head official of the mosque was the *imam*, who led the public prayers, administered the mosque, celebrated marriages, recorded divorces, arbitrated in disputes concerning religious law or ritual practice, and provided religious instruction to all ages. Other officers were the *khatib*, who gave the sermon at the Friday service, and the *bilal*, who chanted the call to prayer. None of these offices required formal schooling or certification, though their holders had likely studied under a Qur'anic teacher, attended a pesantrèn, or even been to Mecca and acquired the title of hadji. No superordinate organi-zation administered the mosque. It was built, and its officers selected, by the villagers. The villagers also supported the officials through paying the *zakat*, the tithe.

The pattern of Islam just described is conveniently called *santri*, taken in its broadest sense to denote a pious orthodoxy in the practice of the Muslim faith.[7] The santri are those Indonesian Muslims who strongly endeavor to carry out the five prescriptions or "pillars" of Islam and who are devotees of a strongly Muslim and rather Arab style of life. The santri have taken the oath "There is no God but Allah, and Muhammad is his prophet." They faithfully pray five times daily, pay the religious tax, fast during the month of Ramadan, abstain from eating pork and drinking alcohol, and make the pilgrimage if health and fi-nances permit. They learn at least enough Arabic to chant the Qur'an, they study the doctrine and texts, and they are devoutly loyal to Muslim theology and ethics as a guide to proper living. They may affect quasi-Arabic styles of dress, enjoy Arabic music, dance, and poetry, and punc-tuate conversation with such pious Arabic utterances as "If God wills . . ." or "God, God, God . . . ." Because of their Arabic affectations, which strike many of the non-santri Indonesians as rather comical,

the santri are lampooned, criticized, and sometimes insultingly called
simply "Arabs." They are largely, however, genetically and ethnically
Indonesians.

THE ABANGAN PATTERN[8]

In all regions of Indonesia, Islamic culture joined with the indigenous
to form a syncretic religion, but purity and piety were strong in the
coastal areas. In the central Javanese heartland of Hinduized civilization,
on the other hand, Islam took a form different from that adored by
the santri. Islam was syncretized with Hinduism, Buddhism, and the
indigenous animistic beliefs to form a blend known as *abangan*. Abangan Muslims may have taken the oath, but they fulfill none of the
other five pillars. They do not practice the five prayers, do not fast
during Ramadan, eat pork (with apparent enjoyment), pay no tax, and
have no desire to make the pilgrimage to Mecca. What is worse, from
the standpoint of the devout, they dilute the pillars so as to render
them flaccid and weak. Abangan mystics have broached the idea that
one can do the five prayers simply by thinking about doing them, and
that an acceptable way of making the pilgrimage is merely to take a
vacation trip to any place that offers peace of heart. At the center of
the abangan religious life is the *slametan*, a feast shared by neighbors
that combines Arabic and Javanese chants to worship Allah, placate
the spirits, and unify the participants so that they are all peaceful and
secure (*slamet*). Abangan ascribe the origins of such un-Muslim items
as the shadow play, the sacred dagger (*kris*), and the Javanese orchestra
(*gamelan*) to mystical and legendary "saints" of Javanese Islam. Abangan
religion is so motley a mixture of the Islamic and the indigenous as
to horrify the santri.

After Madjapahit's demise and collapse (which must have been
gradual, for the Portuguese found the empire still alive though ailing
as late as the sixteenth century), power shifted from eastern to central
Java. During the rule of Sultan Agung from 1613 to 1645, the central
Javanese kingdom of Mataram became the great power on Java. Defeat-
ing and subordinating the north-coast Java sultanates, Mataram absorbed
elements of the maritime Islamic culture into the florid, inland Hindu-
Javanese courtly life, creating in the process the most powerful organizational expression of abangan syncretism ever to exist.[9]

Agung sent ambassadors to Mecca who returned in 1641 with a
document that confirmed his Islamic title of sultan, yet he also claimed
legitimate succession from the Madjapahit king, Hajam Wuruk, and
continuation of the policies of Madjapahit's great minister, Gadjah
Mada, and he assumed the indigenous title of *Susuhunan*. Endeavoring

to harmonize the shift from maritime to inland, Agung sought legitima-
tion from the holy Sunan Kalidjaga, the mystic prince and legendary
saint of syncretic Javanese Islam; Kalidjaga's tomb was made a shrine
and a quintessential source of magical power for the kingdom of Mataram. More purely Islamic accretions entered courtly life as well.
Agung's son, however, reacted against the Islamic overlay. During his
rule (1645–1677), he dropped the title of sultan, abolished his father's
Islamic courts, and slaughtered several thousand Muslim teachers
whom he had invited to the palace for that purpose. Yet the syncretic
character of Mataram continued, embodied in calendars mixing Hindu
and Muslim systems of reckoning time, in ceremonies uniting mosque
and palace, and in a royal bureaucracy based on Hindu concepts yet
incorporating Muslim khatibs.

The king of Mataram resembled the king of Madjapahit and the
other Hindu-Buddhist empires. Islam allowed no man to be a god, but
the king was *kalipatullah*, God's representative on earth. He was still
a sacral figure from whom shone the holy light (*wahju*) in the form
of seven moons and whose divine fragrance wafted through the palace
corridors, out the gates, down the streets, and over the countryside.
He should meditate, like the saint Kalidjaga, until roots grew over his
head, and he might hope that his body would be penetrated by the
divine light in the form of a "child as small as a kris-handle, shining
like the sun."[10] His duty was to maintain a harmonious accord between
state and cosmos, as is reflected in his title *hamengku buwono* (still
borne by the Jogjakarta sultan, who is also Indonesia's secretary of
treasury), which means "He who holds the world on his lap."

No definite borders bounded the kingdom of Mataram. Like Madjapahit it was conceived as a series of concentric circles rippling outward
toward the hinterlands. The innermost circle was the palace, the *kraton*,
a vast complex of buildings and courtyards, enclosed by walls and moats,
and oriented according to the four cardinal directions. In that circle
lived the king, his queens and concubines, officials, royal dancers,
hordes of servants, and a corps of female guards who protected the
king's person from human touch.

Outside the walls of the kraton extended a series of further circles,
the first surrounding the immediate kingdom, the next the region of
Jogjakarta and Surakarta, and the third most of Java. The fourth
circle stretched to include the outer islands, the countries beyond, such
as Champa and Cambodia, and the dense jungles which absorbed the
distal rays of wahju.

In details of administration as in broadly conceived design, the
society was cosmicly ordered. At the lowest level, each village was supposed to be a center surrounded by four hamlets, each located at one

of the four cardinal points. At the highest level, the chief minister was regarded as the central control over four subdistrict officers, two of the left side and two of the right. Four plus one made five—the four cardinal points plus a center—a sacred number and design found throughout Hindu Southeast Asia.

Outside the palace the lords and the prijaji carried the burden of administration. The lords had hereditary rights to their territories, which they loosely subordinated to the kingdom. The prijaji were officials of the king who typically acquired hereditary rights to those territories which they administered in the name of the king. In practice, the two authorities, the lords and the prijaji, functioned similarly, and both may be designated by the term "regent." They lived not by salaries received from the king, but from tribute which they collected from peasants who farmed the territories they administered. Each regent was privileged to appropriate village labor for his own field, kitchen, and court, which was called *dalem* and patterned after the kraton. Since the king quartered none of his soldiers in the territories (though he might send expeditionary forces), each regent kept his own militia.

With their autonomy, the regents were potentially rebels against the king. To check their power, the king resorted to strategies practiced by patrimonial rulers throughout history. He retained influential regents at the court for long periods in order to prevent them gaining power in the provinces, he married them to women in the royal family in order to bind their loyalties to him, and, of course, he executed them. By appointing commoners to the status of prijaji, the king introduced into the provinces loyal officials who could compete with the local gentry. More significant than any of these measures, however, was the Javanese-Hindu world view, which made a cult out of loyalty and service to the king.

A basic concept was that of *gusti-kawula*, the bond between lord and servant. The gusti-kawula concept strikes chords within the Javanese soul that are given overtones by such symbols, attitudes, and experiences as the mystical sense that God is lord and man is servant; the sacral figure of Semar who is both god and servant; poignant memories of kneeling before one's father on Lebaran day to ask his forgiveness in the stately Sanskritized language known as *krama*; and the custom of addressing rulers as "father." The sacral character of the gusti-kawula bond between king and prijaji is expressed in the Mataram custom of prijaji gathering in the court to perform the *seba*. Squatting unmoving for hours in the shadows of the inner palace courtyard, they would fast, meditate, and await orders from their king.[11] As members of the knightly satriya caste, they should emulate the halus asceticism of Ardjuna and cleanse themselves of any motive but service to the ruler.

The prijaji learned his post through adoption and apprenticeship. As a boy of 12 to 15 years he lived with a family of higher status than his own, often performing the menial tasks of the servant in order to experience the humility of service. Through respect for those of higher birth than himself, he learned the halus etiquette. He should, in his youth, master the gentle arts of dance, music, and reciting of poetry, and the gentlemanly skills of riding and weaponry. He should spend a time in study with a religious hermit and, ideally, in his old age he himself would, like Airlangga, become such a recluse. At the same time, he was to some extent encouraged to emulate the lives of such heroes as Sunan Kalidjaga, to spend his youth in pursuit of the joys of the flesh, and even to turn to crime. As an adult he might marry a daughter of an official or nobleman in order to increase his chances for a good position. Next he might apprentice himself to some dignitary without pay, and serve with unquestioning obedience for years. As a mature official, he was expected to continue his cultivation of the spirit by attending dances, shadow plays, and court ceremonies, and by competing in the horseback jousts at the weekly tournaments of kraton or dalem.[12]

Mataram was hardly an organizational and economic *tour de force.* Its only economic support was from peasant agriculture, its transport, communications, and marketing systems were rudimentary, and it achieved little administrative integration of periphery and center. Yet in its prime, before the middle of the seventeenth century, it boasted the strongest Javanese royal dynasty that had ever existed. The integrative force of Mataram was not organizational but cultural, the cult of royalty, and that cult was in its basics not Muslim but abangan.

Within the shadow of the palace, however, were santri enclaves, usually built around the rural pesantrèn. The kiai and his followers were themselves syncretists, probably Sufists; nevertheless, they stood for a more purely Islamic life style than did the abangan. In Islamic doctrine the kiai found a transcendent ideal in terms of which to criticize and condemn the syncretic impurities of the governmental establishment, and the kiai sparked several rural uprisings directed partly against the court. Most significant was the 1825–1830 Java War led by Prince Diponegoro.[13] Born a lower nobleman, Diponegoro was offered the throne in a Mataram court but refused it in favor of his younger half-brother who was of higher birth. Abandoning the court, Diponegoro took to the wilderness to meditate. There he fell under the influence of a kiai. After the Dutch tactlessly angered Diponegoro by violating treaties concerning his ancestral lands, he adopted the Muslim turban and flag, and led the Java War not only against the Dutch but, by implication, against their aristocratic supporters as well. The rebellion failed but at the cost of millions of guilders to the Dutch and hundreds of lives on both sides.

ISLAM AND SOCIAL CHANGE[14]

The Indonesian merchant who converted to Islam was set free from his local community and tribe and made a member of the interisland network of ports and riverine kingdoms united by commerce and Islam, and he joined the international community of Muslims, the *umat*. These social transformations carried special meaning in the context of the Indonesian commercial town. Such a town was not a body politic like the city-state of classical antiquity but more like the Middle East emporium: a polyglot and transient commercial citizenry under the rule of a local prince and band of administrators. Living in separate quarters, speaking different languages, the traders from one nation or ethnic group met with those of another only in the marketplace. United only by their common quest for gain and by the condition that one could sell what the other would buy, the tradesmen formed a functioning system but no moral community. The merchants who joined the international community of Muslims were united, however, by religion, and they now met in the mosque as well as at the market.

Well adapted to the commercial world was the Muslim view that all believers were equal; Hindu notions that the higher caste possessed intrinsic advantages could limit the free give-and-take of bargaining and the free operation of the law of supply and demand. Islam also preached an ethical universalism, a belief that all believers should deal honestly and impartially with one another. Obviously, even among the faithful, practice deviated from the ideal, but the Arab, Indian, and Indonesian merchants could doubtless trust one another more after they had converted than before. The greater trust extended the range of transactions into which a trader would enter and the variety of people with whom he could confidently deal.

Muslim symbolism was simple. Proper ritual required only the mosque, the bath, and God; if the third were present, the first and second could be done without. Such simplicity was convenient for the transient merchant, for he could practice his faith anywhere he went. Under Javanese and Balinese Hinduism, with its palaces and temples, its elaborate pomp and ceremony, and its fusion to the local community and place, the religious baggage was too bulky for travel, and the Hinduized Javanese and Balinese have indeed been less peripatetic than the Muslims.[15] The Muslim trader also enjoyed the assurance that, during the lonely journeys, he could worship his God immediately and directly, without the intercession of the elaborate ceremony and priesthood of Hinduism. Finally, if the peddler died on the road or sea, he could still go to heaven, for the Muslim celestial realm was not attached to any particular earthly locale.

Islam, unlike Hinduism, explicitly idealized the vocation of trade. Trade was, after all, the vocation of the prophet during his early manhood. Bourgeois commercial values such as frugality, diligence, honesty, and dependability were praised by Islam, whereas under Hindu-Javanese, bourgeois trade was a necessity but not a virtue, and it was actively discouraged by Mataram. The most glorious life style for the Javanese Hindu was modeled after that of the god-king who expressed his greatness by ostentatious display and haughty indolence. Though he could not be a god-king, the Hindu-Javanese official could emulate him to an extent fitting to his own station, and his own devotion to duty did not imply the frugal efficiency of the ideal modern civil servant.

The greatest abangan fear was that some particular ceremony, the doctrinal meaning of which was of little concern, might be left undone; the consequence might be disturbance of heart and community by the swarming spirits. The santri, though obsessively following the ritual of the five prayers, was generally less concerned with ritual than with formulating God's word as a system of ethical principles that could guide his life. One outgrowth of this santri bent toward doctrinal systematization was the Muslim law, sjariah, which inevitably conflicted with the rites and customs, the adat, imbedded in the kinship and community organization of the local tribes. A second outgrowth was Indonesia's first system of mass education, the system of pesantrèn, which taught not only mystical theosophy but also the language, the texts, and the doctrine of Islam. In association with the pesantrèn stood the militant intellectual, the kiai, who threatened to rebel against the courtly hierarchy in the name of that doctrine which he taught. The Indianized Javanese kingdoms had their Hindu-Buddhist hermits and monks, but they served as tutors for the kings, and they do not appear to have opposed the court so militantly.[16]

Islam imagined history as linear. History flowed from Adam to Abraham, from Moses to Jesus, climaxing in Muhammed and resolving on Judgment Day. The Hindu-Javanese concept of history was cyclical rather than linear; history would pass through four phases, followed by the destruction of the world, after which the cycle would begin all over again. As in the Judeo-Christian conception, Muslims believe that God interceded in history, to punish and reward by plague and deliverance, but never could He be incarnated as an earthly king.

Linear too is the Muslim notion of the individual life history. The Hindu may be reborn repeatedly, and each rebirth awards an opportunity to live his life so as to raise his status in the next life. The Muslim, having but one life in which to gain his salvation or doom himself to eternal damnation, is called to a tense struggle: during this one life he must prove that he deserves heaven instead of hell.

Islam would seem to have encouraged a certain dynamism among Indonesian teachers, defiant holy men, and traders. Especially the traders gained from Islam a sense that their vocation was meaningful and legitimate, and in this way Islam stimulated the growth of trade; to this day, most of the devout Indonesian Muslims are merchants, and most of the successful indigenous Indonesian merchants are devout Muslims. Observing the correlation between being Muslim and being a merchant, and between the coming of Islam and the rise of trade, one might suggest a similarity to the thesis expounded by Max Weber in *The Protestant Ethic and the Spirit of Capitalism.* Weber observed the tendency for European capitalists to be Protestants, and the correlation between the eruption of Protestantism and the rise of capitalism in seventeenth-century Europe.[17] A close examination of Weber's thesis and the Indonesian case suggests, however, that the parallel is spurious in both its economic and its religious aspects.

Indonesian commerce was not "capitalistic" in Weber's sense. Workers were not free wage earners employed in factories, but peasants, artisans, and slaves. Businessmen were not rising industrialists of the capitalist–Calvinist prototype, but patrician princes or itinerant merchants. Production was not in mechanized factories but in peasant fields or cottages. Business was not the methodical, rationalized life way of Weber's ascetic capitalist but of an adventurous, get-rich-quick variety, often depending on piracy.

Nor was Indonesian Islam "Protestant" in Weber's sense, though it was certainly more so than Javanese Hinduism. Early Indonesian Islam was strongly Sufistic and syncretic. Its attraction lay partly in mystical ecstasy, magical charms, and theosophic schemes. It deviated from the egalitarianism of original Islam to treat the kiai as a sacral, charismatic figure and to award exalted status to him who claimed to be a *sayyid*, a descendant of the Prophet. Instead of drawing his own conclusions from the scripture, as the Protestant was supposed to do, the Muslim should submit to the authority of such a figure. Early Protestantism in Europe, especially Calvinism, encouraged the decline of kingship and aristocracy, but Islam supported the rule of sultans. In short, early Indonesian Islam, by comparison with the Calvinistic Protestantism from which Weber drew his image of the Protestant ethic, was more feudal than egalitarian, more mystical than scripturalist, more magical than purist, and more medieval than modern.

Closer than the parallel with the Protestants is that with their predecessors, the medieval European mystics such as those of fourteenth-century Germany. The German Gottesfreunde movement,[18] which included such figures as Meister Eckhart, Heinrich Seuse, and the Johannes Tauler who inspired Martin Luther, flourished, like Sufism, along the trade routes and among merchants. Like the Sufis, the Gottesfreunde rejected the ossified hierarchy of medieval religion, its canon law, and its priesthood, but they retained certain feudal loyalties and, indeed, drew monks and patrons from the patrician and noble classes. Like the Sufis, the Gottesfreunde taught stages of meditation leading toward an ecstatic union with the transcendent. Some of the Gottesfreunde, notably Eckhart, developed rich speculative philosophies elucidating the inner nature of the creator and his bond to the created. The Gottesfreunde resembled the Sufis in bringing a fresh spirit of dynamism, individualism, subjectivism, and freedom to a society that stressed the static, the hierarchical, and the ceremonial. Freeing the inner life, the Gottesfreunde, like the Sufis, did not directly attack the structure of feudal society.

In Europe, the mystics and merchants soon gave way to the Protestants and the capitalists. The resulting surge of capitalistic expansion into oriental seas resulted, ironically, in the Indonesian-Malayan commercial and mystical phase being followed by colonialism. The Dutch arrived at the turn of the seventeenth century, and the Muslim reformation was postponed until the twentieth.[19]

REFERENCES

[1] J. D. Legge, *Indonesia* (Englewood Cliffs, N.J.: Prentice-Hall, 1964), p. 43.

[2] G. W. Drewes, "New Light on the Coming of Islam to Indonesia," *Bijdragen tot de Taal-, Land-en Volkenkunde*, Vol. 124 (1968), p. 443. Drewes' article is a comprehensive review of evidence and theory on the coming of Islam to Indonesia. Also see W. F. Stutterheim, *Cultuurgeschiedenis van Indonesië*, Vol. III: *De Islam en zijn komst in de archipel* (Groningen: J. B. Wolters, 1951).

[3] The following remarks on Sufism derive from Anthony H. Johns, "Sufism as a Category in Indonesian Literature and History," *Journal of Southeast Asia History*, Vol. II, No. 2 (1961), pp. 10–23.

[4] G. W. J. Drewes, "Indonesia: Mysticism and Activism," in Gustave E. von Grunebaum (ed.), *Unity and Variety in Muslim Civilization* (Chicago: Univ. of Chicago Press, 1955), p. 298. Drewes vividly describes the development of Islamic education in Sumatra and Java.

[5] B. Schrieke, *Indonesian Sociological Studies, Part II: Ruler and Realm in Early Java* (The Hague: Van Hoeve, 1957), pp. 249–253.

[6] Drewes, "Indonesia: Mysticism and Activism," pp. 298–299.

[7] The term "santri" originally denoted the student in a *pesantrèn* but

now refers to all Muslims in Java who piously practice their faith; the "abangan" fail to do so. Though the terms "santri" and "abangan" are Javanese, the behavioral types they denote are pan-Indonesian; it is useful to employ the widely publicized terms "santri" and "abangan" to refer to the pan-Indonesian patterns. Descriptions of the contrast between santri and abangan appear in Clifford Geertz, *Religion of Java* (New York: Free Press of Glencoe, 1959), Chap. 10; R. M. Koentjaraningrat, "The Javanese of South Central Java," in George Peter Murdock (ed.), *Social Structure in Southeast Asia*, Viking Fund Publications in Anthropology (Chicago: Quadrangle, 1960), pp. 88–115; Robert Jay, *Religion and Politics in Rural Central Java*, Cultural Report Series 12 (New Haven, Conn.: Southeast Asia Studies, Yale University, 1963).

[8] For details on the abangan, see Geertz, *Religion of Java*, Part 1.

[9] The following description of Mataram is taken from Soemarsaid Moertono, *State and Statecraft in Old Java: A Study of the Later Mataram Period, 16th to 19th Century* (Ithaca, N.Y.: Modern Indonesia Project, Cornell University, 1963); and from David Joel Steinberg et al., *In Search of Southeast Asia: A Modern History* (New York: Praeger, 1971), pp. 80–86.

[10] Moertono, *State and Statecraft*, p. 57.

[11] *Ibid.*, p. 97.

[12] *Ibid.*, pp. 96–97.

[13] Justus M. van der Kroef, "Prince Diponegoro: Progenitor of Indonesian Nationalism," *Far Eastern Quarterly*, Vol. 8, No. 4 (1949), pp. 424–450.

[14] This section draws on ideas presented in W. F. Wertheim, *Indonesian Society in Transition: A Study of Social Change*, 2nd rev. ed. (The Hague and Bandung: Van Hoeve, 1959), Chap. 8; and Clifford Geertz, *The Development of the Javanese Economy: A Socio-Cultural Approach* (Ann Arbor, Mich.: University Microfilms, 1956), pp. 88–93.

[15] Hildred Geertz, "Indonesian Cultures and Communities," in Ruth T. McVey (ed.), *Indonesia* (New Haven, Conn.: Southeast Asia Studies, Yale University, 1963), p. 69.

[16] See Theodore Pigeaud, *Java in the Fourteenth Century: A Study in Cultural History*, 5 vols. (The Hague: Nijhoff, 1960–1963), Vol. IV, pp. 95–100.

[17] Legge, *Indonesia*, p. 47, imputes to Clifford Geertz the view that Islam in Indonesia plays "a role not unlike that ascribed by Weber to Protestantism in Europe—the role of handmaiden to a commercial class." Actually, in the source cited by Legge, Geertz does not explicitly parallel European Protestantism and Indonesian Islam. In fact, he refers to Weber only to indicate that Indonesian commerce was *not* capitalistic in Weber's sense, but instead *pre*-capitalistic. (See C. Geertz, *Development of the Javanese Economy*, p. 90 and n. 111.) Here Geertz seems to *deny* the relation between the Indonesian case and the Weber thesis, since Weber argued not that Protestantism was "handmaiden to a commercial class," but that it encouraged something quite distinct from mere commerce, namely, "rational, bourgeois, capitalism." See

Talcott Parsons, *The Structure of Social Action* (Glencoe, Ill.: Free Press, 1949), pp. 503–513; for a brief overview, see James L. Peacock and A. Thomas Kirsch, *The Human Direction* (New York: Appleton-Century-Crofts, 1970), pp. 208–216.

[18] Relevant aspects of the Gottesfreunde movement are reported in James L. Peacock, "Mystics and Merchants in Fourteenth Century Germany," *Journal for the Scientific Study of Religion*, Vol. VIII (1969), pp. 47–59.

[19] In tracing sources of interpretations presented in this chapter, special mention should be made of the Dutch writings on Indonesian Islam which long ago introduced most of the concepts employed by contemporary Indonesianists. A classic is Snouck Hurgronje's "Brieven van een Wedana Pension" in his *Verspreide Geschriften* (Bonn and Leipzig: Kurt Schroeder, 1924), vol. 4, part I, pp. 111–249. Published originally in 1890, Hurgronje's well-known essay explicitly elaborates the distinction between "santri" and non-santri Javanese (as well as Sundanese) while expertly portraying the major religious patterns of these groups. Other Dutch writings have elucidated aspects of the "santri" which are more subtle than those discussed in this chapter or in other English-language writings. See Th. Pigeaud, *Javaanse Volksvertoningen* (Batavia: Volkslectuur, 1938), pp. 471–472 or Koes Sardjono, *De Botjah-Angon (Herdesjongen) in de Javaanse Cultuur* (Leiden: unpublished dissertation, Rijksuniversiteit te Leiden, 1947).

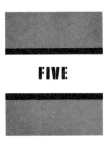

FIVE

EUROPEAN PENETRATION

By 1500 the South Malay port of Malacca was a cosmopolitan city of Indians, Persians, Arabs, Chinese, Malays, and Indonesians, altogether some 15,000 merchants. Travelers of the day report that more ships were anchored in Malacca than anywhere else in the world and that more commerce was carried on there than in any port of Europe. The Portuguese D'Albuquerque was so impressed by Malacca's wealth and acitvity that he wrote, "If the city could be wrested from the Moors, Cairo and Mecca would be impoverished, and Venice dependent on the spice trade from Lisbon."[1] In 1511, the Portuguese did wrest the city from the Moors, and, though hard pressed by raids from the Indonesian Buginese, managed to hold onto it for the next half century. From the Malaccan base, the Portuguese endeavored to monopolize trade in spices issuing from the so-called Spice Islands, the Moluccas. Unfortunately for them, those islands had recently come under the control of Islamic merchant princes, the strongest of whom were the sultans of the twin mountain isles of Ternate and Tidore. After a half century of struggle with these sultans, who ruled a great portion of the eastern islands, the Portuguese had still failed to achieve dominance in those islands, much less in Indonesia as a whole. The quantity of Indonesian trade was much less for the Portuguese than for the combined shipping of the Chinese, Japanese, Siamese, Javanese, Indian, and Arab merchants.

During the years following the Portuguese capture of Malacca, two Islamic sultanates of significance arose in the western islands: Atjeh and Demak. Atjeh on north Sumatra across the strait from Malacca took over Malacca's role in the Muslim trade around the straits, and through a series of "holy wars" achieved a monopoly of Sumatran pepper production and commerce. In the sixteenth century, Atjeh extended its control to the west coast of Sumatra, converting the state of Minang-kabau to Islam.

Demak, a sultanate on the north coast of Java, had developed commercial connections with the Moluccas during the reign of Malacca, and it continued to exploit those islands even after the Portuguese takeover. Bantam, on Java's west coast, became Demak's ally, and together they controlled trade on the Java coast and even in the Java interior until the seventeenth century when Mataram subjugated the north-coast kingdoms. After trade on the Java coast was destroyed by Mataram, some Javanese merchants retreated to Borneo and the south Celebes state, Makasar, which then experienced its golden age of commercial and cultural florescence. Mataram continued to forbid trade by private merchants under penalty of death, and by 1657 Java, formerly known as the "granary of the East," could no longer undertake the shipment of rice; by 1677 the Javanese were regarded as an agrarian people, ignorant of the sea. Before the beginning of the seventeenth century, the Javanese had been capitalists on a par with the Europeans in the sense that both were at an early but potentially dynamic stage of development. But with the seventeenth-century suppression of trade by Mataram and the seventeenth-century surge of economic expansion by the Dutch, a great gulf developed between the Javanese and European economies. The one became increasingly agrarian and conservative, the other increasingly capitalistic and progressive.

Four Dutch ships arrived in Bantam, Java, in 1596. They were cordially received, and subsequent years saw a succession of Dutch ships brave the rigors of the trip to the Indies (a quarter of each crew could expect to die en route through such inconveniences as water so polluted that sailors preferred to drink their own urine). The Dutch joined the Portuguese, the English, and the Spanish in the search for profit within Indonesian waters. In 1602 the Dutch formed the Netherlands United East India Company or VOC (Vereenigde Oostindische Compagnie), the organization through which, in succeeding years, they would push their European rivals from the Indies.

Even after eight years of trading, however, the situation was hardly encouraging for the "Gentlemen Seventeen" who were the directors of the VOC. They had not yet succeeded in paying a single dividend to stockholders, and certainly they did not dominate trade in the archipelago. They were small fish in the eastern oceans, a mere thread in the oriental tapestry woven largely by the Chinese, Indians, Arabs, and other Asians. The Dutch merchants were treated just like any other traders who engaged in petty transactions with the locals; they would shop for peppers on the open market in Bantam, bargain for cloves at the house of a rich man in Ambon, pay taxes to a ruler of Atjeh. The transactions of the Orientals dwarfed those of the Dutch. As late as 1625 a Chinese junk could earn in a single shipment a tenth of the VOC's total annual capital, and a merchant of Masulipatham could sell in one transaction a third of the VOC's total cloth sales for an entire year.[2]

Yet by the last quarter of the seventeenth century, the Dutch had accomplished much. They had achieved some measure of control over virtually all island commerce, they monopolized spice trade in the eastern islands, and they had eliminated much of their indigenous and foreign competition. Stubborn hard work, comparatively rational business organization, and the Calvinist ethic probably had something to do with the Dutch success, but crucial too were their stronger cannons and faster ships.[3]

The efficient, diligent, shrewd, and ruthless Jan Pieterszoon Coen sailed for the Indies at age 21 as a second merchant of the VOC. By the age of 28 he was author of a plan to give the Dutch a monopoly over all trade in Southeast Asia, and by 31 he was governor-general of the company in the East Indies. When Coen took office in 1618, the Bandanese were grumbling about Dutch efforts to monopolize the spices, and several Dutchmen had been assassinated. Coen proceeded to secure the monopoly by personally leading an expedition of warships, practically exterminating the Bandanese population, and carrying the bulk of the survivors to Batavia (present-day Djakarta) as slaves. Monopolizing the spices, the Dutch periodically chopped down spice trees in order to hold the supply low so that prices would remain high, a procedure that reduced the islanders' ability to produce and crippled their formerly blooming economy.[4]

In 1668 the Dutch crushed Makassar in the southern Celebes, which had served as a last stapling point for Javanese and other merchants smuggling spices out of the Dutch-controlled Moluccas. Bantam remained free of Mataram domination and operated as a busy emporium until, during the years from 1682 to 1684, the Dutch aided the son of the Bantam sultan in a revolt against his father. Once in control of Bantam, the Dutch drove the British and the Portuguese out of that port and nearly everywhere else in the archipelago. Through exploiting local conflicts in the fashion of the Bantam affair, the Dutch gained control of a great number of Indonesian communities and they imposed a variety of restrictive commercial treaties on lesser trading states along the entire route of the Java Sea. By the late seventeenth century, the VOC was the "paramount naval power from Atjeh to the Moluccas—dominating trade in these waters, carrying all the lucrative cloves and nutmegs, half or more of the tin and pepper, and much more besides."[5]

Meanwhile, back on Java, Coen had founded Batavia in 1619. In a series of attacks, Sultan Agung of Mataram had endeavored to oust the foreign irritant from the motherland. He launched a massive campaign in 1629, marching tens of thousands of soldiers and carrying tons of equipment through the exceedingly difficult terrain stretching several hundred miles between central Java and Batavia. Agung unfortunately chose to transport the army's food on ships sailing along Java's east coast. Coen, employing the superior Dutch navy, attacked and destroyed some 200 of these transport ships, so that the besieging army was threatened with famine. After a few weeks of sporadic attack on Coen's garrison in Batavia, the starving army of Mataram was forced to retreat in a long, miserable march home, leaving many dead men and buffalo along the way.

In 1645 Sultan Agung died, and in 1646 his son presided over a treaty between Batavia and Mataram. Mataram gave the VOC *de facto* recognition in exchange for 60,000 guilders per year to be paid to the sultan as tribute. In 1674 Trunadjaja of Madura revolted against Mataram, causing Susuhunan Amangkurat to escape to east Java while the Madurese took over the capital. Dying from exhaustion during his flight to the coast, the susuhunan advised his son to enlist Dutch aid in repulsing the rebels. The son did ask for help. The Dutch obliged, they crushed the rebels, and the new ruler of Mataram received his crown from the hands of a Dutch soldier. In return for their military aid, the Dutch made Mataram practically a vassal of the VOC. Subsequent intercessions gave the Dutch more and more of the territory of Mataram. Concluding a treaty with that kingdom in 1705, the Dutch became masters not only of the sea but also, in effect, of Java.

By the mid-eighteenth century, cloves, nutmeg, and pepper were no longer the economically important prizes. Far more important was the coffee that was now being cultivated by the several million inhabitants of Java. Transferring its attention from the seas and spices to Java and the coffee, the VOC reduced its navy and ceased to control interisland trade and shipping. During the next century, the Dutch would be concerned primarily with agrarian Java.

SOCIETY AND CULTURE
IN JAVA, 1750–1870[6]

During the mid-eighteenth century, the kingdom of Mataram was divided among three houses located in the two principalities of Jogjakarta and Surakarta. Though largely autonomous in their internal affairs, the rulers of Mataram along with those of certain other kingdoms were controlled by Batavia through treaties and Dutch-appointed ministers (*patih*). The rest of Java was VOC territory, ruled either directly by the Dutch or indirectly through the local lords and prijaji in their own lands. This Dutch-dominated structure was to remain essentially intact until World War II.

As before, the native regents extracted agricultural tribute from the peasants. But now they turned it over to the VOC instead of the sultan or king. In the Prianger region of west Java, the regents were subjected to the so-called "Forced Delivery" system introduced in 1723. Required to deliver specified annual quotas of coffee to the VOC, they received as payment the right to collect from the peasants their traditional taxes of labor and rice. In other areas prijaji or even Chinese were hired to collect produce for the VOC. Thus the hierarchy existing under Mataram remained, but now the regents could look to the stable and powerful rule of the VOC to back their authority; and, of course, profits now flowed into the Dutch treasury.

The VOC had replaced Mataram in political and economic position, but it did not rival it in culture and style of life. The Dutch capital, Batavia, which Coen had founded in 1619, was a settlement designed to imitate the Dutch towns. Poorly adapted to the tropics, Batavia's multistoried, closely packed houses were stuffy, its canals stagnant and disease-ridden, its square fort steamy and ill-smelling. The puritanical Dutch wore heavy woollens in the tropic heat and they reportedly bathed but once per week at best. The governor-general, Coen, and his staff of fever-stricken and underpaid clerks labored in the unhealthy innards of the fort from 6:00 A.M. to 6:00 P.M., after which they broke for dinner, then returned to work into the night if work remained to be done. The death rate of eighteenth-century settlers of Batavia was greater than that of modern soldiers in battle, and Coen himself died of a tropical disease when he was still in his early forties, at the conclusion of his defeat of the sultan of Mataram in 1628.[7]

Social and cultural life in Batavia is best described as raw and mestizo. Since few Dutch wives were brought to that frontier town, the Dutchmen took Makassarese, Balinese, or other native concubines, and their mestizo offspring usually spoke Portuguese or Malay, rarely Dutch or Javanese. Few Javanese lived in Batavia, which was largely inhabited by Chinese, Portuguese-Indians, and Indonesians from the outer islands, both freed men and slaves. Though Batavian religious life was sparsely developed (few of the cynical realists of the VOC saw much point in Christian missions), its status system was based on religious affiliation. Of highest status were the Christians (Dutch, mestizos, and enfranchised Christian slaves). Next highest were the Chinese, after them the native non-Christian population.[8] Western education and the arts were not prominent in Batavia, though the first poet of America's New York, Jacob Steendam, did live there as manager of an orphanage,[9] and historians record the existence of a scientific society and a few moralistic theatrical performances.

Rendered politically impotent by the Dutch, the Mataram courts left to them the task of empire-building and turned inward to elaborate and refine the civilization inherited from Madjapahit. The century after the founding of Batavia is regarded by some as the period of greatest florescence of Javanese art. During this period the *bedojo ketawang* was introduced, according to legend, by the goddess of the South Seas, as she sang and danced before Sultan Agung to express her love for him.[10] The *serimpi* dance, performed exclusively by maidens of the royal family, became fantastically fluid, graceful, and stylized. Crafted by noblewomen, the hand-printed, wax-molded designs of *batik* fabrics became ever more splendid, intricate, and richly colored. The percussion orchestra (*gamelan*) developed special systems such as the three-tone scale that played during the *sekatèn* ceremony to commemorate the birth and death of the Prophet. The sultan himself introduced a new dance drama, the *wajang wong*, in which humans (*wong*) imitated the movements of puppets of the wajang kulit. The repertoire of the wajang kulit itself expanded, the form of the puppets achieved their present refinement, and new instrumental and vocal wajang composi-tions were created. Most striking of all, in this "Byzantine time . . . the modern Javanese court etiquette and the modern Javanese court language obtained their perfection and polish."[11] The sanskritized high Javanese language called *krama* was consciously developed to aggrandize the status of the elite, and the Javanese language became a system of graded sublanguages ranging from ultra-refined *krama inggil* down to the earthy and everyday *ngoko*. Speaking the high language to his superi-ors, the low to his inferiors, the Javanese perfected a linguistic instru-ment of immense subtlety and precision for delineating gradations of rank.

Lacking medieval Europe's strong middle class of traders and artisans to criticize and oppose the courtly tradition and to mediate between court and peasant, Javanese society allowed courtly forms to penetrate popular life far deeper than in the West. The villager became adept at the graded Javanese language whose higher levels he should speak to those of exalted status, such as the regent. Lowering his body as well as elevating his language, the peasant was most worshipful toward the regent, who was the highest representative of the court and govern-ment with whom most peasants dealt. The gusti-kawula relationship between king and regent held, at a lower level, between regent and peasant. In time, however, the regents would come to be stripped of the more obvious facets of their sacral status and transformed, to a degree, into functionaries of the Dutch bureaucracy.

DEFEUDALIZATION OF THE REGENTS

A year before the end of the eighteenth century, the debt- and corrup-tion-ridden VOC collapsed. Its properties were appropriated by the Dutch government, as Holland allied itself with revolutionary France and a Bonaparte became its ruler.[12] Eventually a Napoleonic marshal, Herman Daendals, was appointed the new governor-general of the Indies, a post which he assumed in 1808. Daendals, in his early life a dedicated revolutionary, now became a bullheaded administrator, and he was determined to strip Java of its traditional, patrimonial structure. After his rule ended in 1811, the English took over Java and appointed as governor-general Sir Stamford Raffles. Later to found Singapore, Raffles was tireless, brilliant, scholarly, ambitious, and as dedicated an opponent of traditional "feudalism" as the corpulent Daendals. After Dutch rule was restored to the Indies in 1816, a decade and a half of governor-generals held reformist and rationalist persuasions similar to those of Daendals and Raffles; the first quarter of Java's nineteenth century was a period of liberal reform.

Daendals, Raffles, and their successors strove mightily to transform the native social hierarchy into the rational bureaucracy and society of French Napoleonic and British Liberal ideals. In twenty years the new governor-generals of Java reduced the regents' retinues to a tenth of their former size; they stripped them of ranks, titles, and the parasols that had served as their symbols of authority. They prohibited the feasts that invited the people to participate in the regents' magnificence at circumcision, marriage, and promotion.[13] They denied the regents' hereditary succession, and instead of allowing the regents to collect their customary tribute in labor and produce, they paid them salaries. Finally, Raffles initiated a "land rent" system. Under that arrangement, the peasant would cease to pay tribute in kind to the regent, but would pay instead a tax in cash. It was expected that this requirement would encourage the peasant to raise his production so that he could market enough to pay his tax, fill his needs, and still reap a profit.

REFEUDALIZATION

The exalted status of the regent, deeply embodied in Javanese culture and bolstered by a century of VOC authority, could not be abolished overnight by law. Nor did the Europeans themselves find it easy to change the old arrangements. Through the regents, after all, coffee and sugar had been delivered and profits had been made. The liberal policy introduced by Raffles was given the final ax by the Java War of Prince Diponegoro. Financially weakened by the great costs of the war, the colony of the Indies desperately needed agricultural productivity to regain solvency. The new governor-general of 1830, Van den Bosch, determined to regain such productivity through the Cultivation System, which was a new version of Forced Delivery.

Under the Cultivation System, the villager grew export crops on his rice fields. In theory, production of these export crops would require no more labor or land than did rice and would be limited by law, but in practice this was not the case. The quotas of exportable crops that the villagers were required to deliver to the Dutch as a form of taxation were raised above the legal level. Villagers were compensated for the export crops, but living costs rose faster than the compensation, hence the lot of the peasant under the Cultivation System was worse than before. In addition, the villager was required to build roads, dikes, and do other compulsory and unpaid labor for the regents and the government. Feudal tendencies reasserted themselves as titles, ranks, and ceremonials for officials were prescribed by government regulations.

Although payment in cash for agriculture could have stimulated native economic initiative, the process was short-circuited by the presence of the overlord between farmer and market. The overlord—the government—kept the price fixed even though international market prices fluctuated. The farmer's goods brought high prices on the international market, but under the Cultivation System profits entered the treasury of the Dutch government, not the pockets (or *sarong*) of the Indonesian farmer.

In spite of the money the Dutch made from the Cultivation System, it came under fire in the Netherlands. Liberals argued that even more gain would come from a system of free enterprise, and they demanded that the colony be opened to European entrepreneurs. Humanitarian and religious groups deplored the hardships that the Cultivation System caused the natives. The humanitarian position was strengthened by the 1860 publication of *Max Havelaar*, written by the former colonial official E. Douwes Dekker under the pseudonym Multatuli ("Much I have suffered").[14] That novel excoriates the Dutch authorities and satirizes the Dutch bourgeois while exposing the abuses experienced by the native under the Cultivation System. Bruised by attacks from many quarters, the system finally expired with the institution of the Agrarian and Sugar Laws of 1870. These laws were designed both to encourage free enterprise and to protect the native from its excesses.

By the end of the Cultivation System, the outlines of a bureaucracy—that system which caused Multatuli such discomfort—were apparent. It was a dual system based on race, with top statuses reserved for Europeans. The highest officials were the Dutch residents, responsible for coordinating the tasks of government in territorial divisions called "residencies." Each residency comprised several regencies formerly headed formally by native regents, but these regents were advised and supervised by their "big brothers," the Dutch controllers, who frequently carried the real power while the regent bore the golden umbrella of status. Responsible to the regent were Indonesian district and subdistrict officers who linked the government to the village, which was headed by a *lurah*. Regarded by the Dutch as functionaries within a bureaucracy, the Javanese officials continued to be perceived by the Javanese as a literati representing traditions of kingship and nobility—in a word, as the prijaji.

Race was the basis of status in the wider society as well as in the bureaucracy. Europeans composed the top stratum, of course. Indo-Europeans gained at least legal membership in that stratum if they descended from a Caucasian father either as his legitimate child or as his illegitimate child whom he recognized as his own. The lowest stratum was that of the natives or "inlanders." Only the native was subject by law to compulsory service and forced labor. The native mother of a child fathered by a European had no rights to guardianship of that child on the death of his father. In social as well as legal respects, the natives were regarded as a category of creature below the European.[15]

The in-between stratum was occupied by the Chinese and the half-caste or Indo, and the Indo too failed to gain full acceptance by the Europeans. The Europeans scorned not only the Indo's color, but also such tell-tale signs of impure origin as his "Indische" (Indies) speech. In the early days of the VOC, the Indo had spoken a pidgin Portuguese that was subsequently replaced by Malay mixed with Dutch. Ultimately the Indo spoke Dutch itself, but with an accent and grammar showing the influence of Malay. Multatuli describes the ill-educated Dutch businessman who jeers at the Indo's Malayized Dutch which does not conform to his own gutter dialect; and the Indo's sensitivity to his accent is revealed in an Indo woman's recent recollection of her pride at being mistaken for a Dutch woman at the other end of the telephone.[16] Within the Indo caste itself were substrata based on the extent of Hollandization of clothing, manner, and speech, and on skin color, the gradations of which were denoted by such slang phrases as "coffee and cream."[17]

Daendals had initiated the movement of Dutch elite out of Batavia to the cooler and more spacious suburbs of Weltevreden. In Weltevreden the stuffy canal houses gave way to airy, roomy, country villas inspired by palaces and mansions of the native regents. The bourgeois ethic of Holland, which hid the cozy parlor behind a frugal facade, was replaced by a pseudo-aristocratic Indische love of external display. The neo-prijaji Dutch officials and planters adopted sarongs, ceremonial umbrellas, retinues of slaves and servants, and elaborate rice dishes. To complete the mestizo pattern, they married Javanese wives or kept Javanese mistresses.

During this period the native regents apparently were less influenced by the Dutch than the Dutch by them. They were discouraged from speaking Dutch until late in the nineteenth century, and they were supposed to be addressed in Malay; according to one observer, in 1900 only four regents in all of Java spoke Dutch.[18] Few regents had acquired a Dutch education or much appreciation of Western culture and technology. Most were still absorbed in the florescence of Javanese culture itself, which centered in the courts. The day had not yet come when "the regent who formerly included in his retinue his horse, sitting mat, and betel seat [now preferred] a motor car, a leather armchair, and a cigarette case."[19] Nor had deeper change appeared: Dutch culture and Dutch language had not yet induced modes of thought that veered radically from those absorbed through native upbringing.

NON-JAVANESE PEOPLES, 1750–1870

As Java's coffee and sugar replaced the outer islands' cloves, nutmeg, and pepper as the prizes of world trade, the flow of commerce among the outer islands diminished. With that winding-down, the spread of Islamic and Malay culture slowed too. No major unifying trend like that produced through the fifteenth-, sixteenth-, and seventeenth-century spread of Islam, commerce, and the Malay language and culture is apparent in the eighteenth- and nineteenth-century history of the outer islands, and the history of these regions during this period becomes a mosaic of apparently unconnected local histories. Yet nineteenth-century developments occurring among certain non-Javanese peoples, notably the Chinese, the Minangkabau, the Batak, the Ambonese, the Minahasans, and the Buginese, can be viewed as preparing them for crucial roles in the modern history of Indonesia and adjacent regions.

The Chinese of course, had played crucial commercial roles throughout Indonesian history. Originating largely from the southeast China provinces of Fukien and Kwangtung, they were at Srividjaja both as merchants and as pilgrims. They had traded in the Javanese coastal centers, allegedly founding Semarang, and they had sailed down inland rivers such as the Brantas. Some even intermarried with Javanese from whom are descended families of the prijaji. When the Manchus overthrew the Ming Dynasty of 1644, anti-Manchu inhabitants of the overcrowded southeastern provinces felt a special incentive to migrate, and many came then to the Indies, the men still wearing the flowing dress and long-tressed hair style of the Ming period. In ports such as Bantam they distinguished themselves by their industry and shrewdness in trade, and they owned the most substantial homes in the city. The VOC found the Chinese useful as complements to the regents for collecting crops and taxes from the villages in east and central Java, and in all places the Chinese established themselves as middlemen between natives and Europeans. Neither the Dutch nor the Chinese were convinced of the moral uprightness and good taste of the other, but they

maintained cordial relationships on a commercial basis except for such
incidents as the Batavia massacre in the mid-eighteenth century, an
unfortunate occurrence initiated by a Dutch threat to enslave and exile
Chinese who could not prove themselves gainfully and honestly employed. In reaction, Chinese who were living in Batavia erupted into
rebellion, provoking a harsh government repression and the deaths of
thousands of Chinese in Batavia and elsewhere in Java.[20]

Where the Chinese settled in densely populated and highly developed societies such as that of Java, they tended to specialize in commerce, fitting themselves into that middle-level occupational niche left
unfilled by the natives, who, as in most agrarian and archaic societies,
tended to be either rulers or peasants. In these circumstances, the Chinese assimilated much of the native civilization and began to follow
native social customs. When the Chinese moved into relatively empty
areas, they naturally formed a larger proportion of the local population
than in the populous areas, and in many regions the Chinese were
in the majority—for example, in northeast Sumatra, the Riau and Lingga
archipelago, the islands of Bangka and Billiton, and in large parts of
western Borneo where the total Chinese population had grown to some
50,000 by 1850.[21] Settling into these sparsely populated and rather underdeveloped regions, the Chinese did not merely specialize in trade, but
diversified into all occupations including those of farming, fishing, mining, and lumbering. They retained, however, a strong Chinese identity.

From the sixteenth through the eighteenth centuries in Java, and
later elsewhere, male Chinese immigrants typically married local
women rather than Chinese women, for few Chinese women migrated
to Indonesia before World War I. The offspring of such unions married
among themselves, and an Indo-Chinese society became stabilized and
distinct. Such Indo-Chinese were called in Java *peranakan tionghoa*
(Chinese children of the Indies), and they absorbed native culture,
modifying their Chinese customs accordingly, in spheres ranging from
kinship to language.[22] Nevertheless, since the father was Chinese and
family names were inherited through the father, the distinctive Chinese
family name was retained as a badge of ethnic identity. Later, in the
twentieth century, the influx of female Chinese immigrants, the rise
of Chinese nationalism, and the creation of Chinese schools combined
to produce a new emphasis on pure Chinese identity, and there came
to exist the *totok* (immigrant), usually first or second generation, who
was more oriented toward China than toward Indonesia and who retained most of his Chinese customs. In Java the peranakans outnumber
the totoks two to one; in the outer islands totoks outnumber peranakans. In connection with their assimilation into the native culture,
the peranakans became somewhat less oriented toward trade than the
totoks, and more toward bureaucracy and aristocracy. But both types

of Chinese continued to dominate the Indonesian economy at every level below the macro, which was dominated by the European, and above the micro, which was the realm of the Indonesian.

Eighteenth-century Indonesian waters were infested with pirates. Especially fearful were the Moros from the Philippines. The Moros built three-storied galleys in the old Roman style, rowed by 150 men, that dared attack even the heavily armed vessels of the VOC. The headhunting Iban of Borneo engaged in piracy too, joining Arab and Malay coastal chiefs subordinate to the sultan of Brunei, and in the histories of such swashbucklers as Rajah Brooks, the white ruler of Sarawak, one hears much of such characters. But of greatest historical importance were piratical and seafaring activities of the Buginese. Under the harsh monopolies of the VOC, indigenous trade was stifled in the eastern waters, and the once thriving port city of Makassar was falling into decay. Out of the nearby kingdom of Bone swarmed the pirate fleets of the Buginese. They established themselves on Borneo's east coast, they helped the sultans of Borneo's west coast fight their destructive wars, and they threatened the Dutch in Malacca.[23] Ranging far from their kingdom of origin, the aggressive and status-conscious Buginese played a dominant role in Malayan politics, and in such Malay states as Johore and Selangor they became the ruling families, remaining so to this day.

Resembling the Java War in the use of Islam to oppose both colonialism and traditionalism, the Padri War was fought between 1821 and 1845 in west Sumatra. The Minangkabau of that region differed from the Javanese in their matrilineal tribal structure, their relative lack of Indianization, and their provinciality, but they were similar in their wet-rice agriculture, in certain modes of organizing and symbolizing their patrilineal kingdoms, and in their early syncretization of Sufist Islam with native custom or *adat*. Sufi orders had made a strong impact on the Minangkabau, and such practices as the seven stages of meditation leading to ecstatic union with the divine found avid devotees among them. Around 1800, however, Minangkabau pilgrims returning from Mecca brought anti-Sufi, antisyncretist ideas that were drawn from the Wahabite fundamentalism, a warlike movement sweeping Arabia. The returning pilgrims became fiery reformers. They called for the purification of Islam and the purging of such evil practices as gambling at cockfights, drinking, and smoking. Their movement was called *padri*. Adat chiefs reacted against the movement, since the customary order on which they based their power was threatened. War ensued. The Dutch, as was their wont, seized the opportunity to support the adat against Islam. Acquiring ruling power through the local divisiveness, they gained such authority among the Minangkabau that by 1840 they had managed to establish a system of compulsory coffee cultivation there as on Java.[24]

In the interior highlands of northeast Sumatra were concentrated the Batak tribes, who traced their origin to the scenic mountain lake Toba. A rugged, patrilineal, warlike people with massive stone statuary and barricaded villages, the Batak had had little contact with alien cultures other than that of the Malays in the towns and at the mouth of the navigable rivers flowing from the Sumatran highlands to the coast. The Portuguese governor of Malacca had tried to establish relations with the Batak during the middle of the sixteenth century in order to gain their help against the Atjehnese, but the first significant European contact did not come until the 1860s when German missionaries and Dutch administrators entered the highlands. At the same time the lowlands were being transformed through the coming of Western plantations into a vast estate that cultivated tobacco, rubber, palm oil, tea, and coconut. The work was done by wage labor, at first Chinese but later Indonesian. The plantations did not penetrate Batak lands, but a railroad was built from the coast to their borders, and eventually Batak began to migrate to the lowland city of Medan, which grew at the convergence of the plantations. Missionaries succeeded in converting many hundreds of Batak to Christianity, and they opened Christian schools from which Batak acquired the rudiments of a Western education. Thus equipped, the Batak later became prominent in positions of business and government throughout the archipelago. The same became true of the Minangkabau, whose Muslim reformism and Western education apparently affected them much like the Protestantism and schooling of the Batak.[25]

In the Moluccas, the Ambonese were a tribal group of headhunters until they were dominated by the Muslim sultan of Ternate, who introduced a regional rather than tribal form of society, and converted some villages to Islam. After the Muslims came the Catholic Portuguese, then the Calvinist Dutch, and the latter enjoyed considerable success in converting the Ambonese to Christianity (it was said that Coen spread bags of rice around the church to seduce the Ambonese natives into it, thus causing them to be labeled "rice Christians"). Because the Dutch made the town of Amboina their administrative center for the Moluccas and because the missionaries were diligent educators, there came to be a large group of educated Ambonese who were distributed throughout the Indies in the civil service, the schools, and the hospitals. The Ambonese also formed an important part of the Netherlands Indies army. After the revolution, many chose Dutch citizenship and were expatriated to Holland where some established a republic-in-exile in protest against the rule of the Indies by Indonesia. So Westernized were the Ambonese that they lost their indigenous language, which was replaced by Malay and Dutch. Similarly Westernized were the Minahasans of northern Celebes, who were headhunters before the

middle of the nineteenth century but were transformed in several dec-
ades into peasant and entrepreneurial farmers with a Christianized culture and a pidgin Dutch language. They too played a prominent role
in the Indies bureaucracy and army, and they perform similar roles
in modern Indonesia.[26]

The common theme running through the eighteenth- and nineteenth-century experiences of these diverse peoples—the Chinese, the
Buginese, the Batak, the Minangkabau, the Ambonese, and the Minha-
sans—is their dislocation from parochial roots. The dislocating forces
varied from seafaring and commerce to Christianization and colonization, but all introduced a cosmopolitanism, an involvement in international trade, Western culture, and colonial bureaucracy. Equipped with
such experiences, these non-Javanese groups, usually of less complex
cultural background than the Javanese, appropriated important roles
in the emergence of modern Indonesia.

REFERENCES

[1] J. C. van Leur, *Indonesian Trade and Society* (The Hague: Van Hoeve,
1955), p. 161.

[2] *Ibid.*, p. 203.

[3] *Ibid.*, p. 181. Van Leur denies that the Calvinist ethic or rational organization had anything to do with the Dutch success. I believe that he overstates
the case.

[4] George Masselman, *The Cradle of Colonialism* (New Haven: Yale Univ.
Press, 1963), pp. 229–253.

[5] David Joel Steinberg et al., *In Search of Southeast Asia: A Modern History* (New York: Praeger, 1971), p. 56.

[6] The thrust of this section owes much to Steinberg et al., Chap. 18.

[7] Masselman, *Cradle of Colonialism*, p. 453; Bernard H. M. Vlekke, *Nusantara: A History of Indonesia*, rev. ed. (The Hague and Bandung: Van Hoeve,
1959), pp. 187–190.

[8] W. F. Wertheim, *Indonesian Society in Transition: A Study of Social
Change*, 2nd rev. ed. (The Hague and Bandung: Van Hoeve, 1959), p. 136.

[9] Vlekke, *Nusantara*, p. 193.

[10] Claire Holt, *Art in Indonesia: Continuities and Change* (Ithaca, N.Y.:
Cornell Univ. Press, 1967), p. 116.

[11] D. H. Burger, *Structural Changes in Java: The Supra-village Sphere* (Ithaca, N.Y.: Modern Indonesia Project, Cornell University, 1957).

[12] Vlekke, *Nusantara*, pp. 236–254, gives a good account of the political
events of this unruly period.

[13] D. H. Burger, *Structural Changes*, pp. 15–19.

[14] *Max Havelaar*, trans. Roy Edwards, foreword by D. H. Lawrence (New York and London: House and Maxwell, 1967).

[15] Wertheim, *Indonesian Society in Transition*, pp. 137–138.

[16] Paul W. van der Veur, "Race and Color in Colonial Society: Biographical Sketches by a Eurasian Woman Concerning Pre-World War II Indonesia," *Indonesia*, No. 8 (1969), p. 75.

[17] Paul W. van der Veur, "Cultural Aspects of the Eurasian Community in Indonesian Colonial Society," *Indonesia*, No. 6 (1968), p. 38.

[18] D. H. Burger, *Structural Changes*, p. 17.

[19] *Ibid.*, p. 18.

[20] Victor Purcell, *The Chinese in Southeast Asia*, 2nd ed. (London: Oxford Univ. Press, 1965), pp. 404 ff., describes the Batavia riot. Purcell, Part VII, gives a general account of the Chinese in Indonesia during the colonial period.

[21] This paragraph derives from W. F. Wertheim, *East-West Parallels: Sociological Approaches to Modern Asia* (Chicago: Quadrangle, 1965), pp. 43–49. Also see James C. Jackson, *Chinese in the West Borneo Goldfields: A Study in Cultural Geography* (Hull, England: University of Hull, 1970).

[22] G. William Skinner, "The Chinese Minority," in Ruth T. McVey (ed.), *Indonesia* (New Haven, Conn.: Southeast Asia Studies, Yale University, 1963), pp. 105–110.

[23] Vlekke, *Nusantara*, p. 206.

[24] Steinberg et al., *In Search of Southeast Asia*, p. 145.

[25] Edward M. Bruner, "Urbanization and Ethnic Identity in North Sumatra," *American Anthropologist*, Vol. 63 (1961), pp. 508–521, and "Medan: the Role of Kinship in an Indonesian City" in Alexander Spoehr (ed.), *Pacific Port Towns and Cities* (Honolulu: Bishop Museum Press, 1963), pp. 1–12.

[26] Hildred Geertz, "Indonesian Cultures and Communities," in McVey, *Indonesia*, pp. 92–94.

SIX

SOCIAL CHANGE: 1870–1940

With the instituting of the 1870 Agrarian Law, Indonesia was opened to private entrepreneurs, and the so-called "liberal" period in Dutch colonial history began. Under the Agrarian Law, foreign capitalists could acquire land in the Indies from the colonial government or by lease from Indonesians. The dream of quick wealth from plantations in a tropical land of opportunity soon caught the European imagination. Formerly many Europeans who populated the Indies were the misfit and ne'er-do-well whose presence was not appreciated in Europe, but now the lure of the East attracted some of the more dynamic, able, and venal men of the West. By 1872 some 36,467 Europeans and Indo-Europeans inhabited Indonesia; by 1892 there were 58,806. Before 1870 most of the Europeans in the Indies were colonial officials, by 1892 the officials were far outnumbered by entrepreneurs, planters, and clerks, who came to profit under the thriving economy. Economic growth under liberalism dwarfed that occurring under the Cultivation System. Between 1870 and 1930, the exports from the Indies increased from 107 million to 1,160 million guilders.[1]

Economic growth was accompanied by territorial expansion. European enterprise and government spread to the outer islands. The east coast of Sumatra, formerly populated largely by Malays who fished and hunted turtles in the marshes, now was open for vast plantations. Governmental authority was consolidated in Borneo, the Celebes, the Moluccas, and the Lesser Sundas. Through treaties encouraged occasionally by blitzkrieg-like raids of highly mobile and lightly armed special forces, some 300 states were brought under control by 1910. The Netherlands Indies came to stretch, as Sukarno later put it, from Sabang (in northern Sumatra) to Merauke (in western New Guinea). Worthy of note is the late date of governmental consolidation of the outer islands.

Those who speak of 350 years of Dutch rule are correct only if by "rule" they mean limited claims and vague influences. Before the twentieth century, relations between the Indies government and states on the outer islands were more international than domestic.

Even in the late nineteenth century, resistance to Dutch control was strong in some areas. The state of Atjeh put up the strongest fight, and only after 25 years of tortured struggle that cost much money and many dead were the Dutch able to pacify the Atjehnese. The force behind Atjehnese resistance was Islam. The Atjehnese, who were pious Muslims, saw the war against the Dutch as a holy one, and their struggle was applauded by santri throughout the islands. An Islamologist, Snouck Hurgronje, became aware of this sentiment while living in Mecca disguised as a Muslim in order to make a scholarly study of the holy city and its Indies pilgrims. Back in the Indies, Hurgronje lived for six months in Atjeh, wrote a detailed tome on their customs, and discovered the source of the Atjehnese holy war: the religious teachers. He noted that many of the secular authorities, the adat chiefs, had surrendered early in the war, after which leadership was assumed by the teachers, who had constructed forts and collected contributions, appealing to the people by envisioning the struggle against the Dutch as a path of paradise.[2] Following Hurgronje's advice, the Dutch managed to disengage the adat chiefs from the influence of the teachers. After pacifying the chiefs, they persecuted the teachers, pursuing them into their remotest hiding places. Resistance was broken and the war was won by about 1910.

Territorial expansion was accompanied by advances in transport. In old times the journey overland from Java's west to its center took weeks, as in Sultan Agung's tragic and laborious march to Batavia. Travel on the sea by junk or *perahu* was faster but undependable, for the vessel could be marooned for days in windless seas. The problem of wind was solved by the steamship, and a steamship line, the KPM, came to connect most of the islands. An extensive railway and one of the best road systems in Southeast Asia was constructed on Java, through a sometimes gruesome exploitation of forced peasant labor.

As interisland transport developed, Indies administration became centralized. The guilder became the standard national currency after 1900,[3] replacing the wildly varying local coinage. Taxes, laws, and systems of banking were standardized. Commonplace in the contemporary urbanized world, such centralization had great import in the more populated areas of Indonesia. It remained true that remote islands used bronze gongs as currency and that diverse tribes enforced justice according to their particular adat (customary law), but the dominant trend was toward interisland integration.

Like the rest of Southeast Asia, the Indies colony was an exporter of tropical raw materials and an importer of foreign manufactured goods. Few native industries developed to challenge the quantity, quality, price, and prestige of Western imports, nor did the colonial government encourage such development. Few natives became entrepreneurs in the extraction and distribution of raw produce either, for Westerners and Chinese dominated this field.

CAPITALISTS: INDONESIAN, CHINESE, AND WESTERN[4]

It would be wrong to depict the Indonesian peasant as too numbed by custom and tradition to react to economic opportunities of the liberal period, but it is true that he was part of a culture and society that discouraged the methodically individualistic quest for gain. The typical peasant was settled in a subsistence way of life, producing more or less what he needed and bartering for the rest, plus producing his quota for the regent. Entangled in interwoven obligations—to gods, spirits, regents, kinsmen, and neighbors—he could not pursue profit freely even if he desired to do so. Ecological limits imposed themselves too, especially in central Java where land was already too scarce for the peasant to expand easily into new types of cultivation.

In the more open and sparsely populated areas such as Sumatra, the peasant was more responsive to economic opportunity but still within his traditional pattern. He would plant a little rubber on already-cleared swidden plots before moving on. Once planted, the rubber trees grew like other secondary forest, requiring little tending before being tapped. Unfortunately the colonial government endeavored to preserve the solvency of the large plantations under depression conditions by grossly discriminating against the small holders. Many were ruined. Nevertheless, by 1938 some 800,000 small holders in Sumatra, Malaya, and Borneo supplied more than half of the Netherlands Indies rubber export,[5] which was a large part of the world's rubber production.

Most peasants, though willing to farm for profit, preferred the stability of the village to the roving life of the middleman who transported crops to distant markets. The middleman role was usually left to the Chinese and other aliens. The santri merchants, however, did compete successfully against the Chinese in the role of seagoing peddler. In areas such as west Sumatra and eastern Sumbawa santri dominated trade, and even in Java they monopolized marketing at the lowest levels of carrying and handling. Javanese santri showed a capitalistic spirit by leading in the manufacture of batik cloth and, for a time, of clove cigarettes. Many of these small entrepreneurs were wiped out by the depression of the thirties, but they were staging a comeback at the close of the colonial period.

The santri merchants operated on a smaller scale than the Chinese. Short on capital, the santri peddler willingly expended labor in great quantity for a small profit, as when he walked or sailed a long distance to sell a few goods.[6] No santri achieved the large organizations and ramified networks of the most successful Chinese businessman. The Chinese had the advantage of their clans, families, secret societies, and dialect groups which furnished a basis for pooling capital, forming corporations, and making deals. Such informal social bases for trust were important in a society lacking a strong civil code and court system to enforce contracts among the natives. The santri were perhaps too individualistic to effectively organize. The Javanese lacked the clans of the Chinese; the Minangkabau, who had the clans, nevertheless built their commerce on the tradition of the bachelor peddler's long, lonely journey, the *merantau*. Undeniably important too were Chinese ethos and tradition. In spite of the commercial values of Islam, the Chinese impressed most observers as more industrious, experienced, shrewd, and single-mindedly ambitious than the santri.

As for the kings and prijaji of Mataram, they partook of the Hindu world view which ranked the merchant as the lowest of vocations (so did the Confucian doctrine of China, but the Chinese who came to Indonesia were of a class, region, and culture that was peripheral to Confucianism). Nor were the coastal sultans exactly model entrepreneurs. They had exploited the tradesmen, but few of them cared to enter trade themselves, at least not in the direct sense of getting into the rough and tumble of the marketplace.

Colonial Indonesia simply lacked a broadly based and well-entrenched indigenous bourgeois capitalist class like that of the Western nations. A picture of the small (though growing) place of commerce in indigenous society during colonial rule is given by the statistic that in 1905 only 1.87 percent of the natives were engaged in trade, and in 1930, 2.27 percent were so engaged.[7] Most of these were petty tradesmen, such as hawkers of snacks on the street.

The Chinese were the major group to occupy the commercial role left vacant by the natives, especially in Java. Beginning in 1870 the Chinese came not only as merchants but as indentured laborers, owing passage money to their employers. Such Chinese came to work in the eastern Sumatra plantations, on the docks, in sawmills, in ricemills, at jobs that did not yet attract the Indonesians. But many Chinese who came as laborers saved their wages and eventually became shopkeepers and merchants.

If the Chinese specialized in the distribution of goods, the Westerners specialized in production. They produced in large units that required much capital. By the early twenties practically all mining was carried out by the large and heavily capitalized Western firms, and the great volume of agricultural export came from the large Western-run plantations and mills for sugar, coffee, tobacco, and rubber.

PEASANTS

Dutch economist J. H. Boeke[8] was so impressed by the gulf between the capitalist sector, especially the Western, and the peasant sector of the Indonesian economy that he coined the term "dualism" to emphasize the disparity between the two. In Boeke's formulation, the capitalist constantly strove to exploit scarce resources in. order to reap profit, and he responded rationally to economic pressures such as those imposed by the law of supply and demand. The peasant did not respond so rationally, for he was stuck in the cake of custom and his wants were social rather than economic. The peasant was less interested in saving and investing than in gaining status among his kinsmen and neighbors through giving away his profits in the form of gifts and celebrations.

Critics of Boeke dislike his theory because it exaggerates the distinction between the Indonesian and the European. It also blames the native's economic irrationality or lack of economic initiative on his village traditions rather than on the stifling oppression of colonialism which, in the opinion of some, is the true culprit. Boeke's theory is essentially pessimistic since it roots the Indonesian economic stagnation in ancient and enduring patterns of social life. The view that colonialism was to blame is more optimistic, though not necessarily more realistic, for it is clear to see that colonialism has now disappeared.

A modern theory that resembles Boeke's in pointing to a traditionalism of the peasantry, but which traces that traditionalism directly to the impact of colonialism, is that of anthropologist Clifford Geertz. Geertz notes the effect on landholding patterns of Java's enormous growth of population (from 17 to 48 million) between 1870 and 1940. Holdings shrank until the average farmer cultivated a plot of only a couple of acres. More and more labor was absorbed and supported by smaller and smaller plots of land, yet subsistence remained adequate. This balance could be maintained only by raising the productivity of the land. Remarkably productive through volcanic ash and irrigated agriculture, the land was made even more productive through intensive use. Pregermination, transplanting, land preparation, planting, weeding, harvesting, and flooding were done ever more fastidiously. Fields were extended ever closer to the volcanoes. Maize, soya beans, and other crops were fitted between the rows of the old fields, then of the new ones. More labor was absorbed into less land by ever more complex arrangements of tenancy, subtenancy, and sub-subtenancy. These measures constituted what Geertz calls "involution." The basic pattern did not change but was elaborated into an ornate, rococo form.

The involution could be seen as reflecting a traditionalistic attitude like that described by Boeke, but Geertz asserts that this attitude "which Boeke took to be the cause of dualism was in great part its result."[9] That is, colonialism bred poverty which in turn evoked traditionalism and involution. Geertz supports this argument by a provocative comparison of Java and Japan. He shows that the two islands were strikingly similar in their demography and agriculture in 1870. During the next 70 years, however, Japan increased its agricultural productivity more than Java and, most importantly, funneled that productivity into support of its astounding industrial development. Java's agricultural productivity was diverted into the world market in order to finance the development of Holland. All of Japan's population growth was fed into her industrial sector, while the constant number of farmers increased productivity per field as well as per person through such techniques as fertilizing. Java's population growth was absorbed by her agrarian sector, so that the productivity per field increased but productivity per person did not: more people had to be supported by each field. To ensure that these increasing numbers of people were supported, agriculture became increasingly involuted, and peasant patterns became perhaps more conservative and traditionalized.

Suggestive as Geertz's comparison is, it does not prove his assertion that a traditionalist mentality was the result rather than the cause of economic dualism in Java. Such a mentality could have been itself a factor in the difference between Javanese and Japanese development, as Geertz implicitly admits when he mentions that the two cultures differ in "culture," "world views," and "religiously supported patterns of political loyalty."[10] Indeed, it could be argued that such differences influenced the very response of each culture to the threat of colonialism. Consolidating its nationhood under a Tokugawa warlord, early seventeenth-century Japan banned Western influences, except for a small group of Dutch traders kept quarantined on an island in Nagasaki harbor. But the Japanese had been assiduously studying the technology portrayed in the Dutch books, and had even established special laboratories to explore industrial applications of such Western knowledge. During the same period, the divided Javanese kingdoms were selling their power to the Dutch in exchange for tribute or aid in local wars. Geertz's argument would hold fully only if Java and Japan were wholly alike before the onset of colonialism; that this was not the case would seem indicated merely by the striking difference in their initial response to the Dutch. Of course, perfect comparisons, where all factors remain constant except that in which one is interested, are rarely possible in historical studies. Though Geertz's analysis is imperfect, it is still extremely valuable in probing the question of the influence of colonialism in stifling the development of the Javanese economy and bringing about a pattern of involution.

PROLETARIANS

Not all peasants sank into involution, of course. The penetration of capitalism lured some to become landless proletarians. The Agrarian Law of 1870 theoretically prohibited the peasant from selling that portion of his land which was necessary for his subsistence, but if he could not sell, he could still lease.

A typical tragedy starred the peasant who had been induced to lease his sawah to a plantation, but spent the advance payment and then had to go to work for cash to gain an income until the next rice harvest. Such a peasant did not really become a proletarian since he still owned his land and was only temporarily employed for wages. Nor was the landless peasant who worked for a landed peasant a proletarian, for he still remained in the village context. The true proletarians were those peasants who left the village, perhaps to migrate to a Sumatran plantation to work as a coolie (which Javanese did in increasing numbers after 1890) or to seek his fortune in a city as a laborer, bricklayer, or carpenter for a construction firm, as cook, gardener, launderer, chauffeur, or servant for a European family. Living in the plantation camp or the city *kampung* (shantytown), such an immigrant peasant was deprived of his traditional village solidarity. In the kampung, he would find certain cooperative rites and groups, but fundamental features of village life such as communal ownership of land and exchange of labor were lacking.

Material conditions were poor for the Indonesian worker. The Coolie Ordinance of 1880 guaranteed the plantation laborers certain minimum—very minimum—wages and rights, but at the same time it virtually enslaved him to his employer. Reminiscent of *Uncle Tom's Cabin*, Medan newspapers advertised runaway coolies. If the coolie were caught, he could be imprisoned for a term and still have to complete his contract when he got out. Under the harsh conditions of the Sumatran plantation, the European manager did not hesitate to use force to sustain his godlike authority. Supposedly reliable accounts relate how it was regarded as natural for the Europeans to slap and beat the natives or even to shoot them if they should run amok. In the virtually all-male society of the plantation, the white planter had first rights to those

few women who happened to be available. The native woman of lowly status apparently considered it a privilege to serve as the planter's mistress and servant.

Wages on the Western plantations were kept low, approximately 16 guilder cents per day, for cheap wages were what allowed great profit. The workers were nourished at a level considerably below that now considered minimum, though their nutrition equaled that of the peasant living in a village. According to one study, the average member of a family of plantation coolies consumed 1,282 calories per day compared to 1,391 for the peasant.[11] The Food and Agricultural Organization of the United Nations calculates that the minimum daily requirement for a Southeast Asian is 2,270 calories per day (the average American or Western European consumes over 3,000 calories per day).[12] Some estates offered pensions and health services, but the pensions were small and the health services frequently token, as in the case of the estate clinic whose medication consisted of spoonfuls of cheap patent medicine.

For workers in enterprises owned and run by the natives themselves, material conditions were even worse than in the Western enterprises. A laborer's pay in native Indonesian industry averaged around 2½ guilder cents per day in 1933,[13] and servants for Javanese families were paid practically nothing except room and board. The worker was perhaps partially compensated by the privilege of working for a boss who shared his culture and understood his feelings, and the servant was to a degree "treated like one of the family"—except that he had to squat on the floor while his master sat, kneel when he served him, and behave in ways that appear to the outsider as childish, dependent, and obsequious. One should remember, however, the peculiar place of the servant in Javanese ideology. In both classical and popular drama, *wajang* or *ludruk*, the servant is a clown who is, to be sure, childish, dependent, two-faced, and sexually hermaphroditic or impotent. But he is also marvelously wise and clever. In the case of Semar, the clown-servant is a god, and his role on stage is sometimes played by a real-life prince. In ludruk, the clown-servant role is the starring one, usually played by the troupe leader.[14] This exaltation of the servant role is not merely idealized compensation for its actual wretchedness, but a humorous and poignant appreciation of the profound meaning of finding a place, any place, in the social hierarchy.

BUREAUCRATS

By 1900 both liberal businessmen and humanists in Holland were worried about the decline of native welfare and the disintegration of native communities provoked by the spread of capitalism in the Indies.

Liberals had professed to believe that free enterprise would work for the good of all, native as well as European, but things had not turned out that way. Native poverty bothered the social conscience of the humanists and disappointed the economic hopes of the businessmen who had hoped for prosperous natives who would buy Dutch goods. After much criticism from many quarters, the liberal policy was replaced by the "ethical policy," which promised health services, assistance in agricultural development, and schools for the peasants—all to be provided by funds from the Netherlands treasury.

The ethical policy was, by comparison with most colonial policies of the day, ethical indeed, but also a bit unrealistic and hypocritical. The limited social reform which the government was willing and able to finance barely began to correct the extensive social problems brought about by colonization and modernization. And reforms could be shown to serve the interests of colonialism and capitalism as well as those of the native. Still the programs of the ethical policy were planned and executed with consistency of purpose, efficiency of administration, and knowledge of local culture and conditions that are impressive by comparison with the majority of programs sponsored by development agencies today. What is more, Dutch administrators of the ethical persuasion took an intense personal interest in certain Indonesians, especially those of the nobility and intelligentsia, and worked with them for years as patrons and friends rather than merely as administrators. With all its virtues, however, the ethical program failed to significantly repair the economic and social damages of capitalism and colonialism and to mold a meaningful framework within which Indonésians could move in orderly fashion toward modernity. One of the most important consequences of the ethical policy was in part unintended; it fostered the growth of an indigenous intelligentsia, who were later to spearhead the movement toward Indonesian independence.[15]

More welfare services necessitated more bureaucracy, and more bureaucracy required more bureaucrats. As these could be supplied from Holland only at prohibitive cost, the government endeavored to train native Indonesians to perform the new technical jobs, such as vaccinator, teacher, and agricultural-development agent. It also strove, once again, to defeudalize the native regents to prepare them for the modern function of coordinating the technical bureaucrats in their regencies. Cleavage and conflict emerged between the regents, the "old prijaji," and the technical bureaucrats, the "new prijaji."[16] Defeudalization of the regents proceeded, but the Dutch administrators increasingly treated them as museum pieces having no useful function and no real power. Especially was this the attitude of the type of Dutch administrator who appeared with the ethical system. The old Indische-style adventurer-exploiter had gained considerable feel for the native society, and he appreciated the wide meaning of the regent's status which he, in fact, emulated in his own "Indische" style of life. The new breed of Dutch administrator was less involved in native life in the visceral sense, in part because he brought his family from Holland instead of keeping a native mistress. He was more idealistic, less patient with the feudal *accoutrements* of the regents, more eager to get things done. Hence he was more likely to turn to the technical man, the new prijaji. Since the old prijaji considered themselves superior to the new by virtue of their superior birth and upbringing, the snub must have been galling.

European primary schools had existed in Java since 1816, and since that time a few Indonesian aristocrats had been selected to attend them. Also, European families had occasionally brought young prijaji into their homes to learn European tradition and manners. Beginning in 1848, Dutch schools were founded to train Indonesian clerks and administrators, and they drew their students exclusively from the hereditary prijaji. This elitist pattern changed in 1851 with the establishment of schools to train native teachers and vaccinators. Sons of lesser prijaji, heretofore excluded from European education, were admitted to these vocational schools. Seizing the chance to gain government posts through such training, they formed the beginning of the "new prijaji" who based their claim for status on education. Shortly after 1900, the European schools were formally opened to qualified Indonesians, and such ethical reformers as Snouck Hurgronje made special efforts to get sons of the elite into them; by 1920 some 6,000 natives were enrolled in these schools. Hurgronje and others like him became patrons and mentors of Indonesian protegés who gathered at their homes to absorb ideas of progressive social philosophy at the same time that they assimilated the European education at school. As the need for technicians and professionals grew, the *Dokter-Djawa* (vaccinator) school was transformed into a full-fledged medical school to train native doctors, a veterinarian school was founded in 1907, an agricultural secondary school in 1903, and a law school in 1908.

Most significant, perhaps, was the system of schools that provided primary education in Dutch for natives; these were the Dutch Native Schools (Hollandsch-Inlandsche Schoolen), which were instituted between 1907 and 1914 by General van Heutz. Enrolling some 20,000 students in 1915 and 45,000 in 1940, the Dutch Native Schools provided the first mass opportunity for natives to acquire the Dutch language that was necessary for a post in the colonial government. Quick to grasp the opportunity were the lesser prijaji who were still excluded from the elitist schools and posts.

What the Dutch language schools created was a class hierarchy based on education rather than birth or wealth. Throughout Indonesia there emerged a new middle class, an intelligentsia, a new prijaji basing its claims on the diploma and the white collar. With a diploma, the lesser prijaji or even the son of a villager or trader could obtain a white-collar post not only in the swelling bureaucracy of the ethical government but also in the Western plantations and mills, which needed accountants, draftsmen, and clerks. Indonesian families proved themselves willing to make great sacrifices to educate their sons, to the extent that expenditure for education exceeded all others in some households. The prestige of the diploma was so great that in many circles the ordinary Western-educated school teacher ranked above the kiai or even the native regent. Competition for white-collar jobs was so intense that the Indo-Europeans, who had formerly monopolized such posts, sank to the level of the kampung if they fell behind in the race to acquire education. If the young prijaji were of the fortunate minority to graduate from the European system, he might even study in Holland, or become a lawyer, doctor, or engineer by attending the colleges of law, medicine, and engineering that became firmly established in the twenties in Batavia and Bandung. That the ambitions of even the nobility were thusly focused is revealed in the story of a son in a court in Solo who, upon being asked to what occupation he aspired when he grew up, replied, "Doctor-lawyer-engineer."[17]

Like intelligentsia everywhere, those of Indonesia suffered from alienation and discontinuity. Graduates of the second-class Dutch Native Schools learned Western subjects and Western languages, and they were taught such Western methods as the examination to evaluate individual achievement—a shocking innovation from the group approach of the pesantrèn. But after all this, the second-class school graduates received no diplomas. Lacking that essential credential for the government post, they were naturally disposed to form a dissatisfied semi-intelligentsia. Even those Indonesians who got the diploma and the position were confronted by discrepancies between their education and their existence. Living on low wages in cities, they were often forced to reside in the urban kampung, whose bad drainage, stinking sewage, and crowded lack of privacy contradicted values of hygiene and conduct which they had laboriously acquired through Western schooling.

More fundamental than these special problems, however, was the general discontinuity between Western education and native world view. The education was solely technical and functional, and Javanese felt it lacked the ultimate significance and meaning of the pesantrèn or the wajang. Traditional Javanese education initiated the pupil into an esoteric knowledge and experience which gave insight into the mysteries of this world and the next. Dutch Native Schools were not only short on native theosophy, but also gave little instruction in Western humanities and philosophy. Noteworthy is the number of Indonesian students who, according to their own reports, became disillusioned with the technical schooling and turned to the mystical and the occult in a search for understanding of the broader significance of existence. Indeed, the first organized movement to revitalize Javanese culture and philosophy, the *Budi Utomo,* found its earliest disciples among Indonesian students at the most technical of Dutch schools—the medical, veterinarian, and agricultural.

REFERENCES

[1] J. D. Legge, *Indonesia* (Englewood Cliffs, N.J.: Prentice-Hall, 1964), p. 79.

[2] James T. Siegel, *The Rope of God* (Berkeley and Los Angeles: Univ. of California Press, 1969), pp. 70–77. See also Anthony Reid, *The Contest for North Sumatra: Atjeh, the Netherlands, and Britain, 1858–1898* (London and Kuala Lumpur: Oxford Univ. Press and Univ. of Malaya Press, 1969). C. Snouck Hurgronje, *Mekka in the Latter Part of the 19th Century: Daily Life, Customs and Learning of the Moslims of the East-Indian Archipelago,* trans. J. H. Monahan (Leyden: Brill, 1931), gives a fascinating account of Indonesians whom he met during his Mekka sojourn. Hurgronje's *The Achehnese,* 2 vols., trans. A. W. S. Sullivan (Leyden: Brill, 1906), is a detailed account of life in Atjeh.

[3] David Joel Steinberg et al., *In Search of Southeast Asia: A Modern History* (New York: Praeger, 1971), p. 208.

[4] This section owes much to Steinberg et al., pp. 217–232. On santri capitalists, see Lance Castles, *Religion, Politics, and Economic Behavior in Java: The Kudus Cigarette Industry* (New Haven, Conn.: Southeast Asia Studies, Yale University, 1967); Clifford Geertz, *Peddlers and Princes: Social Change and Economic Modernization in Two Indonesian Towns* (Chicago: Univ. of Chicago Press, 1963); Alice D. Greeley Dewey, *Peasant Marketing in Java* (New York: Free Press of Glencoe, 1962).

[5] Clifford Geertz, *Agricultural Involution: The Processes of Ecological Change in Indonesia* (Berkeley: Univ. of California Press, 1963), p. 113.

[6] Dewey, *Peasant Marketing in Java,* pp. 16–18.

[7] W. F. Wertheim, *Indonesian Society in Transition: A Study of Social Change,* 2nd rev. ed. (The Hague and Bandung: Van Hoeve, 1959), p. 144.

[8] Julius H. Boeke, *Economics and Economic Policy of Dual Societies as Exemplified by Indonesia* (New York: International Secretariat, Institute of Pacific Relations, 1953); and *The Structure of Netherlands Indian Economy* (New York: Institute of Pacific Relations, 1942). For critical assessment, see Benjamin Higgins, "The Dualistic Theory of Underdeveloped Areas," *Economic Development and Cultural Change,* Vol. 4 (1956), pp. 99–115; M. Sadli, "Some Reflections on Prof. Boeke's Theory of Dualistic Economics," *Ekonomi dan Keuangan Indonesia,* Vol. X (1957), pp. 363–383.

[9] Geertz, *Agricultural Involution*, p. 142.

[10] *Ibid.*, pp. 130, 140.

[11] Wertheim, *Indonesian Society in Transition*, p. 264.

[12] Malcolm Caldwell, *Indonesia* (London: Oxford Univ. Press, 1968), p. 22.

[13] Wertheim, *Indonesian Society in Transition*, p. 268.

[14] James L. Peacock, *Rites of Modernization: Symbolic and Social Aspects of Indonesian Proletarian Drama* (Chicago: Univ. of Chicago Press, 1968), pp. 71–73. A fascinating portrait of another type of clown portraying the proletarian during the colonial period is R. Ahmad Wongsosewojo, "Loedroek," *Djawa*, Vol. 10 (1930), pp. 204–207.

[15] See Legge, *Indonesia*, pp. 79–94, on the ethical policy.

[16] Robert van Niel, *The Emergence of the Modern Indonesian Elite* (The Hague and Bandung: Van Hoeve, 1960), pp. 27–29.

[17] D. H. Burger, *Structural Changes in Java: The Supra-village Sphere* (Ithaca, N.Y.: Modern Indonesia Project, Cornell University, 1957), p. 21.

SEVEN

CULTURAL RESPONSE: 1900–1940

"Rust en Orde" (Peace and Order)
Colonial Dutch slogan for the proper
state of Indies society

The Java, Padri, and Atjeh Wars were all regional in outlook, and the scattered peasant revolts[1] that occurred during the nineteenth century were both regional and lacking in coherent social objectives or programs. Essentially the wars and the revolts were reactive movements, desperate attempts to rid native society of the disruptive colonialism and capitalism. More obviously constructive were the national, peaceful, sustained religious, educational, literary, and political movements that emerged in the twentieth century. Their social programs and goals were relatively coherent, for their leaders and ideologues were largely of the intelligentsia class.

RELIGIOUS, EDUCATIONAL, AND LITERARY MOVEMENTS

The first important organized cultural movement was the *Budi Utomo* (High Endeavor) founded in 1908 by three students from the Javanese Medical School (STOVIA), one of whom was Raden Sutomo, later a prominent leader in Indonesian nationalism. It is interesting that the medical profession and the lesser nobility ("raden" is a lesser prijaji title) were the source of this earliest cultural protest movement; neither doctors nor nobles are ordinarily noted for their radicalism. The explanation is in part that already given, that the medical school was excessively technical, thereby encouraging a mystical reaction among its students and driving them to seek meaning in the theosophical roots of their native culture. A further explanation is that the medical profession provided one of the very few nonbureaucratic elite statuses in Indonesia. By becoming doctors, prijaji sons like Raden Sutomo could acquire a Western education and life style without joining the colonial bureaucracy as their fathers had had to do. The medical members of the intelligentsia enjoyed more freedom from the colonial government than did the bureaucrats, hence with less fear of consequence they could create and join radical movements. Physicians were strikingly prominent in most movements of twentieth-century colonial Indonesia.

Within a year the Budi Utomo had attracted over 10,000 members, though it limited its activities to Java and Madura, and based its guiding philosophy (or theosophy) on the Hindu-Buddhist culture of Java. Budi Utomo hoped that through revitalization of this deeply felt core of Javanese identity, a meaningful and respectable alternative could be found to the values offered by the West. The movement looked to India's Tagore and Gandhi as inspirations in the revival of native culture. Controlled for some time by old and traditionalistic prijaji, Budi Utomo was usually apolitical, and it sought legal recognition from the colonial government.[2]

Budi Utomo, essentially an abangan revitalization, flourished simultaneously with a twentieth-century santri revival throughout the Malayo-Indonesian region. Since 1870 the opening of the Suez Canal and the steamship had encouraged great numbers of santri to make the pilgrimage to Mecca, and the bonds between Indonesia and the Holy City as well as other Middle Eastern centers of Islamic learning were growing stronger. By the turn of the twentieth century, the Indonesian community was the largest of any foreign one in Mecca, and many Indonesians who made the pilgrimage to Mecca remained for years to study in Cairo. By the beginning of the twentieth century, several of the Malay, Indonesian, Arab, and Indian citizens of the Malayo-Indonesian world had come under the influence of the teacher of Islamic modernism, Muhammad Abduh of Cairo's Az-har University. These students returned to Singapore, port of embarkation and disembarkation for pilgrims to Mecca. Founding schools, journals, and associations in that Southeast Asian center for the dissemination of Muslim thought, they later spread into the Malay peninsula and the islands of the Indies. Carrying on their work of reform and education in those places, they were known as the *Kaum Muda* (New Faction) of Malayo-Indonesian Islam.[3]

The Kaum Muda reformists pressed for a return to the fundamental truths of the text and tradition, the Qur'an and the hadith, that were believed to record verbatim the word of Allah. Other authorities were rejected, including the venerated kiai and other Muslim teachers and scholars who taught the ornate philosophies of medieval Islam. These schemes were of merely human origin, said the reformist, whereas the texts and traditions were of divine origin. Believers were exhorted to pursue the method of *itjihad*, to analyze and dissect the original Arabic scriptures in order to read for themselves their divine message.

Paradoxically, a return to the ancient text implied an advance toward modern values. The holy scripture did not mention the animistic and Sufistic rites and beliefs cherished by the abangan, hence such superstitions must be ruthlessly excised from the life of the santri. Properly analyzed, the scripture was believed to include an understanding of economics, science, medicine, law, and politics that was fully adequate for the modern world. Through reformism, then, the santri could rediscover a bedrock of ancient and pure identity while simultaneously equipping himself for the challenges of the twentieth century.

Expressed by several Indonesian organizations, such as Persatuan Islam in west Java and Al-Irsjad among the Arabs, the reformist ideas were most successfully propagated by the Muhammadijah, founded in Jogjakarta in 1912 by Kiai H. A. Dahlan.[4] The father, maternal grandfather, and other relatives of Dahlan were *khatib* (preachers) in the Great Mosque of the Jogjakarta kraton. Dahlan was born (in 1868) and reared in the santri neighborhood (*kauman*) nearby. Like other santri children, he began the study of Islam and Arabic in early childhood and soon joined the pious congregation of santri men in the Great Mosque. Upon reaching adolescence, Dahlan was sent to Mecca by his father, with the aid of funds from a merchant aunt (female merchants are common among both santri and abangan Javanese). Studying for a time in the Near East, Dahlan came under the influence of Muhammed Abduh and returned to Jogjakarta a determined reformist. Assuming the post of khatib at the mosque, he sought to purify its symbolism by pointing out that it was wrongly positioned, according to rules of the holy Qur'an. That and other reformist notions were not applauded and Dahlan was so discouraged that he prepared to board a train out of Djokdja, but was persuaded by friends to stay. Dahlan sought his livelihood through trade as well as religion, and he used his commercial travels to spread the gospel of reformism throughout Java and to organize progressive Muslims of the island. These activities culminated in his founding of Muhammadijah on November 18, 1912. Against unceasing popular resistance and occasional danger to his life, he worked for the advance of Muhammadijah without respite until the day of his death, February 28, 1923.

Muhammadijans were relentless opponents of abangan syncretism. They preached against the worship of spirits and the performance of rituals not decreed by the holy Qur'an, and they succeeded in purging at least their own lives of those abangan practices. Muhammadijans streamlined and purified santri ceremonies as well, reducing the number of bodily movements accompanying certain prayers and rendering the Friday sermon in the vernacular instead of Arabic. Muhammadijah became the most active and effective indigenous social-welfare organization in Indonesia, building clinics, orphanages, and hospitals, and organizing boy scouts, student groups, and a vigorous women's movement.

At the time of Muhammadijah's founding, Christian missionaries for the first time were actively encouraged and subsidized by the colonial government, and some Muslims saw missionaries as suddenly threatening the dominance of Islam in the islands. Competing with the Christians and inspired by modernist ideas from several sources, Muhammadijah organized itself in a Western pattern alien to the santri. It elected a president, appointed a governing council, hired an office staff, formed branches all over Indonesia, held national congresses, and published reports. At the same time, Muhammadijah adhered to the Islamic taboo against receiving monetary interest, and thus opened no bank account.

Financial support for Muhammadijah came partly through government subsidy but largely through contributions from the santri bourgeois—the smallholder farmers of Sumatra, the cigarette manufacturers of Kudus, and the batik entrepreneurs of Jogjakarta, Surakarta, and Pekadjangan. Santri of this bourgeois class were attracted to Muhammadijah ideology because it rendered meaningful and legitimate their struggle to survive and advance in the rapidly changing Indonesian commercial society. On occasion, conversion to reformist Islam and the joining of Muhammadijah even stimulated the emergence of native capitalism. The story is told that Pekadjangan, a small north Java village, was originally a community of thieves who were converted early in the twentieth century by a reformist preacher who threatened hell fire and damnation if they continued their crimes. Joining the Muhammadijah *en masse*, the men of Pekadjangan used their formerly criminal ingenuity to manufacture and sell batik and other fabrics. In that enterprise they were extremely successful. Today Pekadjangan is a remarkably prosperous and industrious village which houses Mercedes automobiles and works its looms during the siesta hours when most of Indonesia sleeps. Pekadjangan remains virtually 100 percent Muhammadijan and is faithful in its financial support of that movement.[5]

Attacking the mysticism, scholasticism, and syncretism of the rural Javanese Islam, Muhammadijah threatened the kiai's status and the identity of his devoted rural santri worshippers. These rural santri reacted by branding Muhammadijans infidels, Christians, or proponents of the heretical doctrine of Ahmadiyya (which claimed that not Mu-hammad but the Pakistani reformer, Hazrat Mirza Ghulam Ahmad, was the last prophet of Islam). In 1926 the traditionalists founded (with the blessings of the Dutch, Muhammadijans claim) the *Nahdatul Ulama* (Union of Muslim Teachers) to withstand the threat of reform-ism. Ruled by a conservative dynasty which still controls a famous pesantrèn in east Java, the N.U. soon outstripped Muhammadijah in attracting support of the rural masses. N.U.'s activities have been largely political and religious rather than social and educational. N.U. has not equaled Muhammadijah in the building of hospitals and schools, but it controls the Ministry of Religion of the Republic of Indonesia.

The Indonesian Muslim reformation differed from the European Protestant reformation in that the Protestants had the historical arena more to themselves. As the most revolutionary movement of their era and society, they developed for a time without strong competition from other equally dynamic forces. The Muhammadijans had to compete from the start with movements as dynamic as they—socialists, commu-nists, nationalists. Christian missionaries gave them tough competition too, in the religious sphere, and the giant Western corporations elbowed the santri businessman out of many an economic opportunity. As the excitement of Muhammadijah's early years diminished, and its charis-matic founders were replaced by leaders less fiery, the movement lost some of its dynamism. It became more rigid and conservative, more defensive in the face of threat from Christianity, communism, and secular nationalism. Nevertheless, Muhammadijah continued to grow steadily and work diligently in education, social welfare, and religious reform. Steadfastly apolitical, at least in formal organization, it escaped the governmental repression that cut short the lives of the more radical movements during the colonial period.

Educational Movements

Most important was Muhammadijah's modernization of Muslim educa-tion. The small school which K. H. A. Dahlan as a young man had founded in the Jogjakarta kauman eventually multiplied into some 4,000 schools located throughout the Indies. Muhammadijah schools differed radically from the old-style pesantrèn, which were not graded into classes and taught nothing but Arabic and Islam. Muhammadijah schools were divided into classes and levels that paralleled those of the Dutch government schools, and they taught Western subjects in the Dutch language. Muhammadijah schools also included instruction in Islam, but they varied widely in how much. At one extreme was the Dutch language school which gave only a few hours per week of religious instruction; at the other extreme was the madrasah which taught half religious and half secular subjects. Unlike the other schools, the madrasah segregated boys from girls and required the girls to cover their female charms with white hoods and cloaks. It appealed to the more traditionally pious Muhammadijan who desired his daughter to prepare for motherhood by acquiring sound religious and moral education, and who wished to educate his son to be an Islamic teacher. Even the Western-style Muhammadijah schools retained such Malayo-Muslim customs as learning through chanting, but in many respects they were and are quite modern.

If Muhammadijah was the most significant santri educational movement in prewar Indonesia, *Taman Siswa* (Garden of Learning) was the most significant abangan one.[6] Its founder, Suwardi Surjaningrat, later known as Ki Hadjar Dewantara (Teacher of the Gods), resembled Kiai H. A. Dahlan in being a native of the court city of Djokjakarta. Dahlan, however, was from the trading class; Dewantara was of the nobility. Like Dahlan, Dewantara formulated his educational ideas following a time of study abroad, but his study was in Europe rather than the Middle East. Dewantara's decision to found his group emerged in a thoroughly abangan context—during meditations of a mystical group, some of whose members formed the Taman Siswa's first board of directors.

Taman Siswa was smaller and poorer than Muhammadijah. It lacked the support of an indigenous merchant class, and it refused colonial government subsidies for fear that strings attached would restrict the Taman Siswa nativism. In this nativism, Taman Siswa differed fundamentally from Muhammadijah. Muhammadijah, a reformist movement, rejected local institutions such as the pesantrèn, and determined to substitute alien and modern institutions. Taman Siswa, founded ten years later than Muhammadijah, had seen the discontinuity and alienation resulting from a decade of widespread Western education. Ki Hadjar Dewantara was impressed by such critics of Western schooling as Tagore in India, Froebel and Montessori in Europe. Absorbing their ideas into his own, he favored self-expression, individual guidance, and the adjustment of teaching to the world of the child. He taught the arts—Javanese music, dance, and painting—to encourage the pupil to express and identify his inner self.

Despairing at the loss of traditional bonds and solidarities, Dewantara yearned to restore a base of community. He imagined the Taman Siswa as a "family," and he described charmingly the mutual involvement of teachers and students; the Western school sent the teachers and students their separate ways after a few hours of contact, but Taman Siswa kept them together day and night. Faculty members were supposed to be "brothers in learning" and not to emphasize the distinctions of rank or to amass property which would lead to inequality. Taman Siswa banned explicit politics from the classroom, but the majority of the teachers were leftist, and they supported the nationalist or communist parties.

By 1940 Dewantara had succeeded in building some 250 schools throughout the archipelago. His system narrowly escaped repression by a government "Wild School" ordinance of the middle thirties, but it did survive and, like Muhammadijah, survives today.

Literary Movements

Of somewhat different character from Muhammadijah and Taman Siswa were the twentieth-century literary movements. No single organization coordinated all literary efforts, but two were highly significant: *Balai Pustaka* and *Pudjangga Baru*. Balai Pustaka (Hall of Good Reading), founded in 1917 by the government, was a publishing firm which could gain wide circulation for the work of any Indonesian writer whom it agreed to publish. *Pudjangga Baru (The New Poet)*, a literary journal of very limited circulation, was founded by three young Sumatran writers, Takdir Alisjahbana (b. 1908), Armijn Pane (b. 1908), and Amir Hamzah (b. 1911). *Pudjangga Baru* declared itself responsible for fostering that spirit of dynamism which would create a new Indonesian culture. The editors affirmed their devotion to the Indonesian spirit (semangat Indonesia) which they sought to express through forms that would reveal the "beautiful and noble emotions and thoughts contained in the hearts of our people."[7] Yet the journal was concerned less with the majority of the Indonesians than with the Westernized intellectuals who read its poems and essays (and one novel) in the new Indonesian language. Anti-Dutch but not militant, nationalist but not fanatical, *Pudjangga Baru* by no means rejected all of Western culture; neither could it fully accept the West while rejecting indigenous values.

The writings that came to light through Balai Pustaka and *Pudjangga Baru* certainly do not exhaust the creations of the Indonesians of the period, but they are representative, and they do exemplify the conflict between the Western and the indigenous, the modern and the traditional that plagued most of the intelligentsia. An example is a first group of novels by Sumatran writers, which were published between 1922 and 1933: *Sitti Nurbaja* (a girl's name), *Salah Asuhan (Wrong Upbringing)*, *Karena Mentua (Because of the Mother-in-Law)*, and *Kalau Tak Untung (If Fortune Does Not Favor)*. All of these novels depict the troubles of young people caught between collective constraints imposed by family and tribe and individualistic freedoms offered by school and Western friends. The conflict between the two ways of life is most sharply highlighted by the dilemma of whether to follow one's parents (the traditional way) or one's feelings (the Western way) in choosing a spouse. The outcome is usually tragic, reflecting a pessimistic view of culture contact. Interestingly, especially in light of the vigor of Muslim reformism in the writers' Sumatran homeland, the characters are not strongly Muslim and they do not see Islam as a mediator between the Western and the traditional.[8]

By comparison with such writers as Idrus and Anwar, who were to emerge during the reckless times of the Japanese Occupation, these colonial writers were rather sentimental and turgid, and they tended to schematicize their characters in overly simple categories, such as tribal and modern, Eastern and Western. Still, they were dynamic pioneers, and the sentimentality and stereotyping would be transcended by the cynical Idrus and the wild Anwar.

POLITICAL MOVEMENTS

The Indische Partij (Indies Party) was founded in 1912 by E. P. E. Douwes Dekker, an Indo-European grandnephew of the author of *Max Havelaar*. Dekker's cofounders, Dr. Tjipto Mangukusumo and Ki Hadjar Dewantara, were Javanese, but most of the few hundred members of the party were Eurasian. Condemning the double standards of a colonialism that paid a European more than an Indo-European or an Indonesian who did the same work, Douwes Dekker advanced the notion of equal pay for equal work. He campaigned so successfully that in 1918 a law was passed that established, for many positions, a unitary salary scale which disregarded the employee's ethnic origin. The Indische Partij also protested against rule by the growing number of Dutchmen who came to the islands with the intention of returning home with a pension after 20 years of service. The party coined the slogan: "The Indies for those who make their home there." So radical a threat was this cry for independence and self-rule that the government exiled several of the Indies Party leaders, including Dekker and Dewantara, an action which destroyed the party.

In 1912 was founded the Sarekat Islam (Islamic Union).[9] Growing out of an Islamic merchants' union which had been created by santri batik merchants to block Chinese competition, S.I. shared many points of ideology with Muhammadijah, and many of the S.I. merchants were members of Muhammadijah.

Sarekat Islam soon became more than a businessman's association. It attracted the intelligentsia and the masses as well as the capitalists. The S.I. leader was the charismatic Umar Said Tjokroaminoto. Tjokro was a prijaji educated in the governmental administrator's school

(OSVIA), but he chose, it is said, to work for a time with a traveling wajang show. Many villagers saw Tjokroaminoto as the *ratu adil* (righteous prince) who would liberate them from their colonial oppressors, and some remote communities regarded the S.I. movement as a holy war against the Dutch. The religious aura was sustained by requiring that new members take secret oaths and buy tokens to ensure invulnerability. As word of S.I. spread among the peasants, the village religious authorities stepped forward to organize chapters, and each chapter was seen as a quasi-religious brotherhood.

As S.I. grew into Indonesia's first mass organization, a new faction, the communist, made its appearance. A Dutchman, Hendrik Sneevliet, had come to reside in the Javanese harbor city of Semarang, a center for left-wing movements. Sneevliet founded the ISDA (Indian Social Democratic Association) in Semarang in 1914, and he soon became a sympathizer with the Russian Revolution. Associating himself with a Javanese, Semaun, who was both a Marxist and a member of the S.I., Sneevliet and his friends wormed their way into the core of S.I. to propagate Marxism there, with some effect. Their criticism of S.I.'s bourgeois capitalism caused Tjokroaminoto to begin to speak of "sinful capitalism." "Sinful capitalism," he explained, was foreign, whereas virtuous capitalism was indigenous.[10]

Under communist influence, S.I. shifted, after 1917, from peaceful opposition to violent hostility toward the colonial government. Led by Semaun and others, S.I. organized a workers' union and strikes. Unfortunately for S.I., the government had just ended its "ethical policy" of tolerance. The government exiled members of the S.I. and ISDA, harassed S.I. branches, and repressed the strikes. Conservative bourgeois merchants, averse to communism and revolution, left the party. Tjokroaminoto came under harsh criticism, and the communists moved to take over the S.I. Attacked from the left, from the right, and by the government, S.I. seemed ready to disintegrate.

The santri leaders of the S.I. rallied, however, around the banner of Islamic modernism and pan-Islamism, that international movement which dreamed of a world Muslim empire with a Turkish caliph as its ruler. At the sixth national S.I. congress in October 1921, Hadji Agus Salim, the shrewd, Dutch-educated Minangkabau Muslim, mounted a powerful attack on the communists, showed them to be atheistic opponents of the core S.I. ideology, and the communists had to leave the party. With the expulsion of the communists, S.I. lost the support of the laboring class, and it never regained its mass following.

The communists, who had adopted the name PKI (Indies Communist Party) in 1920, went against the advice of their highest Indonesian agent, Tan Malaka, and planned to stage uprisings in west Java and west Sumatra in 1926 and 1927. The revolts, led in most areas by local PKI members, miscarried. The outbreaks were easily crushed by the Dutch government, which exiled over a thousand participants to the malarial swamps of the upper Digul River in New Guinea.

The communists were destroyed, the S.I. had declined, and Indonesian politics were now dominated by more purely nationalist factions. Especially important were the students, for whom experience of study abroad had proved a fertile source of nationalistic sentiment. Visiting Holland, the Indonesian student became aware of the tiny size of the country that ruled his own vast territory. He saw white men doing menial labor. He met Dutch opponents of Indies colonialism. And icy winters in Europe must have reminded students from the varied island groups of their tropical commonalities. As early as 1908 students at Indies and Dutch universities founded the Indies Association (Indische Vereeniging), later named the Indonesian Union (Perhimpunan Indonesia). Other students founded additional groups, seeking a constructive method to prepare Indonesian intellectuals for self-government. One of the founders of Perhimpunan Indonesia, Dr. Sutomo (the same Raden Sutomo of Budi Utomo), hit upon the idea of the Indonesische Studieclub (Indonesian Study Club), which he founded in Surabaja. Instead of limiting itself to discussion of issues, the club sought to do good. It founded schools, banks, health clinics, and orphanages. It was politically neutral. The concept of the study club spread, and in 1926 a young man named Sukarno, who had just graduated from the engineering college in Bandung, founded a club in that city. Unlike the Studieclub of Sutomo, that of Sukarno had no interest in social work; it was strictly a political organization and it agitated for Indonesia's immediate independence.

Sukarno,[11] second child of a poor teacher from the lower Javanese nobility, was born in an east Javanese town in 1901. His mother was a Balinese of the Brahmin-Hindu caste. His formative education was from the wajang kulit. Enamored with the flitting shadows on the screen, Sukarno fancied himself a satriya, an identity which his father encouraged by changing his name from Kusno to Sukarno, after the fearless Karno, satriya hero in the Mahabharata.

In adolescence, Sukarno was sent away to study in the Dutch Hogere Burger School in Surabaja. He lived in that lively port city at the house of Tjokroaminoto, leader of the Sarekat Islam. According to Sukarno's recollections, these were years of poverty and of mistreatment by the Dutch, who taunted him at school and crushed his romance with one of their daughters. But his poverty and alienation were mild compared to that suffered, for example, by Hitler in his Vienna days. Sukarno nourished his dreams by watching movies, acting in folk plays, and imagining himself as one or another hero of history. He retained his identity as a satriya, and he was later nicknamed Bima, the fearless Pandawa warrior. From Tjokroaminoto he acquired a Marxist view of capitalism and colonialism, and from him, as well as from his deeper Javanese roots, he acquired a desire to join apparently irreconcilable viewpoints into a unity.

After marrying the daughter of Tjokroaminoto, Sukarno left Surabaja and matriculated at the Technical College of Bandung. During his studies there he divorced his first wife and married his landlady, who was several years older than he. Alongside his domestic life, Sukarno studied, and he remembers himself as a good student in drawing, poor in mathematics. Receiving his diploma in 1926, Sukarno refused to enter the service of the colonial government. Founding the PNI (Perserikatan Nasional Indonesia) in 1927, he oversaw the party's adoption of a resolution condemning cooperation with the Dutch.

Orating and writing against the colonial government for many months, Sukarno was finally arrested and sentenced to prison in December 1930. Enriched, perhaps, by the Javanese myth of the savior in seclusion, Sukarno's reputation grew rather than diminished during his imprisonment. Adulation of him reached its peak during his first important appearance after his release at the Greater Indonesia Congress held in Surabaja at the beginning of 1932. Masses jammed railroad stations as he rode from Bandung to Surabaja, and 6,000 ecstatic admirers were on hand to meet him when he arrived. In his opening speech, Sukarno drew on his beloved wajang imagery to compare himself to Kokrosono, a wajang figure who, when he reappears from seclusion as a hermit, is at once happy and sorrowful. He is happy because he has won the miraculous weapon Nanggala, with which he will overcome the demon Kongso; he is sorrowful because he has been forced to watch from afar while two of his children suffer great danger. The children in the story represented the members of the PNI; the great danger was the strife and disunity into which the movement had fallen during Sukarno's absence.

After a flurry of inflammatory oratory, Sukarno was arrested again. This time he was exiled, in which state he would spend the remaining years before World War II. First he was kept on the island of Flores where he broke his solitude by organizing a local theater. Later he was removed to the Sumatran port of Bengkulen. There, in spite of his abangan background, he joined the Muhammadijah. His relations with that organization were typically flamboyant. He walked out on the first meeting he attended in protest of a screen placed between himself and the female members. He made vague efforts to synthesize the Muslim faith with such diverse orientations as socialism and nationalism but succeeded only in irritating purist Muslims who found his understanding of Islam extremely superficial.

Since he was in exile, Sukarno did not accomplish much organizationally during the prewar period. He did, however, create symbols of enduring power. Under his leadership the nationalist movement acquired the concept of a nationalist language, "Bahasa Indonesia," a red and white flag, an anthem, "Indonesia Raja," and it popularized the name "Indonesia." All these symbols were central during the postwar Indonesian revolution, and all are official national symbols today.

Sukarno's prewar life history, which is closely intertwined with the prewar history of the PNI, is organized in a episodic rhythm. Periods of fiery oratory and violent struggle alternate with periods of repression and exile. The rhythm of K. H. A. Dahlan's life history is much more sustained and systematic. Several points can be drawn from the contrast. Dahlan was santri, Sukarno abangan. Dahlan was reared according to the systematic logic of the Qur'anic doctrine, Sukarno through the dramatic adventures of the shadow play. Might the one type of education dispose the personality to seek constant and systematic unfolding of the life history, the other foster a disposition toward dramatic ups and downs? Obviously it is difficult to prove such gross linkages between cultural background and life history, but just as obviously some linkages do exist. The simplest explanation of the difference between Sukarno's episodes and Dahlan's constancy is that Sukarno was a nationalist, hence subject to periodic and sudden governmental repression. Dahlan, a neutral, was allowed to develop his movement methodically and undisturbed.

The colonial government did, of course, exercise a powerful influence on the course of nationalism during the prewar period. The government itself tried to provide political participation for the natives in the Volksraad or People's Council inaugurated by Governor-General Van Limburg Stirum in 1918. Composed of Europeans, Indo-Arabs, Indo-Chinese, and Indonesians, the members of the Volksraad were both elected and appointed. A series of reforms eventually brought the number of Indonesian seats to 30 as against 25 Europeans. The population of Indonesians from whom a vote was taken numbered approximately 1,000, the Europeans some 500. Limited in its power, the Volksraad served primarily as an advisory group and an arena for the airing of opinion.

During the 1920s the Indies economy prospered, reaching its peak in 1928. Profits went mainly into the pockets of Europeans and Chinese, but Indonesians gained too, as is suggested by the number who made the pilgrimage to Mecca. In 1927 the Indonesian pilgrims numbered 52,000, most of whom were able to pay their own expenses. Attracted by the prosperity, an increasing number of Netherlanders migrated to the Indies; by 1930 some 40,000 Netherlands-born Dutchmen lived there. Popular opinion came to emphasize a distinction between the "trekkers," the Dutchmen born in Holland who planned to return home after their term of service, and the "blijvers," the Dutchmen who considered the Indies their home. The blijvers seemed to involve themselves more with Indies affairs and to associate more with the natives. As the proportion of trekkers rose, the Dutch population became more alienated from the Indonesians. That alienation as well as considerations of policy encouraged the Indies government's increasingly suspicious, fearful, and repressive attitude toward native movements.

As the government became more repressive, nationalist movements became more cooperative. Nationalists reasoned that a stance of non-cooperation resulted merely in arrest and exile. The conservative Budi Utomo and Persatuan Bangsa Indonesia, a study club, united to form the Parindra (Greater Indonesian Party) in 1935, and in 1937 the moderate left established the Gerindo (Indonesian People's Movement). In the same year the Muslim reformists and conservatives united in the MIAI (Great Islamic Council of Indonesia). All these groups endeavored to work within the colonial framework by seeking representation in the Volksraad.

Indonesian faith in cooperation was shaken, however, in 1939. In 1936 an Indonesian member of the Volksraad had submitted a plea for a meeting of the Netherlands and the Indies to discuss the possibility of independence for the latter. Holland waited three years to respond, then gave a discouraging reply. Despairing of cooperation, the Indonesians united the varied nationalist factions into a single party, GAPI, and began to press more vigorously for independence. Holland promised in 1941 to hold a conference but could not give the matter her full attention since she had been occupied by Germany since 1940. The nationalists achieved little before the Japanese invaded and occupied the islands in 1942.

SOCIAL AND CULTURAL ASPECTS
OF PREWAR NATIONALISM

The Western-educated Indonesian was caught between the native culture, to which he could not comfortably return, and the Western culture, which he could not fully join. His biculturalism was reflected most vividly in his bilingualism. Reared from infancy to speak some tribal or ethnic tongue, he was educated in school to speak, write, and even think in the Dutch language. Yet Dutch could never be "his" language.[12] What bicultural and bilingual Indonesians craved, at least some of them, was a synthesis of the two poles, the Western and the native. Such a synthesis would embody both the traditional qualities of the native and the modern qualities of the West and it would be the Indonesian's own property, his own culture, his own language. The most successful cultural synthesis of this type was Bahasa Indonesia, the national language. Elaborated from the Malay which had served the islands for centuries as a lingua franca, Indonesian drew both on the regional languages and Western languages, yet it was distinct from both. It was first officially adopted in 1928 by a congress of Indonesian youths, reflecting the usual association between youth and the search for identity.

The Indo-European would seem nicely designed for a mestizo culture and language, for he was racially as well as culturally mestizo. Some Indos did express the view that by straddling the native and the Western, they could serve as the keystone that united the two in a political coalition. Neither Indonesian nor European responded enthusiastically to that Indo bid for Indies leadership, and the typical Indo was not enthusiastic either. The Indo was too compulsively bent on gaining acceptance by the European stratum to seriously develop the native half of his identity. Most Indos sided with the colonial power against the nationalist movements, and when Indonesia got its independence in 1949 the majority of Indos opted for Dutch citizenship and emigrated to Holland.

The Javanese and Minangkabau were both leaders in prewar nationalism, but in different ways. The intellectual leaders were largely Minangkabau and the charismatic leaders Javanese. The Javanese Sukarno and Tjokroaminoto were the two prewar leaders with the greatest mass appeal. Each had as his righthand man a Minangkabau intellectual; Tjokroaminoto had his Hadji Agus Salim and Sukarno his Muhammad Hatta and Sutan Sjahrir. That a Javanese was a mass leader is not surprising, for the masses were largely on Java, and only a Javanese could speak their language and manipulate their symbols. Why the intellectualist leaders should have been Minangkabau is a more difficult question, but several influences suggest themselves. Reformist Islam had been especially successful among the Minangkabau; although Muhammadijah was founded on Java, the Minangkabau were represented disproportionately in its leadership, and the earliest important system of reformist Muslim education was created in Minangkabau. Western education had great impact among the Minangkabau, too; they boasted one of the highest colonial Indonesian literacy rates. The Minangkabau tradition of bachelors going on the *rantau* (wandering) had combined with other factors to create a class of cosmopolitan men with a bourgeois, commercial turn of mind. These traditions and experiences would seem to have fostered the shrewd, rational, pious, and puritanical character that a Hatta or a Salim deployed as a useful balance to the charismatic and mystical personality of a Sukarno or a Tjokroaminoto.

The Sumatrans dominated the prewar florescence of literature in the Indonesian language. The obvious explanation is that the Sumatran languages such as Malay and Minangkabau resemble Indonesian more closely than does the Javanese. Not only in its vocabulary and in certain aspects of its grammar and phonetics, but also in its spirit, Indonesian language is alien to Javanese. Both in its refined, elevated, sanskritized krama and in its onomatopoetic, sensuous, and hilarious ngoko, Javanese is a remarkably rich medium, beautifully molded to express either the civilized pomp of the aristocrat or the earthy resilience of the peasant. Bahasa Indonesia is a language of alienated and bureaucratic intelligentsia who seek meaning through abstract ideology; to Javanese, Indonesian must have seemed, by comparison with their own rich language, peculiarly turgid, humorless, awkward, mechanical, and bereft of emotion or sensuality. They were understandably reluctant to abandon their own Javanese in favor of Bahasa Indonesia, although the post-World War II era would see a renaissance of Indonesian literature in which Javanese writers played an important role.

Certain classes of Indonesians were more disposed than others to support nationalism. Since the aristocrats and regents would lose their high position through the erasure of colonial rule, one would expect them to be conservative. The merchants stood to gain by nationalism since their competitors, European and Chinese, were foreign. The same was true of the intelligentsia; they were in competition with the Europeans and Indo-Europeans for the top bureaucratic and governmental posts. The masses supported such revolutionary movements as the S.I. and PKI, but most nationalist and communist leaders were of the "new prijaji" intelligentsia class. Even activist rank and file tended to be from this group, as is shown by a study of the social backgrounds of persons arrested in the 1926–1927 strikes.[13]

Capitalism and colonialism encouraged nationalism and communism by destroying patterns of traditional identity and community. A report on Minangkabau at the time of the PKI uprising of 1926 provides a telling example. Caught up in the commercial boom, Minangkabau were selling their ancestral land and their matrilineal kinship system was breaking down. Western education was producing Minangkabau youth who did not respect the uneducated adat chiefs. Muslims and communists alike saw capitalism as the source of these disruptions, and they joined forces to condemn it and to glorify communism as a path to a renewed community.[14]

The most consciously alienated members of Indies society were the intelligentsia. Whether prijaji Javanese or tribal Minangkabau, the Indonesian intellectual had been reared to inherit a position in a relatively stable and deeply meaningful local community. Entering a Western school, opting for a white-collar job, he was shorn of his traditional status yet not securely wedded to a modern one, for he earned the new status only through educational, political, social, or technical achievement. And he could lose it; biographies of the nationalist intelligentsia of the colonial era supply numerous instances of Indonesians who were trained for jobs in the civil service but never got the job or did not keep it, then drifted unemployed or employed at some unstable pursuit such as journalist, spiritualist, or, in the case of Tjokroaminoto, member of a traveling show.

Equipped through their education to articulate their alienation and to envisage a solution, the intelligentsia dreamed of a society of a communal rather than capitalist cast. That their visions took this turn was doubtless due to their bureaucratic rather than commercial training and experience, but deeper psychological processes may have been at work too. Such processes are suggested by the symbols through which the intelligentsia expressed their ideologies. Sukarno and some others came to envision the nation as a supervillage, united by such village institutions as *gotong-rojong* (mutual cooperation). The Indonesian constitution itself described the nation as a "family," and in political circles leaders were addressed as "father" and "mother," followers as "brothers." What is suggested here is simply that in formulating their ideas of nationhood, the Indonesian intelligentsia sought to include some of the familial, tribal, and village identity they had lost by becoming intelligentsia.

REFERENCES

[1] An excellent account of a peasant uprising is Sartono Kartodirdjo, *The Peasants' Revolt of Banten in 1888, Its Conditions, Course and Sequel: A Case Study of Social Movements in Indonesia* (The Hague: Nijhoff, 1966). See also Harry J. Benda and Lance Castles, "The Samin Movement," *Bijdragen tot de Taal-, Land-en Volkenkunde*, Vol. CXXV, No. 2 (1969), pp. 207–240; and The Siauw Giap, "The Samin and Samat Movements in Java: Two Examples of Peasant Resistance," *Revue du Sud-Est Asiatique*, No. 2 (1967), pp. 1073–1113; No. 1 (1968), pp. 303–310.

[2] On Budi Utomo, see Bernard H. M. Vlekke, *Nusantara: A History of Indonesia*, rev. ed. (The Hague and Bandung: Van Hoeve, 1959), pp. 348–391.

[3] On reformism in Indonesia, see Harry J. Benda, *The Crescent and the Rising Sun: Indonesian Islam under the Japanese Occupation, 1942–1945* (The Hague: Van Hoeve, 1958), Chaps. 1, 2; on reformism in Malaya and Singapore,

see William R. Roff, *The Origins of Malay Nationalism* (Kuala Lumpur and New Haven: Univ. of Malaya Press and Yale Univ. Press, 1967), Chaps. 2, 3; on reformism in west Sumatra, see Taufik Abdullah, *Schools and Politics: The Kaum Muda Movement in West Sumatra (1927-1933)* (Ithaca, N.Y.: Modern Indonesia Project, Cornell University, 1971).

[4] Dahlan's life is reported in *Riwajat Hidup K. H. A. Dahlan, 'amal per-djoangannja* (Djokjakarta: Pimpinan Pusat Muhammadijah, 1968). The most detailed English-language compendium of facts and sources on Muhammadijah is Alfian, *Islamic Modernism in Indonesian Politics: The Muhammadijan Movement during the Dutch Colonial Period, 1912-1942*, unpublished doctoral dissertation (University of Wisconsin, 1970). A summary of Muhammadijan doctrine is Howard M. Federspiel, "The Muhammadijah: A Study of an Orthodox Islamic Movement in Indonesia," *Indonesia*, No. 10 (October 1970), pp. 57-80. Several of my remarks regarding Muhammadijah are based on research among the contemporary Muhammadijans which I carried out from January to July 1970 in Jogjakarta and other regions of Indonesia.

[5] This account was related to me by one of the converted criminals who led the movement to industrialize and Muhammadijahnize Pekadjangan.

[6] Ruth T. McVey, "Taman Siswa and the Indonesian National Awakening," *Indonesia*, Vol. 4 (October 1967), pp. 128-149.

[7] Quoted in Heather S. Sutherland, "Pudjangga Baru: Aspects of Indonesian Intellectual Life in the 1930's," *Indonesia*, Vol 6 (1968), p.111.

[8] This paragraph follows closely Anthony Johns, "The Genesis of Modern Literature," in Ruth T. McVey (ed.), *Indonesia* (New Haven, Conn: Southeast Asia Studies, Yale University, 1963), pp. 410-437. The most complete Indonesian literary history is A. Teeuw, *Modern Indonesian Literature* (The Hague: Nijhoff, 1967). Modern Indonesian literature in English translation can be read in Faubian Bowers (ed.), "Perspective on Indonesia," *Atlantic Monthly Supplement*, Vol. 197, No. 6 (1956), pp. 97-168; John M. Echols, *Indonesian Writing in Translation* (Ithaca, N.Y.: Modern Indonesia Project, Cornell University, 1956); Rufus S. Hendon, *Six Indonesian Short Stories* (New Haven, Conn.: Southeast Asia Studies, Yale University, 1968); Burton Raffel, *The Complete Prose and Poetry of Chairil Anwar* (Albany: State Univ. of New York Press, 1970) and *Anthology of Modern Indonesian Poetry* (Berkeley: Univ. of California Press, 1964); Lionel Wigmore, *Span: An Adventure in Asian and Australian Writing* (Melbourne: Cheshire, 1958).

[9] Robert van Niel, *The Emergence of the Modern Indonesian Elite* (The Hague and Bandung: Van Hoeve, 1960), pp. 101-159, describes in detail the career of Sarekat Islam. A detailed account of movements during the prewar era is J. M. Pluvier, *Overzicht van de ontwikkeling der nationalistische beweging in Indonesie in de jaren 1930 tot 1942* (The Hague and Bandung: Van Hoeve, 1953).

[10] Bernard Dahm, *Sukarno and the Struggle for Indonesian Independence*, trans. Mary F. Somers Heidhues (Ithaca, N.Y.: Cornell Univ. Press, 1969).

[11] This account comes largely from Bernard Dahm, *Sukarno and the Struggle for Indonesian Independence*, but also from Cindy Adams, *Sukarno: An Autobiography* (New York: Bobbs-Merrill, 1965).

[12] A suggestive analysis of the sociocultural meaning of the Dutch, Indonesian, and Javanese languages is Benedict Anderson, "The Languages of Indonesian Politics," *Indonesia*, No. 1 (April 1966), pp. 89–117.

[13] Van Niel, *Emergence of Modern Indonesian Elite*, pp. 233–236.

[14] B. Schrieke, *Indonesian Sociological Studies*, Part I (The Hague and Bandung: Van Hoeve, 1955), pp. 83–144.

EIGHT

REVOLUTION AND INDEPENDENCE

> . . . berdjuanglah mati-matian dan
> membating-tulanglah habis-habisan
> seolah-olah kita ini malaekat-malaekat
> jang menjerbu dari langit! (Struggle and
> work your fingers to the bone like angels
> striking from the skies!)
> President Sukarno, Independence Day
> speech of August 17, 1960[1]

The Dutch, who had fallen to Germany in 1940, were ill-prepared with troops or weapons for the Japanese invasion of the Indies in 1942. As the Dutch were rapidly defeated by the Japanese forces, herded into concentration camps, and forced to engage in degrading work, their prestige fell in native eyes. Dutch internment left administrative posts open. Some of these posts the Japanese filled with the Indonesian intelligentsia, but the pangreh-pradja, the traditional prijaji civil service, retained the most important Indonesian positions.[2]

What the intelligentsia gained during the occupation was not so much bureaucratic position as organizational skills and opportunities with which they could sow the seeds of a national society and culture. Nationalist leaders, such as Sukarno and Hatta, were returned from exile by the Japanese and were asked to cooperate in propagandizing for the Japanese cause. Exploiting the extensive organizational resources which the Japanese put at his disposal, Sukarno traveled the countryside, speaking to the people and building mass support for Indonesian nationalism. From the Japanese, Sukarno and other nationalists acquired new ideas for dramatizing and ritualizing politics. Japanese techniques of propagandizing, sloganizing, and staging mass rallies, shows, and song-fests would later serve Indonesia by sustaining the revolutionary spirit of 1945–1949. And the Japanese experience encouraged Sukarno's view of revolution as a romantic adventure, his obsessive fear of Western cultural penetration, and his search for an Asian national identity. Younger Indonesians found the violent and romantic symbols of the Japanese military regime an appealing alternative to the stolid and color-less colonial bureaucracy of their fathers.

The Dutch fear of pan-Islamism had forced them to keep tight reins on the Muslims, but the Japanese saw themselves and Islam as having interests in common. They hoped to persuade the Islamic teach-ers to join them in the holy war against the unrighteous Western infidel. Some teachers were rigidly and heroically uncooperative, as in the in-cident where Hadji Rasul, a famous Minangkabau reformer, refused at an important ceremony to bow in the diretion of the imperial palace. Others were more cooperative, and Bagus, a Muhammadijan colleague of Rasul, accompanied Sukarno and Hatta to Tokyo in 1943 to accept a decoration. The Muslims enjoyed more freedom to organize politically under the Japanese than under the Dutch. Eventually the conservative and reformist elements of Indonesian Islam united to establish the Masjumi Party.

The Muslims did not, however, replace the prijaji in the bureauc-racy. Rural Muslim teachers enjoyed ceremonies of honor and special courses, but their dissatisfaction with Japanese rule is suggested by the fact that two of the three revolts against the Japanese were by them. The failure of Muslims to gain real power during the occupation is indicated by their initially weak position in the postwar nationalist coalition that was heavily dominated by nationalists and bureaucrats.

Indonesian youths were indoctrinated and drilled in school, and they studied the Japanese and Indonesian languages. Through such military groups as the Japanese-trained PETA (Defenders of the Father-land), Hizbullah (Army of God), and the HEIHO, an auxiliary corps, the youths got experience in leadership which most of them, especially the Javanese, were denied under the Dutch. Since the defeat of Ma-taram, respect for the military had been lacking among the Javanese, and throughout the colonial period most Indonesian soldiers had been recruited from such outer-island groups as the Ambonese and the Mina-hasans. Under the Japanese, imbued with traditions of the Bushido (Way of the Warrior), a military ethos flourished. The military youth (*pemuda*) groups later became a force in the nationalist movement that could not be subordinated to the civil service or the political parties.

The Indonesian literary movement took a dynamic turn as the chaotic and disordered occupation produced two of the most creative writers in Indonesian literary history: Chairil Anwar and Idrus. Idrus's prose accounts of the decomposition of life during the Japanese period were written in an incisive, vigorous, and sardonic style (suggested by such story titles as "Oh! Oh! Oh!"). Anwar wrote poetry of ferocious intensity, expressing passionate and wild feeling. His 1943 poem "Me" ("*Aku*") ended by shouting a desire to live a thousand years, but his reckless way of life resulted in his death from syphilis, tuberculosis, typhus, and cirrhosis of the liver at the age of 27.[3]

Under conditions of war and occupation, export industries collapsed, unbacked currency caused galloping inflation, and rationing led to black markets, hoarding, speculation, and rampant corruption. Hundreds of thousands of peasants were marched off to die in slave labor on projects resembling the "Bridge on the River Kwai." Youths were drafted into the military and police. Villages were returned to the system of forced deliveries. Many areas suffered critical shortages of rice, the population of rats and bedbugs exploded, and death rates rose. There was torture and harsh despotism. The "Rust en Orde" of the colonial empire was destroyed, and from the ruins rose the Indonesian revolution.

REVOLUTION[4]

As their defeat became imminent, the Japanese set up a preparatory committee to draft a constitution for Indonesian independence. The grant of independence had not been received, however, at the time of Japanese surrender in mid-August 1945. Sukarno and Hatta, the older nationalists, preferred to wait; they were not yet convinced that Japan would surrender, they felt that the Indonesian underground was not yet able to muster sufficient strength to overthrow the Japanese, and they feared that a useless bloodbath would ensue. But Sukarno and Hatta were kidnapped by some of the Pemuda Indonesia, the impatient and militant All-Indonesia Youth Organization, and these youths prompted them to declare independence immediately. After some argument, they agreed, and Sukarno, sleepless and feverish, broadcast the declaration on August 17, 1945.

The new nation had barely finished establishing a rudimentary organization, with Sukarno as president, Hatta as vice-president, a cabinet and a constitution, when the first British troops began landing in Jogjakarta (formerly Batavia) to reclaim Indonesia for the allies and the Dutch. Thus began the four years of chaos and struggle known as the Indonesian Revolution.

In the center of the uproar were the pemuda, whose bands were frequently remnants of the Japanese-trained military groups. Declaring their own independence as well as that of Indonesia, the youth gangs toted guns, looted stores, and decorated walls with anticolonial slogans on daggers dripping red to express their defiance of the Dutch authorities. PETA units attacked Japanese posts and conquered some Japanese units, and, inspired by the seductive voice of a certain Bung Tomo, they ferociously fought the British during the battle of Surabaja in November 1945. By 1946 the pemuda groupings, building on the PETA groups that had refused to comply with Japanese orders for disarmament, were slowly coalescing into a national army.

Robber bands of fanatical Islamic persuasion were roaming the countryside of west Java. Throughout the islands, Dutch, Chinese, Eurasian, and Ambonese procolonialists were persecuted, raped, and killed. At the same time, roving patrols of trigger-happy Dutch and Ambonese of the KNIL, the Royal Netherlands Indies Army, were shooting and kidnapping Indonesians. Local revolutions, spearheaded by the pemuda in such places as north Sumatra, resulted in violent overthrow of aristocrats formerly supported by the Dutch.

During the tumult, the leaders, Sukarno, Hatta, and Sjahrir (head of the first cabinet), were endeavoring to negotiate with Holland. They strove to achieve independence through diplomacy rather than violence, especially through the mobilizing of international opinion in favor of Indonesia. In these diplomatic strategies Sjahrir was more effective than Sukarno. Negotiations were difficult since the radical pemuda favored an uncompromising revolutionary stance. Violently opposing each concession, the pemuda repeatedly provoked a public outcry that led to the fall of a succession of cabinets.

In the fall of cabinets, the Muslims played their part, too. From the beginning of independence, they had opposed Sukarno's Pantjasila, the "philosophical basis of the Indonesian state." Pantjasila erred, in the Muslim view, by listing belief in God as merely one of the five principles of the state. What was worse, Sukarno reduced the five principles to one, social harmony. Santri felt that Sukarno exposed his abangan world view in reducing God to a vague notion of society. Desiring an Islamic state rather than a secular one, the Muslims reconstituted the Masjumi Party to represent their cause. The Masjumi opposed each cabinet in turn during the revolution, gaining increased representation as each new cabinet was established.

Muslims opposed communists as well as nationalists on the grounds that the communists were atheists. Lacking God, communists were guided, in the Muslim view, by no positive norms, but merely by the desire to destroy and disrupt. The communists, for their part, regarded the Muslims as hypocritical Arabs who exploited labor through capitalism and women through polygyny. The Muslim-communist conflict was exacerbated in 1948 when the PKI, establishing a rebel government in the central Javanese town of Madiun, razed mosques and otherwise persecuted the santri. PKI appealed to the citizenry of Indonesia to forsake the Republic but the government cleverly provoked a battle before the communists were prepared. Republican troops, supported by some of the santri, destroyed the PKI and killed the PKI leader, Musso. For a time the PKI burrowed underground.

Meanwhile the Dutch had formed a system of states in east Indonesia and had launched a "police action," capturing much of west and east Java as well as oil areas of east and south Sumatra. In captured regions they restored conservatives, including Chinese and Eurasians, to power. In December 1948 they began what they called a second "police action," bombing the temporary Republican capital, Djokjakarta. The Dutch occupied that city, captured Sukarno and Hatta, and then took most of the remaining Republican territory. But Indonesian troops, forced to retreat into the central mountains and jungles, emerged periodically for guerrilla attacks on the Dutch forces occupying the lowland and urban territories. The success of such attacks and the threat of sanctions applied by the United Nations and the United States eventually brought Holland to the conference table. Indonesian independence was granted on December 27, 1949.

Even after that date, sporadic resistance occurred in the outer islands. The south Moluccas, for example, seceded from the Republic and opposed the landing of federal troops. But for the majority of Indonesians, especially the Javanese, the revolutionary experience was a cause for patriotism and *élan* lacking in colonies such as Malaya that were freed without battle. Concepts such as *perdjuangan* (struggle), *merdeka* (freedom), *semangat* (dynamic spirit), and, of course, *Revolusi*,[5] had caught fire during the revolution and were absorbed into the speeches, novels, plays, and dreams of the Indonesians, even to the extent of influencing their image of the ideal thrust of human life.

INDEPENDENCE[6]

When Indonesia gained its independence in 1949, those who came to power were predominantly the leaders of the revolution. Sukarno became the new state's president and Hatta its prime minister. Partly due to Hatta's influence in the army and partly due to his major diplomatic role in bringing the negotiations with Holland to a successful conclusion, Hatta was at the time perhaps more powerful than Sukarno. The next few years reflected his strong and rational if uncharismatic influence. The cabinets under Hatta gave high priority to establishing security, unifying the army, and stimulating economic development.

The press was free; the seeds of a constitutional democracy appeared to have been planted; and, thanks to the Korean War boom, exports increased.

In that encouraging atmosphere, education expanded enormously. The number of elementary-school pupils increased to three times the prewar number, there were fifteen times as many senior-high pupils, and ten times as many students at the universities. New government universities were built at Jogjakarta and elsewhere to supplement those at Djakarta and Bandung. A host of private universities sprang up, sometimes with revolutionary names, flimsy housing, and suspect credentials, to admit those who were not accepted by the governmental institutions. To absorb the hordes of school and university graduates, the bureaucracy swelled to include, by 1953, some 500,000 posts—more than four times the number that had existed under the Dutch. With expansion, the bureaucracy became increasingly sprawling, disorganized, ineffective, and corrupt.

Failing to solve all problems through their practical approach, Hatta and his associates failed also to inspire the revolutionaries who felt that their routine postrevolutionary existence lacked élan and meaning. Hatta's influence declined. In 1953 a cabinet favorable to Sukarno's approach was formed, and Sukarno assumed the dominant role in Indonesian politics.

Accelerated economic decay, bureaucratic inefficiency, and political turbulence marked the Sukarno years of 1953 to 1956. A major political cleavage developed between the parties of the santri and those of the abangan. The traditionalist Muslim group, Nahdatul Ulama, which came to consider the Masjumi excessively intellectual and innovative, had left that party in 1952. With the removal of the traditionalist N.U., Masjumi became increasingly bitter toward the PKI. And the PKI, now recovered from Madiun, joined with PNI to form a bloc opposing Masjumi's plan to create a Muslim state. The abangan-santri split correlated with that between salaried workers and private entrepreneurs, Javanese and Sumatrans, and Sukarno and Hatta. The deeply rooted cleavage between santri Masjumi and abangan PNI-PKI penetrated to the village level as each bloc sought mass support in the elections of 1955.

Distracted by politics from policy-making and problem-solving, the government during these years resorted to unsound economic devices. Inflation accelerated, the bureaucracy became grotesquely bloated, and export production barely increased. The government "Indonesianized" the economy by taking over foreign enterprises in order to heighten the sense of national unity and to gain quick money. The consequence was a sudden and marked drop in the already low production.

The election had been viewed as the solution to all conflict, but the basic cleavages remained. The outer islanders tended to favor the

Hatta-santri-private enterprise-Masjumi bloc. They resented Sukarno's approach, and they were bitter that outer-island profits filled Javanese stomachs. In 1958, army commanders of certain outer-island regions proclaimed a rebel Indonesian government, and a civil war ensued for several years.

Sukarno proposed a solution to strife, his concept (*konsepsi*) of "guided democracy." Guided democracy called for the formation of a single cabinet in which all major parties would cooperate harmoniously and a national council in which the various functional groups—workers, peasants, national businessmen, and others—would unite through consensus rather than the vote. Sukarno's idea was to abandon the "free-for-all," conflict-inducing democracy of the West, and to replace it with the government-by-consensus supposedly practiced in ancient and idyllic Indonesian villages. With the nation in danger of splitting and exploding, few opposed Sukarno's authoritarian system. In fact, many Javanese, accustomed to centuries of Hindu-Buddhist kingship and Dutch colonialism, found guided democracy a more familiar and compatible concept than constitutional democracy.

Implementing his plan, Sukarno dissolved the elected parliament and the cabinet responsible to parliament—agencies that restrained his power. He instituted a 616-member People's Consultative Assembly that seldom met. He set up a cabinet responsible only to him. He also created a 77-member National Planning Council, a 45-member Supreme Advisory Council, and a National Front Organization enrolling 200 political parties, mass organizations, and functional groups, and encompassing, by 1962, a membership of 33 million.

The army, assisting Sukarno in his "guiding" actions, banned communist political meetings, labor-union activities, and activities of parties opposing Sukarno. With the decline of parties and parliamentary apparatus, civil liberties diminished. Strikes and newspapers were banned and legal guarantees were brushed aside. Chinese trading was prohibited in rural areas, British and Indian enterprises were seized, and private-property rights were not highly respected.

While the army supplied the muscle, PKI worked on the mind, drumming up crowds for the Bung's speeches, organizing demonstrations, and shouting about the countryside, "Support Bung Karno's Konsepsi 100%!" PKI publicly subordinated goals of class struggle to those of national unity. Although it was the largest communist party outside the Sino-Soviet bloc by 1963 (it claimed 3 million core members and 12 million members of its mass organizations), PKI was exploited by Sukarno and hamstrung by the army.[7]

"I like symbolism," confessed Sukarno, as he created an abundance of symbols for his "spiritual revolution." Through street-cleaning and earth-hoeing cermonies, he exhorted the people to "retool" for the future. He pled for a return to the Revolutionary Constitution of 1945, that "magically, sentimentally, nationally loaded" document which possesses "soul and spirit."[8] He verbally transformed the malarial swamps of west New Guinea into a paradise to be wrested from Dutch imperialists by lady paratroopers emulating the mythical heroine, Srikandi. A sample of his verbal alchemy is given in the quotation heading this chapter: Sukarno brilliantly converts *kasar* labor into *halus* thrusts of angels from the sky.

Manipol-Usdek, the central ideology of guided democracy, was an acronym coined by Sukarno and his associates. The letters denoted exalted objectives: to attain the "just and prosperous society," organized under "socialism a la Indonesia," financed by "guided economy," and in keeping with the "Indonesian personality." Taught in schools, advertised by newspapers, propagated by song and dance, billboards, and shanty-town gates, Manipol-Usdek was supposed to elicit absolute loyalty. Editors, professors, students, and other intellectuals were made to swear allegiance to it. Civil servants were indoctrinated by courses in it, and those who did not display sufficient devotion to it were "retooled"—that is, demoted or dismissed.

Though inspiring a certain mood of unity and dynamism, guided democracy discouraged efficient administration and development. Scarce funds were diverted from urgent practical tasks into the purchase of such prestige symbols as bombers, destroyers, missiles (ostensibly to defend the motherland against the imperialistic and predatory Dutch and British in New Guinea and Malaysia), nuclear generators, giant stadiums, luxury hotels, the National Monument, and the supreme National Mosque (which is still under construction). While weakening the power of the practical administrators, guided democracy legitimized the power of wielders of symbols. Even those practical administrators who did retain their positions found it difficult to bring about practical reforms, for such achievement possessed little significance or meaning under the ideology and world view of Manipol-Usdek.

At all levels of bureaucracy and society (the two were increasingly synonymous as government expanded under guided democracy), symbolic expression of loyalty to the ruling powers replaced competence in work as a criterion for status and reward. The artist must paint slogans, the scientist must demonstrate how his research reflected Manipol-Usdek. Initiative in private enterprise was not only suspect but actively discouraged by such measures as the sudden and drastic reduction of all bank accounts over 25,000 rupiah.

Prices were tripling annually, government salaries were rising but slowly, and the discrepancy stimulated rampant bureaucratic corruption. Malnutrition, disease, decayed roads, degenerating vehicles, idle

factories, mobs of beggars, gangs of thieves were all signs of economic **91**
and social decline. Political satire by folk singers, jokes by clowns in
folk plays, and the "satanic reversal" of meaning of such formerly charismatic symbols of the revolution as *bung* and *aksi*[9] revealed the despair
of the populace. The regime juggled its slogans and symbols, playing
off the PKI against the army, in an effort to stay in power and preserve
the Republic under the worsening conditions. The devices to get quick
funds and the import of arms provided the government with patronage
to distribute to the competing factions in an endeavor to prevent civil
war like that of the fifties. The xenophobic ideological and military
campaigns against everything from Dutch imperialism to American
rock-'n'-roll (which Sukarno banned) show the familiar pattern of bol-
stering internal unity and morale by external scapegoats. Yet the resort
to symbols was certainly more than irrational response to desperate
conditions. After all, from the ancient Hinduized kingdoms came the
tradition that the regime was in essence symbolic, and that proper
symbolic action by the ruler was necessary to overcome the chaos of
kalijuga.

AFTER SUKARNO

On October 1, 1965, units of Sukarno's palace guard seized and mur-
dered six top right-wing army generals, and announced the formation
of an Indonesian Revolutionary Council. The revolt was quickly broken
by the regular army, which then mounted a compaign against the al-
leged source of the attempted coup, the PKI. Sukarno endeavored to
protect leading communists and pro-communists, but the army and
supporting santri groups killed hundreds of thousands of supposed PKI
sympathizers and their wives and children during late 1965 and early
1966 in central and east Java, Bali, and several other regions. In the
Javanese areas where the number of victims was greatest, Muslim youth
groups took the lead in the slaughter as pesantrèn and madrasah were
transformed into headquarters for the Islamic forces.

Shoved from power in 1966—cautiously by the army, raucously by
mobs of protesting students—Sukarno transferred all executive power
to General Suharto in 1967. In March 1967 Suharto was appointed acting
president while the provisional People's Congress stripped Sukarno of
all governmental powers. The more flamboyant of the Sukarnoist symbols were dropped, but some of the basic ones, such as Pantjasila, were
retained in hopes that their charisma would rub off on the new government.

After the destruction of the PKI, the santri forces enjoyed a revival,
and reformist Muslims prepared to reestablish Masjumi, which Sukarno

had outlawed in 1960. Suharto kept the ban on Masjumi, but he permitted Muslims to form a new party, PMI (Partai Muslimin Indonesia), which was dominated by Muhammadijah. Army leaders who considered Islam an archaic doctrine and feared the rise of an Islamic state managed to prevent the old heroes of Masjumi from seizing leadership of the new party. The army encouraged the installation of PMI leaders who were loyal to the Suharto government.[10]

As the government prepared for the elections of 1971, the political configuration differed from that existing before the elections of 1955: the PKI and Masjumi were both officially extinct, and the military was in control. In the House of Representatives (*Dewan Perwakilan Rakjat*), the largest number of seats (78) were occupied by the PNI, which preached Marxism, nationalism, and Sukarnoism, and appealed especially to abangan bureaucrats. With almost as many seats (75), N.U. appealed to the rural syncretist santri, especially those of east Java. The PMI, with only 20 seats, appealed to the urban Muslim reformists. The armed forces had 75 seats. The PKI was banned, some 120,000 of its members were still in prison, and several of its leaders had fled to India, Albania, and Peking.

To compete with the parties, the government formed a coalition of labor unions, professional organizations, youth groups, technocrats, and even churches, known as *Golkar* or *Golongan Karya*, which means "functional groups." Financed by government funds, Golkar's campaign slogans were "Development, yes; politics, no" and "Development before ideology." Forced to represent the opposite position, the PNI mobilized the oratory of Sukarno's son Guntur and asked its voters to "stab" the *banteng*, the raging bull which was the PNI symbol depicted on the ballots. The votes were cast on July 3, 1971. Golkar won an overwhelming victory. With over two-thirds of the vote, it controlled 335 of the 460 seats in the House of Representatives. N.U. was a distant second with 61 seats, and the other parties won hardly any seats at all, with PNI suffering the most crushing defeat.

Under the Suharto government, the black market virtually disappeared. Inflation dropped from 63.5 percent in 1966 to practically zero. Private enterprise was encouraged under the leadership of a brilliant and pragmatic professor of economics and a technocratic national planning board. Foreign investment was welcomed, and modern Western and Japanese banks suddenly sprang up along a new expressway leading to the foreigner's luxury Djakarta suburb, Kebajoran. Conflict with Malaysia ceased and Indonesia rejoined the U.N. It seemed as if the pragmatic spirit of Hatta had revived and that of Sukarno expired with the June 1970 death of the Great Leader of the Revolution.

[1] "Laksana Malaekat Jang Menjerbu Dari Langit," in *Dari Proklamasi sampai Resopim* (From Proclamation to Revolution, Indonesian Socialism, and National Leadership) (Djakarta: Departèmen Penerangan, 1962), p. 477.

[2] Benedict R. O'G. Anderson, "Japan: 'The Light of Asia,' " in Josef Silverstein (ed.), *Southeast Asia in World War II: Four Essays* (New Haven, Conn.: Southeast Asia Studies, Yale University, 1966), pp. 13–50, provides much of the basis for these paragraphs on the Japanese occupation.

[3] Burton Raffel, *The Complete Prose and Poetry of Chairil Anwar* (Albany: State Univ. of New York Press, 1970), p. xv.

[4] The classic account of the revolution is George McTurnan Kahin, *Nationalism and Revolution in Indonesia* (Ithaca, N.Y.: Cornell Univ. Press, 1952). A vivid local account is John R. W. Smail, *Bandung in the Early Revolution, 1945–1946* (Ithaca, N.Y.: Modern Indonesia Project, Cornell University, 1964).

[5] See Benedict Anderson, "The Languages of Indonesian Politics," *Indonesia*, No. 1 (April 1966), p. 105.

[6] This section follows Herbert Feith, "Dynamics of Guided Democracy," in Ruth T. McVey (ed.), *Indonesia* (New Haven, Conn.: Southeast Asia Studies, Yale University, 1963), pp. 309–410. Essential, too, is Daniel Lev, *The Transition to Guided Democracy* (Ithaca, N.Y.: Modern Indonesia Project, Cornell University, 1966). A popular but absorbing account of Indonesia under Sukarno is Maslyn Williams, *Five Journeys from Jakarta: Inside Sukarno's Indonesia* (New York: Morrow, 1966). Racy but revealing is Willard Hanna, *Bung Karno's Indonesia* (New York: American Field Staff, 1960). An excellent localized study is R. William Liddle, *Ethnicity, Party, and National Integration: An Indonesian Case Study* (New Haven, Conn.: Yale Univ. Press, 1970).

[7] See Donald Hindley, *The Communist Party of Indonesia, 1951–1963* (Berkeley and Los Angeles: Univ. of California Press, 1964). The earlier periods of Indonesian communism are throughly covered by Ruth T. McVey, *The Rise of Indonesian Communism* (Ithaca, N.Y.: Cornell Univ. Press, 1960).

[8] Sukarno, "Penemuan Kembali Revolusi Kita" (The Rediscovery of Our Revolution), in *Dari Proklamasi sampai Resopim*, p. 415.

[9] Anderson, "The Languages of Indonesian Politics," p. 106.

[10] K. E. Ward, *The Foundation of the Partai Muslimin Indonesia* (Ithaca, N.Y.: Modern Indonesia Project, Cornell University, 1970). See also B. J. Boland, *The Struggle of Islam in Modern Indonesia* (The Hague: Nijhoff, 1971); and Allan A. Samson, "Islam in Indonesian Politics," *Asian Survey*, Vol. VIII (December 1968), pp. 1001–1017.

NINE

CULTURAL DIVERSITY IN
CONTEMPORARY INDONESIA: JAVA,
BALI, SUMATRA

*Lain desa, lain adat (for each village, a
different culture).*
Indonesian folk saying

The 3,000 islands of Indonesia contain some 300 groups of the type the
Indonesians call *bangsa*, that is, tribal and ethnic groups distinguished
by name, language, custom, location, ecology, and social organization.
To illustrate something of the diversity among these groups, this chapter
and the next will portray a few of the many, endeavoring to depict
at least one representative from each of the major cultural and geograph-
ic regions of the archipelago. In accord with the book's historical thrust,
emphasis will be placed on those societies that have already been cited
for their important roles in Indonesian history and society: the Javanese
(who comprise half of the entire Indonesian population), Sundanese,
Balinese, Toba Batak, Minangkabau, Atjehnese, Makassarese, Buginese,
Mabonese, and Chinese. A few of the more remote societies from such
islands as Borneo, New Guinea, and the Lesser Sundas will also be
sketched, and it should be said that even these groups are only relatively
isolated; some are Islamized or Christianized, some organized into kingdoms, and some have experienced centuries of contact with the more
"historical" states of Indonesia and have contributed a certain number
of religious or political figures to the wider stream of Indonesian history
and civilization.[1]

THE JAVANESE[2]

Occupying the eastern two-thirds of the island of Java, the 50 million
speakers of the Javanese language are primarily rural peasants who cultivate irrigated rice. Population densities of the rural Javanese are among

the highest in the world, their landholdings among the smallest; Javanese farms average less than two acres in size, and a peasant with five acres is considered a large landowner. Living in bamboo or cement houses tightly packed into clusters in the midst of rice paddies, the Javanese farmers reflect in their settlement patterns a certain communalism; a relevant contrast is with the more individualistic practices of non-Javanese swidden farmers who isolate each farmhouse among its own fields.

An urbanized version of the rural village, found in Javanese towns and cities, is the shantytown or *kampung*. Set in rows along the walkways (*gang*) that burrow inside Indonesian city blocks, the kampung houses resemble those of the rural village, though their cluster is not surrounded by fields. Each kampung reveals its unity in that it possesses a name, which is usually posted on the entrance of each gang and uttered by the kampung dweller in response to the question, "Where do you live?" Entering the gang, the pedestrian trespasses on private quarters; only a few feet from his eyes are the innards of the usually tiny houses, displaying sleeping mats, family quarrels, women stripped down to brassieres, and magical heirlooms on the bedroom wall.

The rural "village complex," called the *kalurahan*, is headed by the *lurah*, a headman elected by the villagers. The kalurahan includes several villages, called *dukuhan* by the government and *desa* by the villagers. The kalurahan in turn is included within larger units, each of which is headed by an official appointed by the central government. The lives and work of the rural villagers are intimately bound to the village and its government. The village acts as a corporate unit holding ownership rights to much of the land on which the villagers farm, and the lurah exercises ultimate authority over the irrigation system. The villager's unit of residence thus controls his tools of production. For the kampung dweller this is not the case; his kampung is merely residential, not productive—a slum version of the "bedroom suburb." Earning his living by working in a shoe factory or lumber yard owned by a capitalist who has nothing to do with his kampung, or selling snacks on the streets outside his kampung, the kampung dweller separates his residential and productive activities.

Both rural village and urban kampung have a *pundèn*, a shrine venerating the community's founder. Though still significant for the rural villagers, the pundèn is ignored by many kampung dwellers, especially those of the younger generation. The villager practices a village-wide ritual, the *bersih désa*, during which offerings are made to the pundèn and the village is purified of dangerous spirits. The kampung dweller's loss of interest in the pundèn and the bersih désa reflects the narrowed, merely residential role of the kampung in his life.

Villagers may unite in mass actions, such as slaughtering a thief, building a road, guarding the village, and harvesting their fields. Just as important as such coordination of effort is the avoidance of strife, a concern expressed in the method of running village meetings: decisions are made by consensus rather than vote. Villagers emphasize that in all affairs they should *rukun*, which means not that they should chummily rub shoulders but that they should tactfully avoid stepping on each others' toes. Unlike the communal village of romantic Western fantasy and ideology, the Javanese désa is not a close-knit group, and neighbors living 150 yards apart may be ignorant of each others' affairs.

As a basis of organizing social life, kinship is not much more important for Javanese than for Westerners. As in Western European tradition, descent is traced through both mother and father—that is, descent is bilateral—and the nuclear family, consisting of husband, wife, and children, usually maintains only loose connections to wider kinfolk. Living in its own independent household, the nuclear family unites with kin only on such occasions as weddings. Exceptions to these statements are found in remote villages, which contain a few households including two, three, or even four families united by bonds between brothers and sisters. Even in such extended households, however, each nuclear family is regarded as a distinct unit, and each maintains its own separate kitchen.

Throughout Javanese society, bonds between sisters remain strong even after they marry and live in separate households. The Javanese household often includes a child "borrowed" from the mother's sister, who may be poor, divorced, subscribe to the traditional belief that children learn halus manners by living in a strange household, or simply have so many children that she "knows not what to do." Not only nieces and nephews but also parents who live with a couple are more likely related to the wife than to the husband. An aged father generally prefers living with his daughter to living with his son, since after early childhood sons treat fathers with great deference and formality. The mother is thus the focus of those household bonds (to *her* sisters and *her* parents, rather than to the husband's) that link her household to the wider family, a pattern sometimes called "matrifocal." Especially in rural areas, this matrifocal tendency is reinforced by a matrilocal one during the couple's early years of marriage, which means that the couple lives with the wife's parents during that time.

The Javanese description of the mother as "minister of the interior" aptly catches the central role played by the mother in the household. She is fully in charge of household finance; the husband turns all of his wages over to her (or is supposed to), and she doles them out to him, the children, and the bill collectors as the occasion demands.

Earning as well as managing money, the mother often occupies herself with trade, whose link to the role of women is symbolized in the Javanese tradition that "playing store" is a game suitable for little girls but not for boys. The mother is usually responsible for disciplining the child, while the father stands aloof. The Javanese view that the house is maternal and feminine territory is expressed in certain traditions: the back and inner rooms are considered female, the guest room or porch, leading to the outside, is considered male, and at wedding parties men sit outside the house while the women sit and work inside.

Marriage among Javanese is traditionally arranged by parents. Despite the attraction of many of the young to the romantic ideal of choosing one's mate on the basis of love, most still follow the traditional pattern of arranged marriage. Rife in the fantasies of the Javanese male, if one may judge from confidential autobiographies as well as from popular drama, is the memory of the sweetheart of his youth whom he failed to marry because he accepted instead the wife chosen by his parents. Associated with the custom of parents choosing a socially acceptable spouse, the Javanese tends to marry within his own social class, high or low. Even stronger is the tendency of the santri to marry among themselves, avoiding marriage to the abangan who, the santri fear, will not faithfully conform to the Muslim faith.

The Javanese rate of divorce is one of the highest in the world; more than half of Javanese marriages end in divorce. Causes cited include the custom of arranging marriages, so that bride and groom do not choose one another and have no chance to test their compatibility before marriage. Relevant too is the Javanese view that divorce is less disruptive of life than a domicile rent by strife. A consequence of the high rate of divorce is that a great many Javanese children have experienced the loss of a parent. Prominent in Javanese songs and stories is the half-orphaned child, a symbol which evokes maudlin pity and tears. Just how the experience of the broken home affects the adult personality—whether, as some have suggested, it inculcates an attitude of avoiding deep and enduring bonds to anyone—is a question answerable only by research sensitive to the Javanese context.

Javanese kinship terms classify kinsmen according to generation; parents and parents' siblings are addressed by the same term, so that one's mother and aunt would both be called "mother." The Javanese system of terms and titles accords great respect to elder kinsmen, and titles such as "father" and "mother" are extended not only to uncles and aunts but also to respected elder persons outside the family. Titles of all kinds are important in Javanese culture. The Javanese should be addressed by his aristocratic or academic title, if he has one, otherwise by a term such as "father," "older brother," or "comrade." To address a respectable Javanese by his name alone is discourteous. To use a title without a name, however, is quite proper. In courtly circles during the colonial period, the custom of replacing name with title was carried to the point that a wife was addressed by her husband's title, as in "Mrs. Subdistrict Officer."[3] Since Hindu-Javanese times, the aristocrat (*prijaji*) has customarily changed both his title and his name when he changes status, suggesting that his name is more a badge of social than personal identity. One may hazard a generalization that, especially for Javanese of the higher strata, names and titles serve less to identify corporate social groups, cement intimate social bonds, or distinguish individual personalities than to *classify* persons according to their place in a rather rigid scheme of society and cosmos. Even more broadly, one could say that, in Java, classification of an individual according to his ethnic group, his rank, his place in the cosmos, is a ritual that must be performed before social interaction begins, and some Javanese conversations never seem to get beyond the endeavor of classification.

Among Javanese, especially those of the abangan type, it is very important to maintain a state of *slamet* (tranquility and order) throughout the life cycle, especially during crises of transition such as birth, adolescence, marriage, and death. To ensure slamet, the Javanese hold frequent *slametans* (communal feasts). Those attending are male members of the household (though the food is prepared by female members), close male neighbors, and perhaps others. Squatting on the floor of the host's domicile, listening to a high-Javanese speech and an Arabic prayer, quietly eating a few mouthfuls of rice, the slametan participants feel as one with each other and with the supernatural figures to whom the speech, prayer, and feast are oriented. The social and cosmic harmony issuing from the slametan soothes the soul of the individual, smoothing its surface so that dangerous spirits cannot penetrate.

Slametans are held at seven months and nine months of pregnancy; then, with variation according to locale, when the baby receives its formal name, when the baby's hair is cut, and when its umbilical cord falls off. On the baby's *weton* day, which is when the Javanese seven- and five-day weeks coincide 35 days after birth, a slametan is sometimes held again, and again on the 105th and 175th day after birth. Later occasions may also prompt the slametan, but certainly one will be held when the abangan boy is circumcised, which is between the ages of 12 and 14 for abangan boys (much younger for santri, who are usually circumcised between the ages of 6 and 9).[4]

The slametan is brought into the marriage festivities, as are other facets of abangan belief; for instance, cosmic calculations determine whether the weton day of the prospective bride and groom jibe and what wedding day is most auspicious. The marriage rituals include a procession of the groom's maternal and paternal relatives to the bride's house to offer wedding gifts before the wedding; a procession of the couple, together with the girl's legal representative, her *wali*, who is a patrilineal male relative deputized by the father to sign the marriage contract for him, and two witnesses, to the Muslim official; and, finally, an *adat* (pre-Islamic, traditional) ceremony at the bride's house. This adat ritual symbolically binds the groom to the bride's family. In the evening the bride's family holds a slametan to bless the union, and then a public dinner party. After remaining in seclusion at the bride's house for five days, the couple visits the groom's house, where his parents give a less lavish slametan and dinner.

Death is mourned by abangan Javanese through slametans held 3, 7, 40, 100, 365, and 1,000 days after the day of death. As in other Indonesian societies, the underlying notion seems to be that the deceased must be ushered gradually into the next life, just as he was brought gradually into this life. Reformist *santri* movements, such as the Muhammadijah, oppose both the slametan sequences that usher in birth and those that usher in death, and many devout Muhammadijans have ceased to practice these ritual sequences.

THE SUNDANESE[5]

The Sundanese, who occupy most of west Java, comprise the second largest ethnic and linguistic group in Indonesia, numbering over 10 million. Their core territory is the central mountainous area known as Priangan, the capital of which is Bandung.

Much of Sundanese culture resembles that of the Javanese. The Sundanese language, though possessing its own script and literature, includes several dialects which shade into Javanese near the highlands' eastern border. The Sundanese enjoy the mask dance, the hobbyhorse trance dance, and the *serimpi*, all of which are popular among Javanese too. The Sundanese have a wajang, but where Javanese use leather shadow puppets, the Sundanese feature wooden, three-dimensional ones. The Sundanese also practice the *pentjak*, the dance of self-defense found in Muslim cultures throughout the Malayo-Indonesian region, and they play a unique bamboo instrument called the *angklung*.

To judge from one contemporary study,[6] landholdings of the Sundanese villagers are small. The average landowner holds one wet-rice paddy with an extent of approximately a quarter acre, and two pieces of dry-rice land with an extent of about half an acre each. Among the Sundanese as among the Javanese, there are no large corporate kin groups, no clans or lineages, and the nuclear family is the basic unit. Natural properties, sacred heirlooms, character traits, powers, and skills are inherited through either the father or the mother—that is, descent is bilateral, as among Javanese. Sundanese society broadly resembles Javanese society in emphasizing hierarchical relationships between high and low, old and young, rather than featuring corporate groups.

The Sundanese *hadjat* resembles the Javanese slametan. During the hadjat, food is offered, incense is burned, formulas are whispered, and spiritual creatures, including local ancestors and Islamic figures, are requested to bless or aid the host. The hadjat ends with a prayer in Arabic language. The participants are men from the host household, close male neighbors, and perhaps others. Like slametans, hadjats are held at critical stages in the life cycle, for instance at the third, fifth, seventh, and ninth months of pregnancy and at the time of dropping the umbilical cord.

Feasts marking death are held on the day of burial, then 3, 7, and 40 days later, and, for some deceased, 50, 100, and 1,000 days later, and then annually. The Sundanese boy is circumcised between four and nine years of age, which is earlier than for abangan Javanese but roughly the same as the age at which santri Javanese are circumcised, to judge from the information on Javanese santri mentioned earlier. The relatively early age of circumcision perhaps reflects the generally greater Islamization of Sundanese culture than of Javanese, for the earlier the circumcision the earlier a Muslim boy is drawn into participation in the pious life cycle followed by the Muslim male.

Marriage is arranged by relatives of the bride and groom. As in Java, the wedding includes a movement of the groom and his family to the house of the bride, followed by an Islamic ceremony (*nikah*) where the bride and the groom, in the company of a religious official and representative of the bride, accept the marriage contract. As in other Muslim societies of the Malayo-Indonesian region, a gift of money is paid to the bride by the groom. Divorce rates in Sunda, as in Java, are quite high.

Sundanese recognize a division between santri and non-santri, and they have supported religiously oriented political parties ranging from the santri Masjumi to the abangan Permai. Generally, however, the Sundanese are considered more strongly Islamized than the Javanese; thus among Sundanese the taboo on eating pork is apparently adhered to by the majority, whereas among Javanese it is only the minority, the santri, who keep the taboo. In some Sundanese regions and at certain periods, rather fanatical movements have flourished; examples are the Bantam uprisings at the turn of the last century and the Darul Islam movement after World War II. Sundanese are less oriented than the

Javanese toward a Hindu-based courtly culture, Sunda boasts no highly
developed courts such as Jogjakarta and Surakarta, and Javanese
consider the etiquette and language of Sunda to be less hierarchical,
refined, and stiff than their own.

THE BALINESE[7]

The two million Balinese resemble the Javanese in that they farm irrigated rice on densely populated land and share Javanese-Hindu artistic
and linguistic traditions—for example, the *kawi* language, the system
of speaking a high-flown vocabulary to high persons and a low vocabulary to the lowly, the wajang kulit and the wajang wong dramas, and
Hindu mythology. Some of the culture of Java must have diffused from
Hindu Madjapahit when its princes and its remaining power were transferred to Bali in the seventeenth century. Despite the cultural similarities and interchanges between Bali and Java, the two societies differ
profoundly. Bali was not deeply penetrated by systems of export agriculture, Islam, or Dutch colonialism, and the contemporary Balinese village
may resemble the Javanese village that existed before these incursions.

Each Balinese inherits from his father a title that indicates his caste
in a system somewhat resembling that of Hindu India. The highest
titles belong to the *Triwangsa* (three peoples), which includes the three
varna (colors) of traditional Hinduism: the Brahman, Satria, and Vesia.
The majority of the Balinese, some 90 percent, belong to the *djaba*
(commoner) caste. Rank and title in the caste system do not guarantee
wealth or power in Bali; indeed, some of the Triwangsa work as hired
help for affluent djaba. A title does assure ceremonial respect. According
to one's title one is addressed in halus or kasar (*kras*) language, one
sits above or below another person, and one can or cannot touch high-
caste persons. The majority of Balinese marry within their caste, and
marriage of a Triwangsa to a djaba would cause the Triwangsa to be
expelled from his caste.

Balinese kinship tends toward the patrilineal—a Balinese regards
as his primary kinsmen those persons related to him through his father.
Balinese tend to reside patrilocally. The wife moves into the household
of the husband, which is typically a noisy, walled compound in which
dwell the husband's parents, brothers, and brothers' wives and children.
The majority of Balinese inherit through their fathers membership in
a clan (*dadia*) which has important religious, political, and economic
functions; one's dadia has its own temple, influences one's membership
in a political party, and may specialize in such work as forging in-
struments of the gamelan orchestra.

Among Javanese, the villager's concern concentrates in his village,
but that is not the case for the Balinese. The Balinese residential group,

his *bandjar,* controls his communal and religious affairs, but not his agricultural ones. His fields and farming are controlled by his irrigation society (*subak*), which unites owners of rice terraces irrigated from a single dam and is organizationally independent of his residential village. " 'We have two sorts of customs,' the Balinese say, 'dry ones for the bandjar and wet ones for the subak.' "[8] Additional groups serve additional functions; not only are there the groups based on ascriptive ties of residence, age, title, or descent, but there are also associational groups called *seka* which bring people together on a voluntary basis simply because they like each other or have some common need.

In his multiple and often voluntary group memberships, each of which defines a specialized set of rights and obligations and controls a special set of activities, the Balinese is, despite his idyllic and pastoral setting, strangely modern. In spite of the modernizing and disrupting forces of Islamization and Westernization, the Javanese, in this respect, is more traditional. The Javanese binds numerous functions, including the agricultural and the residential, into a single unit, the village. To change any one function is therefore disturbing to the Javanese village as a whole. The Javanese would seem to face the choices of totally changing his village, totally resisting change, or simply moving to town, and it is suggestive that more Javanese than Balinese have chosen this latter alternative. The Balinese have created a rural system which ingeniously combines modern flexibility with traditional stability; a change in agriculture, music, or politics can take place within the group specializing in that function without the villager's entire existence being disrupted, a pattern which doubtless has to do with the low rate of migration from rural Bali.

Bali is most renowned, of course, for its rich artistic and religious culture. In Bali, as in Java, the wajang kulit and wajang wong (puppet and human plays) derive partially from such Hindu myths as the Ramajana and Mahabharata and emphasize interplay between halus princes and kasar clowns; in hierarchical Bali the gross caricature of rules of hierarchy by the clowns evoke a cathartic laughter which, according to the whimsical perception of one observer, resembles the laughter at obscene jokes that could be heard in Western society during its days of sexual repression.[9] Balinese gamelan and dance are much livelier than the classical gamelan and dance of Java. Balinese music rises quickly to a climax, and Balinese dance features quick movements of the head and limbs. Classical Javanese music and dance flow gently, projecting a mysterious and tranquil mood. In Java the classical arts are confined largely to the court, to a few professional dramatic and orchestral troupes, and to schools; in Bali, they are practiced every day and night by people from every stratum, whether they be dancers and painters living in peasant villages and working in the fields or princes living in palaces and receiving tourists and heads of state. In Java the arts are introverted, subtle, and profound, part of a mystical quest for inner peace and identity; in Bali the arts are part of a communal and public cycle of ritual and display that harmonizes the community with the gods.

Balinese arts and rites center around the temples, more than 2,000 of which are recorded as existing on Bali. Every village contains several temples, and every villager belongs to a number, sometimes by descent, sometimes by residence, sometimes by magical command. An important temple ceremony is a gala affair of processions and dances, cockfights and crowds, and hundreds of offerings to the gods who are invited guests. The ceremony may boast a dramatic performance such as that enacting the fight between Rangda the witch and Barong the dragon. Male dancers attack the witch with their daggers (kris). She offers no resistance, causing the dancers to fall twitching to the ground, stabbing themselves with their krisses as they enter a deep trance. Rarely is a dancer harmed, however, and the priest of the dragon circulates among them, sprinkling water to restore their consciousness. One interpretation of the action of the trance-dancers is that they are reenacting a deeply troubling experience of early childhood, when the Balinese mother failed to respond to their plea for affection, causing them to turn their emotions inward; the witch represents the mother, the dragon the reassuring father.[10] A more general interpretation of trance in Bali is that it provides an opportunity for spontaneous expression and intense feeling in a formalized, hierarchical society which normally suppresses spontaneity and emotion.

Ceremonies for the Balinese child are held when his navel has healed, when his ears are pierced at 12 and 42 days, and when he receives the blessing of the priest at three months and again at 210 days, which is one Balinese year. After the child is one year old, little attention is paid to subsequent birthdays, except for the third. At adolescence both boys and girls have their teeth filed, although many families cannot afford the expense of the ceremonies at this time and for these children the ceremony is performed later in life. Boys are not circumcised, but girls are secluded at the time of first menstruation, and a feast is given by their families at the end of their seclusion to celebrate their coming of age.

Marriage is usually by elopement. Although the parents of the girl are expected to protest, that is merely part of the ritual, and only when the girl has been stolen against her will is the marriage annulled. Among the most elaborate ceremonies of the Balinese are those surrounding death. The body is buried on an auspicious day, and ceremonies are held for 12 days following the burial and at 42 days after death. Ideally, cremation follows soon after the forty-second day, but the ceremony is extremely expensive and often must be delayed for years. The cremation accomplishes the important task of getting rid of the corpse, because its pollution binds the soul to the material world. Minor ceremonies are held for 12 days after cremation; and the final, major ceremony, *mukur*, occurs 42 days after cremation; the mukur includes offerings and incantations by the high priest and meritorious acts by the participants to help the traveling soul attain its proper life in the afterworld.

THE TOBA BATAK[11]

Nearly a million Toba Batak inhabit the Sumatran mountain valleys near Lake Toba and the lowland farms and cities of eastern Sumatra. Though cultivating irrigated rice, the Batak are also swidden farmers, and they are not so densely populous as the Javanese or Balinese. They partake of a tradition different from that of these Hinduized peoples; indeed, they are regarded by some as originating from a separate racial stratum, or a separate migrational wave. Batak culture lacks hierarchies of rank and title and the complexes of etiquette and arts of Javanese-Balinese Hinduism, and Batak social organization bears a closer resemblance to that of the swidden tribes of highland Southeast Asia than to the irrigated rice societies of lowland, mainland, peninsular, or island Southeast Asia. Until a century ago, the Toba Batak were of the religious persuasion broadly called "animistic," but under the influence of Rhenish missionaries many have converted to Christianity. A number of Batak outside the Toba region have become Muslim.

The Batak belongs to a patrilineal lineage (*marga*), the organization and function of which are quite different from those of the patrilineal clan of the Balinese, the *dadia*. The Batak orients to his lineage more than to any other group, whereas the Balinese regards his clan as merely one of several groups competing for his time. Another broad comparison is between the Batak lineage and the Javanese village: each controls numerous aspects of its members' lives, and owns its members' lands and allocates to them rights to cultivate those lands, as does the Javanese village. But among the Batak, the controlling unit is genealogical, whereas among the Javanese it is residential. The distinction broadly distinguishes tribal from peasant groups throughout the world.

Marriage among the Batak links the bride's lineage (*hula-hula*) to the groom's lineage (*anak boru*) in a highly structured and long-enduring reciprocity. Between hula-hula and anak boru flow such gifts as the buffalo rump which the groom gives his father-in-law and the cloth which the bride gives her mother-in-law. As in many hill-dwelling tribes of Southeast Asia, the Batak feel that the wife-giving group, the hula-hula, is superior, at least in the specific context of the marriage ceremony, to the wife-receiving group, the anak boru. In Batak society this ranking with respect to marriage tends to correspond with ranking in other clans—that is, with the class structure of the total society; the bride's lineage is generally of a higher class than the groom's. The correspondence cannot be exact, however. A wife-giving lineage must also *take* wives, and any lineage is inferior, within the context of the marriage exchange, to that lineage from which it takes wives. A system can thus emerge in which lineage A gives wives to, and is therefore superior to, B; B gives wives to, and is therefore superior to, C; C gives wives to, and is therefore superior to, A. A and B each can claim superiority over the other. To complicate matters further, considerations of kinship as well as marriage determine rank. Thus patrilineal descendants of the lineage founding a given region are termed the region's ruling marga—that marga which controls the land elects the headman. This ranking, determined by kinship, necessarily would be contradicted by marriage in which the ruling lineage took wives from another lineage; in such a marriage exchange, the ruling marga would be classified inferior to the other.

Reflecting patterns widespread among Southeast Asian hill tribes, the Batak decree that a son should take his wife from a lineage from whence came his mother; preferably he should marry his mother's brother's daughter. To marry in the other direction—that is, into the lineage to which his own lineage customarily *gives* wives—would be disturbing to society and to the whole of that existence which roots in those customary rules that the Batak term *adat*. Violation of the adat endangers the natural, social, and cosmic order; obedience sustains it. Something of this idea is retained even by those living in such bustling cities as Medan. Even urban Batak keep the adat alive, kin ties strong, and use mutual aid among kinsmen to advantage in business and other affairs.

THE MINANGKABAU[12]

In the Padang highlands of west Sumatra live the five million Minangkabau, known for their so-called "matriarchal" system of social organization and for the beauty of their alpine mountains and hills on which nestle houses whose roofs resemble the peaked hats of the Minangkabau women. The Minangkabau cultivate both swidden rice and wet rice, constructing irrigation canals and plowing by water buffalo.

The Minangkabau belongs to his mother's clan. Through his mother he inherits the right to use, but not to sell, the lands owned by that clan. Even after marriage, he does not, traditionally, live with his wife but in the household of his mother. In the evening he visits his wife and children in their apartment within the wife's mother's household. The wife is supported and protected by her brother; the husband supports and protects his sisters. The oldest brother of the oldest woman in a house is responsible for its ancestral land (though the woman's husband is expected to help farm that land). This elder brother is called the *mamak*, and his mother's house, including grandmothers, mother, grandmothers' brothers, mother's brothers, and children, is called the "womb" or simply "group."

This household group is affiliated with other such groups that trace descent matrilineally from a common ancestor, jointly composing a unit known as the *kampueng* or by other terms. The leader of such a kampueng, a senior maternal uncle who is traditionally an esteemed personage, is known as the *pengulu andiko*. The kampuengs are grouped into still larger units known as *suku*, several of which compose a village. The heads of the various suku may either form a council or elect a head. The council or the head administers the village in which the suku reside.[13]

Before 1844, Minangkabau society contained a king, the Great Lord, whose position was patrilineally inherited, as were the positions of members of the small, endogamous, royal family. The grafting of this patrilineal royal family onto the matrilineal tribal society is represented in legend by the marriage of a dog, the king, to a tigress which represented the local territories and matrilineal lineages. Among the Minangkabau the royal family never gained the authority and prestige that royalty enjoyed in Java and Bali, and it did not so heavily influence commoner culture.

Between the local, matrilineal society and the royal, patrilineal family stood a mediating figure, the Girl Lord. The Girl Lord, who could be either male or female but in either case should wear a feminine hair style, was responsible for the social and political matters concerning the local, matrilineal groups, while the Great Lord, also known as the King of Religion, dealt with sacral matters of patrilineal significance, such as Islam. Aspects of the Great Lord and the Girl Lord were combined in the person of the Radjo Alam, Lord of the World, who stood for the royal house in its entirety and for the total unity of Minangkabau.

Two traditions existed in local society itself, the one a masculine adat which recognized the power of Muslim law and the jurisdiction of the patrilineal royal family over the entire society; the other a feminine adat which recognized only matrilineal custom and local communities.

These portrayals suggest a principle or theme that, among the Minangkabau, maleness is associated with wider social units, femaleness with localized units. Less elaborately, the same theme is expressed throughout Indonesia, and indeed throughout the world, in that the female governs the household and hearth ("She is the Minister of Interior," as the Javanese put it) while the male deals with the wider spheres of society and cosmos. The ruler of virtually every Minangkabau social unit, ranging from household to kingdom, is male (the exception is the ambiguous post of the Girl Lord), a pattern which refutes the myth that Minangkabau society is ruled by matriarchal amazons.

A second theme in Minangkabau society is the opposition between local custom, the adat, and Islamic law, the *sjariah;* this second theme is linked to the first in that the adat tends to be perceived as more "feminine," the sjariah more "masculine." Symbolized by the *balai,* the village council hall, the adat norms emphasize the collectivist, matrilineal, and matrilocal tendencies of the village community. Symbolized by the mosque, the sjariah emphasizes the individualistic and patrilineal tendencies of the wider Islamic society. At first glance it seems paradoxical and surprising that the matrilineal society of Minangkabau, whose very base would seem to oppose Islam, is historically Indonesia's most dynamically Muslim region, the source of such movements as the Padri, the Kaum Muda, and the homeland of the most influential Indonesian Muslim intellectuals, such as Hadji Rasul and his son, Hamka. The history of the interplay between adat and sjariah among the Minangkabau suggests that the opposition between the two has developed gradually and is by no means absolute.[14]

Early Islam in Minangkabau was Sufist and syncretist, receptive to the magical lore of the local culture and to its adat. In its mode of organization, however, Sufism necessarily undermined the matrilineal base of Minangkabau society. Sufist meditations and chants were practiced in schools scattered about the countryside and run by holy men and male teachers. Transmitting their authority and spiritual power to their sons and grandsons, these men wove a patrilineal thread into the matrilineal fabric of Minangkabau society. At the same time the schools challenged the position of the royal family, which had claimed the patrilineal pattern as a special prerogative of royalty. The Islamic schools thus became, through their organization, a locus of male power which challenged the local adat. Due to their mystical and contemplative orientations, however, the schools were not yet agents of active social reform.

In the mid-nineteenth century, the schools became seats of radical reformism which spurred forward the Padri movement. Led by the Muslim teachers who had come under the influence of the Wahabi purists, the Padri regarded adat society as *djahiliah*—syncretic, unenlightened, and contrary to true Islam—and they fought to change its essential structure. A first result of the Padri propagandizing was that Islam spread more widely and penetrated more deeply into Minangkabau society, becoming itself a special form of adat, the *adat Islamiah*. A second result was the decline of Sufi cults of the traditional syncretist type and a growth in the more puritanical, rationalist type of Islam. A third result was that the adat leaders lost prestige; supported by the Dutch as opponents of fanatical Islam during the Padri War, they appeared to the people as tools of colonialism.

Shortly after the advent of the twentieth century, the Minangkabau purist Muslims established a complex of reformist schools and spearheaded the Kaum Muda reformism that was spreading through the archipelago. In reaction Minangkabau conservatives built syncretist, traditional Islamic schools. Today, in the vicinity of such Minangkabau highland towns as Bukit Tinggi and Padan Pandjang, nestling side by side in the hills, the two types of schools contrast markedly. In the reformist girl's school, unadorned, white-cowled puritans teach similarly ascetic girls seated under the scowling portrait of a stern, feminist builder of their dormitory which is surrounded by a moat to keep out the boys. In the traditionalist girl's school, nubile maidens clad in colorful sarongs and kerchiefs sing romantic songs to the accompaniment of flashing eyes and snapping fingers as they learn the charms appropriate for a good wife. In the villages, Islam and adat have achieved a certain synthesis. Thus a kinship group may boast not only its adat chief, its pengulu, but also its own malim, khatib, and bilal. And a Minangkabau marriage includes not only the Islamic ceremony, the nikah, but also adat rites that unite the lineages of the bride and groom.

Young men of Minangkabau have long followed the custom of leaving their villages in the hands of elders and women, and embarking on a wandering known as *merantau*. Freeing the young bachelor from the local community, the merantau broadens his experience with the world. The tradition of merantau has encouraged Minangkabau men to trade throughout the islands and Malaya as well, where Minangkabau founded and dominate the state of Negri Sembilan. During the early twentieth century, the wealthy Minangkabau youths would merantau to Mecca, remaining for study there or in Cairo; returning full of the teachings of Muhammad Abduh or even the radical Pakistani Ahmadiyyah, they added fuel to the fires set by local reformers. A few years later, merantau encouraged a Minangkabau export of politicians such as Hatta, Sjahrir, and Salim, who became intelligentsia leaders of the Java-based Indonesian nationalism. Migrating to Java, too, were Minangkabau novelists such as Abdul Muis, Nur Sutan Iskandar, and Selasih, who led the early florescence of Indonesian literature. Renowned for dynamism and shrewdness, the Minangkabau character was doubtless shaped by the tradition of merantau, which in turn found support in the individualism derived from the desert religion of Islam.

Migration and commercialism have resulted in the sale of much ancestral property. As a result the territorial base of the Minangkabau matrilineal and matrilocal society is lost. Migration is fatally damaging to matrilocality. If a couple leaves the village, they can hardly stay with the wife's mother, so naturally they set up their own household in their new community. Dwelling with his children, the husband naturally becomes integrated into the household and he takes on new functions, such as paying for his children's schooling. A consequence of these and other trends is that in many urban areas, in and out of western Sumatra, the Minangabau family is assuming the form toward which modernizing families throughout the world are converging: the independent household, in which husband, wife, and children live as a nuclear family. Through the breakdown of matrilocal, communal society, Minangabau adat loses power. As secularization cuts the power of Islam too, the opposition between Islam and adat may diminish.

THE ATJEHNESE

Islam and such institutions as the Muslim school and the rantau gave power and status to the men of Minangkabau. Among the Atjehnese of northern Sumatra, Islam and the rantau serve a similar function, even though Atjehnese kinship is not matrilineal but bilateral; descent is traced through both males and females. In Atjeh, however, residence is matrilocal, so that children grow up among their mother's relatives. Rules of inheritance favor the male, since they follow the Islamic law which decrees that male heirs get two shares, female heirs one. When women marry, however, they are customarily given a house. Men are rarely given a house before their parents die; as a result most Atjehnese women own the house in which their husbands, their children, and they themselves live.

In one Atjehnese village recently subjected to intensive study,[15] women owned not only the houses but a considerable portion of the rice land, and they controlled and managed virtually all the land, since the men were away most of the year. Most of the men spent their time on rantau in eastern Sumatra, carrying on trade, and returning to the village only for major Islamic holidays. Getting food through their own agriculture, the women depended on the men only for the cash they brought home for gifts of luxuries and baubles.

Growing up for the Atjehnese boy means abandoning the home and community controlled by women, and joining the rantau society controlled by men. Staunch Muslims, the Atjehnese men apparently see maturation as a movement away from childish indulgence of the senses and desires (*hawa nafsu*) toward the Muslim ideal of disciplined rationality (*akal*), which is best practiced in trade. The first step toward maturity is the boy's schooling in the reading and chanting of the Qur'an, a mode of instruction which begins at age six, outside the home, in the company of men and boys only. Around age eight, when he is circumcised, the boy begins to wear pants, and he stops playing with girls. At puberty he becomes obligated to perform the five daily Islamic prayers, and he moves into the bachelor's house, the *meunasah*. Beginning at this stage, the Atjehnese male is rarely seen with women, and so long as he lives he will rarely appear in public with a woman other than his wife. Upon reaching adulthood, the Atjehnese man characteristically leaves the village altogether, traveling East to trade.

Marriage is arranged by parents, but the prospective spouses have some say. Girls may veto a proposed husband, and one of the ideals they seek is the man who is generous in giving his wife and children money that he earns while trading in the East. Boys fear getting a wife who demands too much. Believing that farming is women's work, Atjehnese women scorn men who stay home to farm; men as well as women believe that the male's primary duty is to provide cash for his family, and that trading is the best means to get cash. Atjeh's divorce rate of approximately 50 percent is largely due to conflict derived from the wife's feeling that her husband fails to contribute enough income to meet her demands.

Regarding the husband as privileged to visit his home only because he brings cash, Atjehnese women do not invite him to enter into household decisions. When he hs home, he is indulged like a guest or a child by special cooking and polite deference. But when the cash which he has brought is exhausted, his wife decides that he has overstayed his welcome. She sends him on his way, back to the East to do more business and earn more money.

Puasa, the fast month, is the primary occasion for the men to visit their homes. Anticipating their visit, they speak of it with pleasure, giving little thought to the hardship of fasting. During that month, because the husband is home and special food must be prepared, the wife's duties are heavier than normal, but the husband has little to do. Though women must rise early, the men laze about, rising for the dawn prayer but returning to bed to sleep late. After an afternoon nap, the men break the fast in the evening by a meal of rice porridge served at the bachelor's house. After praying together, the men return home for a feast prepared by their wives, then come back to the bachelor's house to pray again and to recite portions of the holy Qur'an.

When the month ends, the men join their wives in the ritual of asking forgiveness of relatives and others for their sins and errors during the preceding year. Cleansed of sin, they recall their vacation not as a time of indulgence, but as a time when disciplined reason (*akal*) won over indulgence of desire (*hawa nafsu*): they did keep the fast. Back in the realm of akal, masculinity, and Islam, they are ready to leave the household, the village, the women, and the children, as they go back East to trade.

Atjehnese men, then, experience subtle shifts of mood and perception associated with their maturation and movement toward rantau. These transformations work toward an objective that is reinforced by the Islamic religion: the cementing of bonds between men as they transcend their dependence on women. Independence is gained at the expense of a certain alienation from family and community.

REFERENCES

[1] An extremely useful survey, to which this chapter owes much, is Hildred Geertz, "Indonesian Cultures and Communities," in Ruth T. McVey (ed.), *Indonesia* (New Haven, Conn.: Southeast Asia Studies, Yale University, 1963). Essential, too, is Koentjaraningrat (ed.), *Villages in Indonesia* (Ithaca, N.Y.. Cornell Univ. Press, 1967). Concerning Indonesian village-nation relations, see G. William Skinner, *Local, Ethnic, and National Loyalties in Village Indonesia: A Symposium* (New Haven, Conn.: Southeast Asia Studies, Yale University, 1959). Surveys of Indonesia during the colonial period include Raymond Kennedy, *The Ageless Indies* (New York: Day, 1942); and the more scholarly and systematic B. Ter Haar, *Adat Law in Indonesia* (New York: Institute of Pacific Relations, 1948; published in Dutch, 1939).

[2] For references on the Javanese, see H. Geertz, "Indonesian Cultures," pp. 480, 486–491; Robert R. Jay, *Javanese Villagers: Social Relations in Rural Modjokuto* (Cambridge, Mass.: MIT Press, 1969); Clifford Geertz, *The Social History of an Indonesian Town* (Cambridge, Mass.: MIT Press, 1965); Selosoemardjan, *Social Changes in Jogjakarta* (Ithaca, N.Y.: Cornell Univ. Press, 1962). Comments on the kampung are based on my experience of living in one in Surabaja during 1962.

[3] Selosoemardjan, *Social Changes*, p. 118.

[4] This statement is based on a survey of 425 male Javanese in the region of Djokjakarta which I carried out in 1970. All respondents, approximately half of whom were santri, were asked the age at which they circumcised their sons. The differences between santri and abangan were statistically significant, indeed, virtually absolute: most santri reported circumcising their sons between ages six and nine, most abangan reported ages from ten to fourteen. The figure "twelve to fourteen" which most sources list as the age for Javanese circumcision may be based on a largely abangan sample.

[5] Information for this section comes from Andrea Wilcox Palmer, "Situradja: A Village in Highland Priangan," in Koentjaraningrat (ed.), *Villages in Indonesia*, pp. 299–325.

112   ⁶ *Ibid.*, p. 303.

⁷ On Bali, see sources in H. Geertz, "Indonesian Cultures," pp. 481–482, 483–491; also Clifford Geertz, "Tihingan: A Balinese Village," in Koentjaraningrat (ed.), *Villages in Indonesia*, pp. 210–243; J. L. Swellengrebel, *Bali: Studies in Life, Thought, and Ritual* (The Hague, Van Hoeve, 1960); and the more specialized studies of C. Hooykaas, such as *Agama Thirtha: Five Studies in Hindu-Balinese Religion* (Amsterdam: N.V. Noord-Hollandsche Uitgevers Maatschappij, 1964).

⁸ C. Geertz, "Tihingan," p. 212.

⁹ Gregory Bateson and Margaret Mead, *Balinese Character: A Photographic Analysis* (New York: New York Academy of Sciences, 1942), p. 12.

¹⁰ *Ibid.*, pp. 32–38.

¹¹ On the Batak, see sources listed in H. Geertz, "Indonesian Cultures," pp. 485–491. This section relies particularly on Edward M. Bruner, "Kinship Organization Among the Urban Batak of Sumatra," *Transactions of the New York Academy of Sciences*, 22, Series II (1959), pp. 31–40; Edmund Leach, *Rethinking Anthropology* (London: Athlone, 1961), pp. 91–95; and Jacob C. Vergouwen, *The Social Organization and Customary Law of the Toba-Batak of Northern Sumatra*, trans. Jeune Scott-Kendall (The Hague: Nijhoff, 1964). A detailed bibliography is Toenggoel P. Siagian, "Bibliography of the Batak Peoples," *Indonesia* (October 1966), pp. 161–184.

¹² On the Minangkabau, see H. Geertz, "Indonesian Cultures," pp. 484, 486–491; also Harsja W. Bachtiar, " 'Negeri' Taram: A Minangkabau Village Community," in Koentjaraningrat (ed.), *Villages in Indonesia*, pp. 348–386; Nancy Tanner, "Disputing and Dispute Settlement among the Minangkabau of Indonesia," *Indonesia*, No. 8 (1969), pp. 21–67; Taufik Abdullah, "Adat and Islam: An Examination of Conflict in Minangkabau," *Indonesia* (October 1966), pp. 161–184.

¹³ This paragraph attempts to synthesize information supplied in Bachtiar, " 'Negeri' Taram," and in P. E. de Josselin de Jong, *Minangkabau and Negeri Sembilan: Socio-political Structure in Indonesia* (Djakarta: Bhratara, 1960). These two sources seem to disagree on the terms applied to kinship units and their leaders above the level of the household.

¹⁴ The following sketch of the history of the interplay between adat and Islam is drawn from Taufik Abdullah, "Adat and Islam," plus a few observations of my own during a brief visit in the Padang Pandjang and Bukit Tinggi area of west Sumatra.

¹⁵ See James Siegel, *The Rope of God* (Berkeley: Univ. of California Press, 1969); all information cited in this section on the Atjehnese comes from Siegel, but see also the classic ethnography by C. Snouck Hurgronje, *The Achehnese*, 2 vols., trans. A. W. S. Sullivan (Leyden: Brill, 1906).

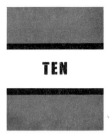

TEN

CULTURAL DIVERSITY IN
CONTEMPORARY INDONESIA: THE
OUTER ISLANDS

THE MAKASSARESE AND BUGINESE[1]

The southern peninsula of the island of Celebes is inhabited by some two million Makassarese and three million Buginese, populations which differ from one another primarily in language. Daring and fierce seafarers, the Buginese swarmed from their kingdom of Bone to colonize small principalities throughout the archipelago. The Makassarese founded the rival kingdom of Goa, situated in the town of Makassar.

The kingdom of Goa was a port kingdom after the pattern of other Malayo-Indonesian Muslim ports. The king made money either by taxing ships that passed through his ports or by sending out his own. The population was in large part alien: Malays, Javanese, Arabs, Indians, Chinese, Englishmen, and the Dutch. As in the other Muslim-Malay kingdoms, the king held power through personal charisma and magical symbols; no godlike Hindu-Java ruler, the king was not worshipped, his men followed only so long as he led, and challengers frequently sprouted from distant branches of the royal family. The Dutch conquered Makassar in 1675, but did not penetrate deeply into royal affairs until 1905 when they began to impose their control much as they had done long before on Java. During the days of colonialism, Makassar was a lively port, the locale of European branch offices for both business and government. A bit quiet and seedy today, it remains an entrepot, with a large Chinese quarter, a harbor filled with sailing vessels, and an inn still known as the Grand Hotel.

Divided into royal, noble, and commoner strata, Makassarese society is open to the social climber. The region offers considerable opportunity to make money, through trade or opening land, and thereby to rise in rank. Both family background and personal achievement determine status, but the crucial outward sign is the amount of brideprice a man receives for his daughters. As in other coastal Malay societies, the prices for each stratum of women are codified and publicized, but setting the price for a particular bride requires much haggling. Because no girl may marry for a price lower than that paid for her mother, and since the groom's family gains prestige from purchasing a high-priced bride, both families gain from setting a high price. Each bride price is ultimately confirmed by the imam of the mosque, whose decision takes account of the total social situation of which the families are part.

The wedding is a gala affair. The feasts last as long as two weeks, with many buffaloes killed, a horde of guests invited, and numerous ceremonies performed to symbolize the high rank of the host. The Muslim nikah is the official marriage ritual, but there are also adat ceremonies to symbolize union of families of bride and groom. Makassarese enjoy an extremely low divorce rate, 7 out of 107 marriages in one village studied; the low rate of divorce is perhaps partly due to, or symptomized by, the high (and presumably nonrefundable) bride-price.

As exemplified in the marriage system, Makassarese males feel a strong drive to gain status. Failure brings shame, insults evoke revenge, and competition is strong among equals. Unequals follow different rules. Subordinates are expected to act submissive and obedient toward their superiors, who should be charismatic, authoritative, and ready to throw big feasts. Such a "big man" may control a kin group, to which members are allied through their mothers, fathers, or marriage. By arranging prestigious marriages for his kinsmen and coordinating their labor and land, the big man may lead such a group toward high status. Such status is symbolized by regalia—flags, swords, umbrellas, and plows that are worshipped through offerings of food, betel, and sacrificial animals. As the big man and his group grows in status, the regalia gain sanctity; as his power wanes, and his followers fall away, the regalia lose their sacredness.

The Makassarese emphasis on hierarchy is reflected in familial relations. A son conversing with his father should not contradict him, but should listen quietly and respond formally. A similar relation exists ideally between older and younger brothers. Relations between mother and daughter, aunt and niece, and grandmother and granddaughter are more egalitarian and cooperative, and brother and sister are particularly close. In Makassarese mythology, a major theme is the hero and his twin sister who are separated, then engage in a kind of wandering as they seek reunion; the American reminded of "Evangeline" should imagine such a story featuring siblings instead of lovers.

In Makassarese society, Islam opposes adat to a degree. The *pinati*, a holy person specializing in the adat ceremonies oriented around the ornaments and ancestors of the kin group, is frequently a female, and there is a notion that the ancestor cult is a religion of men. The equation between feminine-masculine and adat-Islamic oppositions is broadly similar to that pervading such societies as the Minangkabau and the Atjehnese.

A synthesis between Islam and adat is suggested by the fact that, before the coming of the Dutch, the highest princes of Goa and Bone each retained a special royal Muslim official called the *kali* who ranked next to the king himself and who came from a branch of the royal family. A trend toward purifying Islam of its adat undercoating is suggested by the great activism of Makassar branches of Muhammadijah (the national Muhammadijah congress of 1971 was held in Makassar). The more syncretist N.U. also maintains branches in Makassar, noteworthy for their placid and folksy atmosphere by comparison to the dynamic Muhammadijah, which has built hospitals, clinics, and schools in Makassar and the surrounding countryside.

THE WESTERN SUMBAWANS[2]

Expanding into the remoter regions of the outer islands, the Makassarese subdued and colonized the coastal kingdoms of Sumbawa, the third island east of Java, just beyond Bali and Lombok. Since the early seventeenth century, when the newly converted Makassarese used the notion of "holy war" to justify conquest, both east and west Sumbawan kings have been vassals of Makassar and have been nominally Muslim. Royalty continues to signify refinement and rank in the world view of the Sumbawans, and the palaces of the old sultans are still preserved, though that of Bima is empty and dilapidated, and that of Sumbawa Besar is now a slightly rundown hotel.

Sumbawa is divided into two cultural-geographic regions: Bima and Dompu to the east, encompassing some 250,000 persons, and the area surrounding Sumbawa Besar to the west, with a population of some 180,000. Separated by an overnight sea voyage or a painfully rough day-and-night ride overland, the two sides of the island are quite distinct in pattern. The Bimans, who appear shorter, darker, and more hard-boiled than the easterners, speak a language resembling that of Flores and Sumba. The western Sumbawans speak a language resembling that of the Sasak of Lombok, and they look and act more like the people of Bali and Java. The description to be presented here is drawn from a study of a village, Rarak, which is one of many communities in the savannah region of western Sumbawa that support themselves by the cultivation of dry rice.

The year of the Rarak villagers is divided between the dry and the wet seasons, a division which is quite sharp in the rugged and parched islands east of Bali. As autumn approaches, marking the November onset of the wet season, the Rarak villager prepares to clear a field in order to plant rice. Owning rights of disposal to between five and eight parcels of land, he selects that which has been longest fallow, and by the end of August he is wielding a long-handled brush knife and a machete to hack the field clean of shrubs. When the growing season begins, the villager moves himself and his family to the site of his swidden; for the next months, they will sleep and live there, in a drafty, single-roomed hut with a roof of palm leaves.

Invoking the blessings of Allah upon the community and its crops, and announcing the most auspicious date for ceremonially initiating the planting, the *lebé* (mosque head) formally opens the growing season. Now the villager must begin an around-the-clock vigilance against the animals that threaten to eat and destroy his crop—raucous crows by day, wandering horses, goats, deer, and wild hogs by night. As the months of the growing season wear on, the stress and hardship begin to tell. Fatigue, anxiety, and increasing malnutrition are aggravated by sleeping in damp, rickety swidden huts under light cover, and such illnesses as pleurisy, pneumonia, arthritis, and active turberculosis spread.[3]

When his harvest is finally in, the villager returns in relief to his village home, larger and more solid than his swidden hut, and now stocked with bundles of paddy. The villager can enjoy a rest during the dry season, "hunting deer, searching the forests for honey, or combing the upland streams for shellfish."[4] In the company of neighbors and kinfolk, he joins the rounds of feasts, house-raising parties, circumcisions, funerals, naming ceremonies, and major Islamic celebrations.

Cross-cutting the yearly cycle of the community is the life cycle of the individual, which fits the prototype for pious Muslims of the Malayo-Indonesian region. The Rarak male is circumcised around age seven. He probably spends some time in his boyhood studying with an Islamic teacher who instructs him in reading and chanting the Qur'an, and when he acquires some skill, his father may stage a celebration to signify his further coming of age. His first marriage is sealed by the nikah ritual, followed by an elaborate adat feast.

Rarak kinship organization is bilateral, though it displays a slight patrilineal bias in the tracing of descent. Households are small and nuclear; there are no extended families or households embracing two or more married siblings. One's bilaterally traced kindred do not as such form a corporate group. Residence is neolocal.

In Rarak as elsewhere in Indonesia, there is a distinction between the Islamic and adat spheres of culture and power. Islam is represented by a hierarchy of mosque officials, headed by the lebé. These officials apply laws based on both sjariah and adat to such domestic matters as marriage, divorce, inheritance, alimony, adultery, and illegitimacy. The lebé gives Friday sermons at the mosque, and he organizes such Muslim festivals as Lebaran, Idhul Adha, and Maulud. Extending his power in to the realm of adat, he oversees the agricultural ceremonies concerning the time of the first planting, the washing of the new crop, and the first harvest. The lebé is also a shaman, delving into the non-Islamic lore of magic.

The lebé's primary qualification is his ability to read and chant the sacred Qur'anic texts. His income derives primarily from the *zakat*, a tithe collected from the villagers, who pay in kind out of their paddy harvest. Donated with surprising eagerness and regularity, the tithe is apparently felt by villagers to compensate for lax attention to religious duties during the rest of the year.

Just as the lebé sits astride the Islamic pyramid, so the village head-man, the *kepala kampung*, is at the top of the adat hierarchy, the lower levels of which are occupied by his assistants. Just as the lebé must know the sacred Arabic language and texts, so the modern head-man must know the national language and symbols. Such knowledge, plus an acquaintance with the more practical aspects of national govern-ment, the headman likely acquires from school in the lowland. The headman's duties are largely administrative; for example, he must arbi-trate local disputes concerning theft of livestock and claims to land. Like the lebé, he is a shaman, but with different specialties. The lebé specializes in the magic necessary for construction of house and mosque, the headman in diverting sorcery deployed by enemy soccer teams! Traditionally, the lebé and the headman have exhibited comple-mentary personalities: the lebé was scholarly, introverted, and conserva-tive, the headman skilled at *pentjak* fighting and at taking command in tense situations. Since the postwar onset of national independence, however, the headman has become something of an organization man, whose major talent is dealing with governmental red tape and harmoniz-ing opposing factions.

THE ROTINESE[5]

The Rotinese are located to the east and south of Sumbawa; Roti is the southernmost island of the Indonesian archipelago. Exemplifying yet another variant of Lesser Sunda culture, the Rotinese contrast with the Sumbawans in that they are Christian rather than Islamic, and in other respects as well.

Roti is divided into two territorial divisions which reflect dif-ferences in custom, dialect, and topography: the eastern half, known as Sunrise, and the western half, known as Sunset. Cross-cutting the duality of region are eighteen autonomous states, each ruled by its own lord. The population of Roti is approximately 70,000, but some 30,000 Rotinese also live on Timor and Sumba.

A dry, hilly land, "rifted with limestone reefs and marls,"[6] Roti resembles Sumbawa in its distinct division into wet and dry seasons, but the wet season apparently comes later, beginning in the fall or winter, and continues until April. The dry season begins in the late spring and summer, planting occurs from late December through February, and harvest is from April to June. Though some dry-field rice is grown, most rice is cultivated in irrigated fields that are individually owned but tap a joint water supply. Of greater economic importance than rice growing is the tapping of lontar palms to get syrup. Trade is mainly by Chinese and by Muslims; the majority of the Rotinese are Christian.

Although the Sumbawans of Rarak were bilateral swidden farmers, wet-rice farming Rotinese boast lineal descent groups. Clans "own" water and possess the right to appoint a ritual head over the individuals who hold plots of land within a fenced area irrigated by that water. Land, trees, and animals are the property of the individual household.

Descent is ideally "patrilineal" in that names are usually taken from the father's group and the child usually joins that group. If no bridewealth has been paid, however, a child belongs to his mother's group and takes part of her name. Bridewealth is paid in gold, money, or kind—usually water buffalo. Polygyny is permitted and is ideal for the rich and the aristocratic. The preferred match is between cross-cousins, particularly the father's sister's son and mother's brother's daughter, whereas marriage between parallel cousins (father's brother's daughter and mother's sister's son) is forbidden, as in other matrilateral cross-cousin marriage systems of Southeast Asia. Marriage is between lineages of the same clan. Residence is patrilocal for the youngest son, neolocal for the older sons.

Each Rotinese district or domain comprised a number of named clans, which constitute its political units. Ruling each domain is a "male" lord (*manek*) and a complementary "female" lord (*fetor*), plus a number of other lords, one of whom, known as the "head of the earth," is obligated to uphold the adat. Members of the clans of the male and female lords are regarded as the nobility, but all other Rotinese are commoners. Formerly there was a slave class, but it has now been absorbed into the commoner stratum.

Most Rotinese are Dutch Reformed Protestant; a few are Pentecostal and Seventh Day Adventist. The Christianity is interwoven with the adat, which centers on the ancestral spirits and their opposites—malevolent spirits associated with the bush. Major ceremonies are held at marriage and death; minor ones at the seventh month of pregnancy, during the cutting of the baby's hair, baptism, naming, and during the agricultural cycle. The dead are buried on the third day after death. Feasts are held on this day, on the seventh, ninth, and fortieth day, and additional feasts may be held a year or even three years later. The coffin is called "the ship of the dead."

THE IBAN[7]

The Iban are a swidden, animistic, formerly headhunting and aggressively warring tribe that inhabits the interior of Borneo. Migrating northward since the nineteenth century, about 100,000 of the Iban have now settled in Sarawak, Malaysia. The Iban furnish a particularly clear example of the bilateral, seminomadic tribe which is organized into neither kingdoms nor clans and lineages.

Dwelling along the low hills of the jungle, the Iban number only some nine persons per square mile, barely over 0.5 percent of the density of the Javanese. Iban live in "long houses," each of which has a backside composed of a row of apartments for families and a frontside which is a veranda. Each apartment is a *bilek*, and the family that lives in it is also called a bilek. The bilek family is the basic unit of Iban society. It is not submerged into any clan or lineage, nor is it fully absorbed into the long house; indeed, many a long-house community has disintegrated because its constituent bilek units decide to split apart. Within a given long house's territory, all of its bileks enjoy equal rights of access to land, but virgin land that a bilek clears is its own, to use and to pass on to its heirs.

Coming upon a forest area which they wish to clear for farming, Iban men clean the undergrowth with bush knives, fell trees with ax or adze, and burn the rest of the vegetation. They then dibble holes for seeds (over 110 holes per minute at top speed). Women sow the seeds and keep up the weeding after the planting is done, while the men go away on journeys; formerly they went to seek heads in order to enhance their prestige and spiritual power, more recently they have gone as pirates, laborers, or scouts for the British army during the anticommunist campaign in Malaya. The men return in time to help with the harvest. Each bilek is responsible for harvesting its own crops, which may average 20 bushels per acre for 4–5 acres per bilek. The different bileks may exchange labor, but it is strictly a tit-for-tat arrangement, with no bilek giving more than it gets.

The Iban traces descent bilaterally, and he endeavors to balance his allegiance to maternal and paternal sides of his kindred; his dependence on each is symbolized in the important ritual called *gawai-tusak*, in which one of the child's ears is pierced by a relative of the mother and the other by a relative of the father.

The Iban resides ambilocally. A married couple chooses to live with either the husband's family or with the wife's, and statistics show neatly that the Iban chooses patrilocal residence half the time and matrilocal residence half the time. When an Iban is a member of a bilek, he cannot be disinherited or disowned, but if the Iban marries and moves out of the bilek into which he was born, he loses all rights to inheritance from his parents. Moving into his spouse's bilek, he gains rights to inheritance from his in-laws, once the marriage is established, which is usually after the birth of the first child. Adoption demonstrates as decisively as marriage that, among the Iban, rights depend on residence. An adopted child is a member of the adopting bilek and none other, and in all matters of inheritance or succession, claims based on adoption are as valid as those based on birth.

The bilek expands by marriage, adoption, birth, or the return of a divorcee. When a bilek grows too big, someone leaves and founds a new bilek. The new bilek is a separate but equal replica of the old. It is not, as among the Batak or a similarly organized unilineal society, a unit subordinate to a lineage from which it descends.

The usual reason for partition of a bilek is disharmony, as in unequal sharing of labor by siblings' families. Ideally, all siblings but one marry out of the bilek, but often two or more siblings remain together, each with his wife and children. Loyalty to one's wife and children naturally comes into conflict with loyalty to one's sibling, and when quarrels arise, the conjugal bond has primacy. Of 34 bileks that split, 80 percent contained two married siblings, which is to say that in most partitions the Iban goes with his spouse instead of staying with his siblings. It would seem that this pattern is adaptive to the Iban economy, in which the most efficient productive unit is the bilek composed of no more than one child-rearing couple; the split between siblings reduces each bilek to this size.

The head person of a new bilek, as of the old one, is called the *pun bilek*. In exactly half of the cases of partition, this pun bilek was a man, in half the cases a woman, and in all cases the new pun bilek's position is theoretically equal to that of the old pun bilek. Property is split between old and new bileks, and the old property is no more sacred or prestigious than the new, with two exceptions. The original bilek retains the ancestral rice seed, the *padi pun*. The seceding bilek carries the *sangking*, which is the "younger brother" of the padi pun, and the sangking becomes the padi pun of the new bilek. Similar imagery is followed in dividing the ritual whetstone, an instrument crucial in initiating the rites of the farming cycle. Ownership of a bilek's property depends on residence; the Iban insist that whoever lives in a bilek, even if he were an enemy, possesses the valuables, which are Chinese jars, bronze gongs, weapons, the padi, and land rights.

When pioneering new territory, several bileks may join together and build a small long house, closer to new fields than the main long house. During their 15- to 20-year swidden cycle they return periodically to the old house. Even in a joint pioneering enterprise, each bilek is responsible for its own livelihood. One bilek is jurally equal to another, though the more industrious and fortunate bileks accumulate surplus with which they sometimes buy gongs as symbols of their wealth.

Emphasis on the independence of the bilek should not obscure the unity of the long-house community. Most of the residents of the long house are kinsmen as well as neighbors—a pattern that contrasts profoundly with that of the typical Western apartment house, where virtually no neighbors are kinsmen. Iban place great emphasis on making the long house a place of ritual security, and the atmosphere is communal and intimate, resembling that of the

> . . . boulevard. At nightfall, when lamps are gleaming up and down its length, strolling men gather in casual groups to sit and smoke, chew betel, and discuss together the happenings of the day.[8]

In spite of the communal mood of the long house, each bilek stubbornly holds to its autonomy. The diverse bileks do not own common property such as the "village green" of the Polynesian village. Virtually all that is commonly owned is the burial ground and the *tangga*, a huge, notched log offering entry into the long house. Supposedly jointly maintained by the constituent bilek units, the log invariably falls into disrepair, and in one illuminating incident, one of the two long-house headmen, exhorting the member families to unite in fixing the log, is finally forced to do it himself.

Salient features of the bilek, then, are compactness, independence, and ease of movement. The customs of kinship, marriage, inheritance, and partition among the Iban are designed to ensure that each bilek retains these characteristics—that it not grow too large, too dependent, or too sedentary. The portable and ruggedly individualistic bilek is well adapted for the constant expansion into virgin territory that the swidden pattern requires.

The Ma'anjan like the Iban are of the Dajak type found in Malaysian and Indonesian Borneo, the interior of which the Ma'anjan inhabit. Numbering around 30,000 souls, the Ma'anjan also resemble the Iban in their dry-rice, swidden agriculture, in their bilateral, nuclear-family-centered social organization, and in their animistic or Christian religion, which sets them off from their Islamic neighbors to the east and west. Within the Ma'anjan society is a particular group, the Padju Epat, who are distinguished by their practice of a nine-day death ceremony, the *idjambe*. The following description is of the Padju Epat.

The Ma'anjan *dangau* resembles somewhat the Iban bilek. It is the primary social, economic, and ritual unit of the Ma'anjan. Occupying its swidden field house during much of the year, it is composed of husband and wife, their unmarried children, and occasionally, but only temporarily, a married child and his or her spouse and children. The dangau house owns common property, has its own head, and acts as a unit in labor exchange (which appears to be more frequent among Ma'anjan than Iban) in that work given to a dangau should be repaid to the contributing dangau. Like the bilek, each dangau family has its own unique strain of sacred rice.

Each dangau cultivates its own field, which averages about the size of the Iban bilek's field—roughly five and a half acres—and produces slightly over ten bushels per acre. The swidden cycle broadly resembles that of the Iban, but the dangau frequently fails to produce enough rice for its own needs, and the Ma'anjan farmers supplement swidden rice agriculture with such activities as rubber-growing for profit

Somewhat similar to the Iban long house is the Ma'anjan *lewu'*, a village house that combines under one roof several dangau families. Like the long house, the lewu' was formerly quite large, composed of as many as a dozen families. Today they are usually small, reflecting an attitude that to live independently is modern, and that privacy is pleasant. The lewu' group owns its village house, heirloom property, and primary rights to swidden lands. As among the Iban, approximately half of the marriages are matrilocal, half patrilocal, so that half the husbands live in their wives' natal lewu' houses and half the wives in their husbands' natal lewu' houses. Land-use rights are inherited according to membership in a household, as are heirlooms such as gongs, jars, and plates.

Descent among the Ma'anjan is reckoned bilineally, which gives rise to two types of kinship groups: one organized around the contemporary individual, the other around ancestors. A group of the first type is called a "kindred." Each person includes within his kindred a core set of relatives such as siblings, parents, grandparents, grandchildren, and, if living, great-grandparents and great-grandchildren, as well as a more amorphous group that includes cousins and uncles whom the individual barely knows. Should the individual need help in such activities as house-building, he can call together his kindred. No individual shares the same kindred with any other individual, except his full siblings.

The second type of group, known as the *Bumuh*, comprises all the bilineal descendents of an ancestor. If such an ancestor pioneered in clearing a particular territory, all of his descendants inherit special rights to farm in that territory. As a result the Padju Epat lands are divided into hereditary territories of the several Bumuhs that compose the community.

Almost half of the villagers are Christian and the rest are animist except for a small minority of Muslims (who, interestingly enough in light of the general connection between Islam and trade, are virtually all engaged in trade and are the only Padju Epat so occupied). The animists are the most ceremonially active group, and one of their most elaborate ceremonies is the *idjambe*, the cycle of death rituals involving primary burial and subsequent disinterment and mass lustration of the bones.[10] The Padju Epat explain their retention of the idjambe, which other Ma'anjan groups have lost, by the story that a Muslim fanatic, a recent convert, sought to Islamize the Ma'anjan, beginning by destroying the cremation ceremonies and paraphernalia. The story goes that he succeeded in all but the Padju Epat villages, which put up a desperate last-ditch fight. The pattern is like that elsewhere: a conflict between Islam and the indigenous cycle of death ceremonies that ushers the deceased gradually into the next world.

A *tambak* is an elongated, richly carved, iron wood box in which are stored the ashes of bones that have been burned. Such a box is constructed, and a tambak group created, when some person feels that he has achieved such prestige and wealth that he should commission the construction of his own box, to serve as the repository for his own ashes and those of his descendants. Affiliation with a tambak group is ambilateral; if, upon marrying, one cuts one's tie with one's natal tambak group by moving in with one's spouse, one can join the spouse's tambak group.

The ceremonies carried out by a tambak group to honor a deceased person occur seven days after death, 49 days, and then annually for three years; for three years food is taken to the grave following the harvest, with a feast and a cleansing ceremony each time. Until the forty-ninth day, relatives are in mourning, and are excluded from rituals and restricted in their activity, both ceremonial and nutritional.

After some two or three hundred corpses have accumulated, the villagers entertain thoughts of the idjambe, the nine-day cleansing cycle. Arrangements are made, the ceremony is scheduled, and, a day or two before the cremation is to begin, returning emigre relatives appear carrying the exhumed remains of corpses. Progressing through daily incantations, sacrifices, and refreshment with rice beer, the ceremony reaches a climax on the eighth day when peculiar and inverted actions are performed. Boys amuse themselves doing things the wrong way; a buffalo is slaughtered and eaten by women who wail over it as though it were a corpse; a cock fight is held and the winning rooster is beaten to death.

By the ninth day, the bones of the dead have been exhumed and cleaned. Special coffins have been made, and into each have been placed the remains of ten or twelve individuals belonging to the same tambak group. The coffins have been stacked on a boatlike structure, around which are assembled nail and hair trimmings and other paraphernalia to be used in the journey of the dead. On the last day of the ceremony, the coffins are carried to a cremation platform in the forest. Ignited while women wail, the coffins burst open, spilling ashes and charred bones. When these remains have cooled, they are raked up, placed in a bronze gong, and purified. The bones are then carried to the proper tambaks, and their contents dumped in, after the old ashes have been unceremoniously dumped out. The various tambaks are then surrounded with clothes, plates, baskets, and other items that have been rent or smashed, and the participants go back to the ceremonial hall for a last meal.

On the ninth and final night, orators evaluate and interpret the ceremony, discussing in eloquent speeches whether the rules were properly followed. Upcountry relatives return to their villages. Seven and 49 days later, post-cremation ceremonies are held. On the seventh day, lashes, trees, and other items are cut to signal the breaking of ties to the dead, and other rites are performed. On the forty-ninth day, a chicken is killed, and offerings are taken to the tambak as a last remembrance.

THE AMBONESE[11]

The province of Maluku (Moluccas) includes the set of islands east of Celebes and north of Timor, but the Moluccan people are concentrated on the island of Ambon. Racially and culturally as well as geographically, these Moluccans are between the Malay and the Melanesian. On the whole they have darker skin and larger frames than the Malay type of Indonesian, bearing a striking resemblance in some instances to the Negro.

The total population of the Moluccas, according to the 1961 census, was 1,296,033, while that of the core district was 789,534. On the island of Ambon, about half the population is Christian and half Muslim. Most villages are of one or the other of these religions, though a few are mixed. The Ambonese originally were shifting cultivators, divided into small tribes of kinship groups. For hundreds of years, however, the Ambonese have been influenced by forces connected with the international spice trade. Dominated first by the Islamic kingdom of Ternate, they were then penetrated by the Catholic Portuguese and the Calvinist Dutch, remaining under Dutch colonial rule from 1605 to 1949. Ambon today is a mestizo culture, combining European, Javanese, Malay, and Melanesian elements. Contemporary patterns are exemplified by a study recently made of an Ambonese Christian village which we may call "Allang."

In Allang as elsewhere in Ambon, clove and nutmeg constitute the primary cash crops. Subsistence agriculture is usually of the swidden type. Because Ambonese soil is thin and infertile, a plot is usually cultivated for only a few years and then abandoned. Major swidden crops are spinach and other greens, squash and other gourds, sweet potatoes and other root crops—notably cassava, the root from which tapioca is made—and sago, from which flour is made. Ambonese are known throughout Indonesia as root rather than rice growers and eaters, a trait that may correlate with their Melanesian affinities.

The village of Allang encompasses several partilineal, patrilocal clans called *mata rumah*, each of which controls a certain portion of land. A second unit is the *familie*, the bilateral kindred, which is not a corporate group but does gather at such times as birth, marriage, and death. Because membership in the familie cross-cuts membership in the mata rumah, the familie serves to integrate the various lineages that compose the village society.

The village is ruled by a council, which consists of the hereditary ruler plus the eight heads of groups called *soa*, each of which is a collection of mata rumah, and other traditional leaders. The congregation is, in this Christian village, the most viable nonkinship organization.

In Allang, indigenous customs surrounding birth have long since disappeared, to be replaced by infant baptism. Indigenous adolescent initiation ceremonies have given way to Christian confirmation which retains, however, some indigenous features, and is a highly emotional experience for the congregation. Marriage takes place first before the village chief, at his residence or in his office, then at the church, thus conforming to both civil and Christian custom. The adat ceremonies are held afterward; the groom's family and kindred carry the bride-wealth to the bride's family, transferring the bride and her children from her father's to her husband's kinship group.

In the indigenous kinship system, institutionalized linkages between the various lineages of a village ensure that each receives brides from certain lineages and gives brides to others. As among the Buginese, bridewealth is important, and wife-stealing is practiced, apparently to escape the haggling and expense. Also similar to the Makassarese, divorce is rare, and apparently was so before the advent of Christianity as well as after.

Christian funeral services have replaced the adat customs surrounding death and burial. Held at home or beside the grave, the services are preached by a minister or elder accompanied by an orchestra of flutes. Vigils on the third and fortieth days occur less often than formerly.

In other Ambonese villages, whether Christian or Muslim, social life appears to resemble that of Allang, except that in some villages, richer complexes of adat have been retained; one such complex turns around a village priest who placates founding ancestors and gains their help in the cycle of farming.

THE MUREMAREW[12]

West New Guinea, which became part of Indonesia in early 1963, boasts an indigenous population of approximately 700,000, divided into diverse and scattered tribes. Among the several distinctive culture areas is the region east of the Mamberamo River, largest river in the northern part of the island. Peoples of the region tend to be slenderer, shorter, and lighter of skin than tribesmen to the west of the Mamberamo. They have thin lips, narrow nostrils, and crisp, woolly hair.

On the River Marew, tributary of the Mamberamo, is found the village of Muremarew, whose dualistic patterns may serve as one example of those existing in the varied settlements of the vast island. The village of Muremarew is divided into a higher and a lower section, the *peejawoom* and the *tawanawoom*. On the higher level, the peejawoom, are dwellings for married people. Three and a half meters below is the tawanawoom, the site of bachelors' houses, a guest house, and two multipurpose houses. The higher section has a place for meetings, a square for dancing, dance paraphernalia such as drums, feathers, plumes, and shell strings, and the home of the war leader and best hunter, who is also the star dancer. The lower section is no place for meetings and association; no children play there, no shouting or laughter is heard, and men stay away for fear that contact with this inferior half of the community will disturb their hunting.

The dualism extends from the village to the river. The upstream section is peejawoom, the downstream, tawanawoom. Men bathe in the upper division, women in the lower. Distinguishing between the sexes, the two terms also distinguish senior from junior generations, and, indeed, divide the entire universe. Peejawoom is associated with the sky, the sun, elders, kinsmen, males, hunting, and the ancestral hero, Adjaw. Tawanawoom is associated with the earth, the moon, youth, strangers, women, sago, and the ancestral heroine, Jowesso.

Like other villages on the Mamberamo, Muremarew has a majority of males. As a result it has a large number of bachelors. There are 13 of them, 10 of whom are over 21 years of age; by comparison there are only two unmarried and marriageable girls, and one widow. Owing to their numbers, bachelors in Muremarew and other communities of the Mamberamo are developing into a distinct social group with their own norms and customs. They specialize in the hunting of crocodiles, the skins of which they sell to Chinese traders. Enjoying an abundance of such foods as tinned fish and rice, and equipping their quarters with mosquito nets, suitcases, chopping knives, and clothing, the bachelors' conspicuous consumption antagonizes the more honorable but impoverished married segment of the village.

Subsisting largely on sago, which is primarily grown and prepared by women, the village depends on women for food. Animal life is scarce, and hunting yields little food, yet the hunting of game is a manly pursuit; it is an important symbol of virility that is celebrated by rite and myth. As hunters, yet linked to the female portion of the cosmology, the bachelors occupy an anomalous position in this respect as in others.

Composed of antagonistic lineages, the village threatens to split apart. Yet it holds together because it is the only place where the people feel safe; as they put it, "there is no life outside the community."[13] No sorcery is believed to issue from within the village, though sorcerers are assumed to live outside, and the community maintains a strong *esprit de corps*. No chief or elders govern the village, and all villagers have equal say in discussion and decision.

Like other societies of the region, the Muremarew ideally marry by exchanging sisters. Marrying one another's sisters over many generations, a pair of lineages becomes permanent partners in the exchange. Since such an alliance is regarded as the coming together of opposing portions of the society, the cosmos too is imagined to be united; the alliance is not merely between spouses and lineages but between Adjaw and Jowesso, heaven and earth, male and female.

When a Muremarew dies, his corpse is wrapped in banana leaves and left for several months in a tree or a scaffolding made of trees. When the corpse has decomposed, the bones are removed, rewrapped, and buried—the occasion for a big feast. On the feast's opening night, the two opposing halves of Muremarew society, the *Soromadja* and the *Waseera*, exchange betel nuts, arrows, pig's teeth, shells, and other gifts to symbolize their unity. The celebration elicits joy and merriment, dancing and singing, as the villagers express their belief that a great spirit will soon descend to create a new order, after which misery, illness, hunger, and death shall cease.

THE CHINESE[14]

Recent migrants to the archipelago, the Chinese are not so localized as the indigenous groups; though half of them live on Java, the rest of the Chinese population of some three million is scattered throughout the islands. The Chinese are primarily located in urban areas (their rural populations were largely evacuated to the city by the Indonesian government in 1959–1960, and their commercial interests have always kept most of them in the towns and cities). The Chinese render virtually any service that brings profit; an example is the Chinese *tukang gigi* (fixer of teeth) whose skills are advertised in small towns by signs depicting grinning incisors, canines, and molars. The Chinese are doctors, priests, and entrepreneurs, and they run the rice mills, stores, lumber yards, and wholesaling and export establishments. Few Chinese are laborers or peasants, though many worked at such occupations when they first arrived in Indonesia. Few Chinese are in government or politics, and the Indonesian universities impose a quota limiting the number of Chinese who are admitted—a restriction that has not prevented a reasonably heavy representation of Chinese from entering the academic and medical professions. The Confucian philosophy of the Chinese mainland idealized the mandarin and the landed scholar gentry while denigrating the merchant, but like most overseas Chinese, the Chinese in Indonesia regard wealth as the major symbol of status. Elaborate hairdoes and glamorous dresses for women, Arrow shirts, nightclubs, lotteries, and mistresses for the men are among the pleasures afforded by wealth. Sometimes garish in display and reckless in gambling, the Chinese are frugal and industrious in amassing the wealth that allows such indulgences.

The Chinese family name is inherited from the father. In marriage between Chinese and Indonesian, the father was usually Chinese, hence the Chinese name was retained and has served for centuries as a badge of Chinese identity. Since the communist massacre of 1965, however, when communal tensions occasionally exploded against the out-group Chinese, they have begun to adopt Indonesian-sounding names designed to aid their absorption into the nation. Chinese names are frequently transformed into Hindu-Javanese variants, as in "Chandra" from "Chan." Despite the name change, persons inheriting the same surname still worship common ancestors at the surname temple.

The greatest change from the traditional mainland Chinese pattern can be seen on Java, where the culturally mestizo Chinese, the *peranakan*, outnumber the purer ones, the *totok*. The two types contrast in a variety of respects. Totoks are more inclined to go into business and are more interested in getting rich. They place higher value on work, frugality, self-reliance, and commercial daring. Peranakans value leisure, the enjoyment of life, social position and security, values which resemble those of the indigenous Javanese. Totoks live in the central business district in shop/house dwellings similar to those of south China. Peranakans are dispersed throughout the towns, but they prefer Western-style houses like those of the Indonesian elite.

Totoks are patrilocal, patrilineal, and patriarchal, like Chinese of the traditional mainland society. To a degree the peranakans have absorbed matrilocal, matrilineal, and matrifocal tendencies of Javanese society, resulting in a rather bilateral system. Peranakan daughters as well as sons inherit property. In fact, since young peranakan couples sometimes reside matrilocally, the daughter is the logical recipient of the parental house and its ancestral tablets. Peranakan cults tend to venerate ancestors and ancestresses of the mother as well as those of the father. In the traditional patrilocal Chinese household, the son's mother had great authority over his wife, whom he brought home to live in his mother's house. Since peranakan couples live neolocally, in a house independent of the parents of either spouse, the son's mother loses control over his wife. Reflecting the matrifocal influence of Javanese society, many peranakan households now include relatives of the wife as well as the husband, enhancing the wife's authority and status. Peranakan bilaterality is even reflected in kinship terminology; thus, in the generation of parents and grandparents, kinship terms do not now distinguish maternal from paternal relatives.

Rarer now than in the past is the family-owned Chinese shop above or behind which lived the family owners who did all the shop work, from selling to sweeping. Nonrelatives, even non-Chinese, are often employed today, especially in the large stores and enterprises. Nevertheless, businesses are still family-owned to a great extent, and virtually the only way to gain shares in a Chinese company is by marrying into the family that owns it. In many ways the Chinese have accommodated to the local culture, but they have retained that pattern crucial to their economic power and social place—the familial basis of their commerce.

SOCIOCULTURAL TYPES

Struggling to categorize the scattered and diversified Indonesian societies, the observer is likely to notice first the ecological and economic divisions. Such groups as the Javanese, Balinese, and Rotinese are largely sedentary growers of wet rice, while the Sumbawans, Iban, and Ma'anjan are shifting cultivators of dry rice. The Sumatrans carry on both types of agriculture, and the Moluccan and New Guinea "Melanesian" groups tend to subsist on root crops instead of rice. Among the Chinese and the santri-type Muslims, commerce is an important source of livelihood, and Javanese of the Hinduized and aristocratic tradition are particularly numerous in the civil service stationed throughout Indonesia.

Gross correlations may be observed between sociocultural patterning and such ecological-economic divisions. Stratification is more pronounced and more symbolically elaborate among the wet-rice societies, especially those which were Hinduized, whereas the swidden groups tend toward a more egalitarian and individualistic mode of life. Religion does not correlate in any simple way with ecology, since Christian, Hindu, and Muslim societies can all be found practicing wet-rice agriculture, but animism does seem to have hung on more strongly among such swidden groups as the Iban or the Ma'anjan; that may be explainable partly, however, by the isolation of such tribes from the historical movement of the great religions. Islam is associated throughout the islands with a commercial and peripatetic style of life, but the most successful merchants are the largely non-Muslim Chinese.

Classification of the Indonesian societies into such types as matrilineal, patrilineal, and bilineal is likely to be misleading, since these crude labels obscure similarities among virtually all of the Indonesian kinship systems. Among these similarities are those of kinship terms, but perhaps more basic is the fact that the nuclear family is the elementary unit of most Indonesian societies, the Minangkabau being traditionally a partial exception to this generalization. The broad distinction between communities organized around kinship groups and those organized territorially would seem to relate to significant differences in other spheres of social structure. Societies such as the Batak, the Minangkabau, or even the bilateral Makassarese tend to organize their communities around kinship groups and to rank these groups so that the individual's status depends on his kinship membership. In a Javanese village, on the other hand, the organization is territorial—one is a member of a village because he resides there—and the basic criterion of status is land ownership. Oversimplifying, one may say that the Javanese villager distinguishes between the elite villager who owns land and a house, the middle-level villager who owns a house but no land, and the landless and houseless wage laborer. Yet even the Javanese villagers regard the highest stratum as descended from an ancestral group of settlers, indicating a certain emphasis on kinship as a criterion of rank.

Penetration of Islam seems to correlate with changes in the ritualized structure of the life cycle. Circumcision of pious Muslim groups generally occurs in childhood, whereas non-Islamized or partially Islamized groups stage circumcision or other initiation rites at puberty.[15] The difference may reflect a pious Muslim view that early circumcision quickly nudges their sons out of the arms of their mothers and into the Islamic world of their fathers and other pious men.

Combining social, cultural, and ecological criteria of classification, whole complexes of peoples can be distinguished—for instance, the "coastal Malays" and the "interior tribes."[16] The coastal Malays are identifiable by their Islamic, maritime culture that has evolved since the rise of Islam in the fourteenth century. Coastal Malay culture has spread from the Malay-speaking peoples of south Sumatra and the Malay peninsula to north Sumatra, west and east Java, Madura and Lombok, Sumabawa and other islands of the Lesser Sundas, south Celebes, and to parts of the Moluccas. In all of these areas, especially the coastal, groups of pious Muslims carry cultural traits (and to a degree, Arab, Indian, and Malay genes) that spread with the diffusion of Islam, trade, and the Malay language during the fourteenth to the eighteenth centuries. Distinguished less by race or origin than by life style, these coastal Malays tend to enjoy Malay, Arabic, and other Islamized literature, to send pilgrims to Mecca, and to organize their society around a distinction between aristocrats, commoners, and, traditionally, slaves. Where a sultan is in control, loyalty to him has traditionally depended on his charisma and accomplishments, and has been more flexible and pragmatic than among the Hinduized, interior Javanese. Ecologically, the coastal Malays are flexible. Disposed to trade to a greater extent than the other non-Chinese Indonesians, they also occupy themselves by fishing, commercial farming of both irrigated and unirrigated varieties, and even with cottage industry. Many of their characteristics derive from adaptation to the Malayo-Indonesian commercial network that unites the harbor towns. Among the societies examined in this book, the Buginese, Makassarese, santri Javanese, and even the Sumbawans and the Minangkabau exemplify most of these traits, as do the so-called Malays of coastal Sumatra and Borneo. The category is not neat, however, since few of these societies possess all of the traits mentioned.

Similarly loose is the category "interior tribesmen," which is intended to include the staggering variety of tribes found in the interior of Borneo, Celebes, and certain islands of the Lesser Sundas. The interior tribesmen, exemplified by the Iban and the Ma'anjan, have remained relatively isolated from the outside world. Most are swidden cultivators of dry rice, gardners of sago, maize, and root crops on marginal land not sufficiently fertile for wet-rice agriculture. They tend to organize themselves on the basis of kinship bonds, either bilateral or unilineal, instead of patrimonial relationships such as those between peasant and regent or subject and lord. Many have remained relatively uninfluenced by Hinduism and Islam, retaining their animism or recently converting to Christianity. Until recently, many were headhunters.

A third major group would be the Hinduized, hierarchical, wet-rice societies such as those of the Balinese and Javanese. Resistant to Islam, these groups emphasize courtly language, rich ceremony, and refined arts such as the shadow play, the dance, and the gamelan.

Such groups as the Batak, the Chinese, the Rotinese, the Ambonese, and the societies of New Guinea fail to fit neatly these typologies, and most Indonesian societies show mixed features. Considering the rough fit between types and facts, some might consider the effort to construct typologies useless. The historian might regard as a more useful endeavor the analysis of the contribution of each group to the mainstream of Indonesian history—an analysis briefly initiated in earlier chapters. Unfortunately, the brisk pace of the historical narrative allows little pause to examine in detail the structure of each contributing society and culture, and in a nation so diversified as Indonesia, the historian as well as the anthropologist should systematically take such structures into account, by description, typology, or some better means.

REFERENCES

[1] Information for this section comes primarily from Hendrik T. Chabot, "Bontoramba: A Village of Goa, South Sulawesi," in Koentjaraningrat (ed.), *Villages in Indonesia* (Ithaca, N.Y.: Cornell Univ. Press, 1967).

[2] Information for this section comes from Peter R. Goethals, *Aspects of Local Government in a Sumbawan Village* (Ithaca, N.Y.: Modern Indonesia Project, Cornell University, 1961); and "Rarak: A Swidden Village of West Sumbawa," in Koentjaraningrat (ed.), *Villages in Indonesia*, pp. 21–35.

[3] Goethals, *Aspects of Local Government*, p. 29.

[4] *Ibid.*, p. 24.

[5] Information for this section is taken primarily from James J. Fox, "The Rotinese" (unpublished manuscript, n.d.). Also see Fox's "Semantic Parallelism in Rotinese Ritual Language," *Bijdragen tot de Taal-, Land-en Volkenkunde*, Vol. 127 (1971), pp. 215–255. Additional important anthropological works on the Lesser Sundas include Clark Cunningham, "Order and Change in an Atoni Diarchy," *Southwestern Journal of Anthropology*, Vol. 21 (1965), pp. 359–382; Rodney Needham, "Circulating Connubium in Eastern Sumba: A Literary Analysis," *Bijdragen tot de Taal-, Land-en Volkenkunde*, Vol. 113 (1957), pp. 168–278; P. Middlekoop, *Head Hunting in Timor and Its Historical Implications* (Sydney: Oceanic Linguistic Monographs No. 8, University of Sydney, 1963); Cora DuBois, *The People of Alor: A Social-Psychological Study of an East Indian Island* (Minneapolis: Univ. of Minnesota Press, 1944). An important work on a somewhat similar group from outside the Lesser Sundas is Richard E. Downs, *The Religion of the Bare-Speaking Toradja of Central Celebes* (The Hague: Utgeverij Excelsior, 1956).

[6] Fox, "The Rotinese," p. 2.

[7] Information on the Iban comes from Derek Freeman, *Report on the Iban* (London: Athlone, 1970); "The Family System of the Iban of Borneo," in Jack Goody (ed.), *The Developmental Cycle in Family Groups* (Cambridge: Cambridge Univ. Press, 1957); and "The Iban of Western Borneo," in G. P. Murdock (ed.), *Social Structure in Southeast Asia* (Chicago: Viking Fund Publications in Anthropology, No. 29, 1960).

[8] Freeman, *Report on the Iban*, p. 125.

[9] Information on the Ma'anjan is taken from Alfred B. Hudson, *Padju Epat: The Ma'anyan of Indonesian Borneo* (New York: Holt, Rinehart, and Winston, 1972); Alfred B. Hudson and Judith M. Hudson, "Telang: A Ma'anjan Village in Central Kalimantan," in Koenjaraningrat (ed.), *Villages in Indonesia*; and Judith M. Hudson, "Letters from Kalimantan: II," *Indonesia*, II (October 1966), pp. 25–36. Where the 1972 monograph differs slightly from the earlier reports, which were written in the midst of the field research, the monograph is taken as definitive.

[10] Information on the *idjambe* is taken from Alfred B. Hudson, "Death Ceremonies of the Padju Epat Ma'anyan Dayaks," in Thomas H. Harrison (ed.), *Borneo Writing and Related Matters*, Special Monograph No. 1, *Sarawak Museum Journal*, Vol. 12 (1966).

[11] Information on the Ambonese is taken from Frank L. Cooley, "Allang: A Village on Ambon Island," in Koentjaraningrat (ed.), *Villages in Indonesia*; and *Ambonese Adat: A General Description* (New Haven, Conn.: Southeast Asia Studies, Yale University, 1962).

[12] Information on the Muremarew is taken from Gottfried Oosterwal, "Muremarēw: A Dual Organized Village on the Mamberamo, West Irian," in Koentjaraningrat (ed.), *Villages in Indonesia*.

[13] *Ibid.*, p. 166.

[14] See G. William Skinner, "The Chinese Minority," in Ruth T. McVey (ed.), *Indonesia* (New Haven, Conn.: Southeast Asia Studies, Yale University, 1963), for a summary of facts and a bibliography on the Chinese of Indonesia. Also see Donald E. Willmott, *The Chinese of Semarang* (Ithaca, N.Y.: Cornell

Univ. Press, 1960); and Giok-Lan Tan, *The Chinese of Sukabami* (Ithaca, N.Y.: Modern Indonesia Project, Cornell University, 1963).

[15]The correlation between strong Islamization and early circumcision is apparent from data supplied by a survey of forms of circumcision in the various regions of Indonesia. See B. Schrieke, "Allerlei over de Besnijdenis in den Indischen Archipel" *Tijdschrift voor Indische Taal-, Land- En Volkenkunde,* vol. 60 (1921), pp. 373–578, and vol. 61 (1922), pp. 1–94. Schrieke's survey indicates that circumcision occurs latest in the abangan heartland of central Java, particularly in and around Solo, whereas it occurs earliest in the more strongly Islamized regions, such as Sunda, parts of the West and East coast of Sumatra, Banka, Billiton, and Lombok. That the correlation is not perfect, however, is suggested by reports of early ages of circumcision among non-Islamic dajak groups in Borneo.

[16]This distinction between the "coastal Malay" and the "interior tribes" is drawn from Hildred Geertz, "Indonesian Cultures and Communities," in McVey (ed.), *Indonesia*, pp. 58–70.

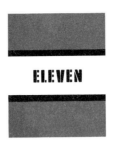

ELEVEN

CONTEMPORARY INDONESIA:
UNITY

Bhinneka Tunggal Ika (Diversity in Unity)
Indonesian national slogan

From the inner islands of Java, Madura, and Bali to the outer ones
such as Ternate, Sumbawa, and Celebes, the traveler encounters a uni-
form urban culture that cuts across the diversity of village, tribe, and
region. Only 10 to 15 percent of the Indonesians inhabit towns and
cities, but many more participate in the urban culture that centers
in and flows from them. A search for unifying themes in Indonesia
might well begin in the urban areas.[1]

URBAN CULTURE

Omnipresent in urban Indonesia is the small Chinese store, the *toko*,
whose front wall is removable to display beads, bangles, and sundries
of a variety found in the general store of early America. In a small
town such as Sumbawa Besar (Big Sumbawa), the shopping district is
little more than a row of such toko. In a large city such as Djakarta,
the toko are squeezed between massive department stores resembling
those of prewar Europe. In these large stores, the fat, gold-toothed, un-
dershirt- or pajama-clad Chinese keeper of the toko is replaced by trim,
young, female clerks in starched white blouses and neat skirts. Behind
the scenes, the owner is still Chinese.

The center of native commerce is the *pasar* or bazaar, a crowded
and noisy complex of stands and booths that sell everything from fruits
and vegetables to rusty daggers and unhygienic haircuts. Pickpockets,
eaters of fire, sellers of medicine, and male or female prostitutes add

flavor to the pasar, as do the snack hawkers, who carry their stoves on their backs and light the evening sidewalks with the glow of their cooking fires. The Westerner will note the incredibly large number of sellers, each of whom displays an incredibly small stock; the pattern reflects the "hidden unemployment" which forces the destitute to devote much time to little profit in a struggle to subsist.

The word "pasar" is said to relate to "kasar," and the pasar is also described as "ramai," which means "cheerfully noisy and crowded." In the pasar, no prices are fixed, and the staccato thrusts and parries of haggling provide relief from the calm and fluid halus etiquette that pervades every Indonesian domicile, whether palace or shack. At the same time, for all but the most hard-nosed santri or Chinese traders, the home provides a cherished retreat from the hustle of the marketplace, the values of which violate those most sacred to the refined Hinduized Indonesian culture.

Distinguishable from the market by its dignified appearance, the cement government office building is enlivened by the hawkers of snacks, drivers of pedicabs, and beggars who squat outside it. Inside, clerks labor (or simply sit) at desks covered with glasses of lukewarm coffee or tea, piles of rubber stamps, and stacks of dusty forms printed on cheap and yellowed paper. Conversation with an official passes across a low coffee table placed near his desk. The government office remains open from 7 A.M. to 2 P.M. and, unlike the store and market, does not reopen after the early afternoon siesta.

In the largest cities are found also the Western embassies. Distinguished from the indigenous offices by their closed doors to contain the air-conditioned coolness and by their lack of the sociable coffee table, the embassies usually conform to the nine-to-five Western schedule. Long after the indigenous civil servant has retired for nap and bath and just before the market tunes up for its evening cacophony, the Western official is whisked by chauffeur to his club or villa for drink and leisure among his countrymen; few spend their evenings with the people.

Night life among the natives tends toward the lurid. A plethora of such tawdry and pornographic Western films as "The Sweet Sins of Sexy Susan" and its sequel "Sexy Susan Sins Again" have virtually driven out the Indonesian-language, Indonesian-produced films popular during the years of Sukarno, and especially the Muslims protest vigorously (but sometimes view secretly) the porno that threatens to poison the indigenous mind. Despite the decline of native film, native theater continues to flourish, especially in Java. Urban commercial performances such as ketoprak, ludruk, and wajang wong in the cities and towns of Java rival the pastoral florescence of dance drama on

Bali; according to one count, Java has more than forty times as many theater troupes per capita as does America,[2] not to mention the even more numerous puppeteers of the classical wajang kulit. In the amusement parks found in such Javanese cities as Surabaja and Surakarta, theater replaces the roller-coasters, merry-go-rounds, tilt-a-whirls, and bumper-cars of the more technologically minded Western nations, and sandwiched into kampungs are rickety bamboo auditoriums that attract huge crowds. Varying in plot from the courtly legends of the Mahabharata to soap opera, popular Javanese theater is always comical since it always stars clowns. Songs by transvestite males, political satire, philosophizing chants, and incredibly accomplished dances are woven through and around the stories and jokes. The ludruk theater is especially interesting from the standpoint of urban anthropology, since it is organized, enacted, and viewed by the kampung-dwelling working class. Uniting the proletariat, ludruk cuts across the ethnic divisions of the pluralistic city by presenting its plays in several dialects as well as in the Indonesian language.[3]

Indonesian entertainment is refreshingly un-Westernized compared to that of such crossroads nations as Singapore. Western dance, banned by Sukarno and detested by many Indonesians, is practiced in only a handful of discotheques, taxi dance halls, nightclubs, and private clubs, most of which are in Djakarta. Possessing few bars, Indonesia has few bar girls. Most prostitutes are in the kampung or skulking about the edge of town, where they do their work in the rice fields. Djakarta boasts a large corps of transvestite male prostitutes. Unionized and aggressive, but beautifully padded, dressed, powdered, and rouged, they parade along the main street and beckon from beneath bridges. Gambling is officially condoned in Djakarta as a means of collecting revenue for urban reform, and Chinese parlors provide lively and expensive games of all kinds. Late at night on quiet corners, pedicab drivers, prostitutes, and workingmen gamble on a smaller scale; in the day, one may buy tickets in the national lottery, an institution which has blossomed into enormous popularity since the downfall of "guided democracy."

Daily conversation in most cities (except Djakarta and Medan) is in the regional dialect. The harangues of the medicine seller, bureaucratic communications, radio programs, political speeches, Friday sermons, billboards, newspapers, and magazines, however, are in the Indonesian language. Djakarta has developed an Indonesian gutter or cockney dialect as a sly, terse, and cynical counterpoint to the pompous, turgid, official acronyms and slogans of the politicians and bureaucrats, and newspapers carry anonymous corner columns which lampoon officialdom in the Djakartanese dialect. The Dutch language, spoken by the Indonesian elite before World War II, theoretically has been replaced by English as the important foreign language taught in schools; unfortunately, the teaching is largely by rote, and the lack of opportunity or need to speak English has resulted in the typical youth's skill in that language being far below that of his father's ability in Dutch.

Not surprisingly, given Indonesia's courtly and colonial history, her urban elite is composed largely of government officials, army officers, and political leaders. A few businessmen, physicians, academicians, and artists enter the elite ranks, usually appropriating one or more political or bureaucratic posts in the process. Wealth, of course, is one symbol of status, especially among the capitalists and the so-called "capitalist bureaucrats" who make money from their government positions: muckraking literature ranging from the novels of Mochtar Lubis to the dramas of the ludruk depict acidly the capitalist bureaucrat whose corruption finances a stylish mistress, a big car, and evenings in the cafe.[4] Just as essential as wealth is a certain cosmopolitanism. The suave member of the elite should speak a Western language, preferably English, know at least the names and slogans of the more famous Western ideologies and philosophies, and possess a university degree, preferably from the West. Oriented more toward the Arabic than the Western culture, the orthodox santri, even the rich and scholarly one, tends to exclude himself from Westernized elite circles by his taste in foreign language, dress, entertainment, and identity. Underneath the Western overlay, the elite maintain indigenous or mestizo private habits. They wear the sarong at home, consume rice as their staple, and bathe by splashing themselves with water from a square tiled basin rather than a shower or tub. Many, however, sit upon the Western-style toilet rather than defecate in the squatting position of the masses.

The urban middle class encompasses middle-level, white-collar workers in government and business, school teachers, the middle ranks of the army and police, merchants, and some artisans. The badly underpaid government worker in the larger city must live in a kampung or makeshift apartment in a dilapidated hotel; he is much better off in the small town, usually managing to live in a neat cement cottage. Below the government worker in status, the merchant and artisan may exceed him in income. Drawing a salary and food allowance adequate for subsisting only a couple of weeks per month, the civil servant, frequently with the thin body and aquiline profile of Ardjuna, somehow maintains his starched white shirt and trousers as well as his halus, if somethat unproductive, courtesy.

At the bottom of urban society is the proletariat—the laborer, servant, pedicab driver, and the ministers to body and soul: the prostitutes and the healers (the status of these last two may rise according to that of their clients). In the smaller towns and cities, the proletarians live in the kampung or, if they are servants, they may live in the houses of their masters. In the metropolis, many are forced to sleep in pedicabs, under bridges, and on the sidewalks, bathing and defecating in the canals and rivers. Many of the urban proletariat are transient, maintaining ties to their villages and returning to them periodically.

Below the bottom, so to speak, are the beggars, much less evident today than during the late stages of guided democracy. At that time the city of Surabaja, for example, was estimated to harbor some 75,000 beggars and vagrants, and certainly hundreds could be seen sprawled on the sidewalks and porch steps after midnight, many of whom would reportedly be dead the next morning. Javanese beggars are polite by comparison with those of India and the Middle East, and most confine their entreaties to quiet pleas; a few are flamboyant, however, such as one stark naked young woman who customarily directed traffic during the noon hour in Surabaja during the Sukarno era. Although the hideous economic conditions of the time were a major source of beggars, a few Javanese tell of deliberately taking up the life of the mendicant for a while, to wander and meditate in search of life's meaning. Beggars today are most notable on the trains, where the horribly maimed swing themselves aboard and twist down the aisles requesting a pittance in return for their moving on out of sight.

The kampung which provides a roof over the heads of most proletarians differs from the slum of Western cities. The kampung grows up as a squatter settlement of shacks and huts. It is never a multistoried tenement building, nor is it confined to a special section of town. The bamboo shacks with *atap* roofs appear in every vacant space, even in alleys behind mansions. Lacking running water and sewers, many kampung are nevertheless kept neat and reasonably clean. The headman of a kampung and his council of youths coordinate periodic clean-ups, bridge-building, and road repairs. In Java, where the pastoral countryside has never been idealized as a retreat for the native elite, existence in an urban kampung is not viewed with as much distaste as one might expect; the Javanese views his kampung as the European immigrant might see his ghetto—a crowded community which nevertheless provides warm fellowship.

In a separate social category are the court cities, Jogjakarta and Surakarta, which supplement the usual urban class structure with that centered around the royal family. The sultan is at the top of the hierarchy, the palace servants at the base. A middle position is occupied by merchants in the village of Kuta Gede who trade in precious metals, lend money, and traditionally serve as Rothschilds to the princes. The two court cities differ in their current position. The susuhunan and prince of Surakarta strove to retain their traditional authority, only to have it stripped since the revolution. The sultan of Jogjakarta, Hamengku Buwono IX, voluntarily relinquished his power, but his democratic reputation made him a national figure, and he is now the minister of finance for the republic. Jogjakarta was selected as the national capital during the revolution, and the sultan's image burnishes that of the Jogjakarta royalty. A portion of the sultan's palace has been transformed into lecture halls for the University of Gadja Mada, but traditional kraton ceremonies continue to attract crowds of thousands during the annual festival of Sekatèn.

Outside the principalities, the royal families have met varied fates. In such remote towns as Ternate or Sumbawa Besar, the sultans have abandoned their palaces and positions. In Bali, on the other hand, kings command great respect, and royal families have taken the lead in commerce.[5]

The notion of "plural" society was first elaborated with respect to Indonesian society, and the Indonesian city or town certainly manifests a plural composition in that its diverse ethnic groups and classes split into separate neighborhoods. The Chinese, especially the totok, have their Chinatown; the Arabs and santri live in a kauman surrounding a mosque; the prijaji live in suburbs with grass and trees; the proletariat live in a kampung. Owing to colonial urban policy, which concerned itself largely with the European elite, and to recent policies and events, the cities have developed few facilities to integrate the various groups. Telephones are rented only by the elite, and the absence of directories constricts the circle of communication, since one can not telephone unless one already knows the number. Public intracity transport, except for the flamboyantly speedy Djakarta bus system (and, formerly, trams in some cities), consists of the pedicab and the horse-drawn carriage. The amusement parks serve a significant function in bringing together the diverse groups, as do massive public ceremonies which have attenuated with the removal of Sukarno.

Trade integrates the urban centers and the villages. By oxcart, bicycle, or the two *pikul* baskets suspended from a pole spanning the shoulders, produce is carried from farm to town. Bulked in the markets, it is then transported by truck or rail to the harbors, by freighter or perahu to such entrepots as Singapore. Interisland trade is not so voluminous as it could be. One might expect that Java would industrialize and export manufactured goods to the outer islands while importing raw materials from them, but the present pattern is for each island to orient individually toward the non-Indonesian market—Singapore and beyond, and ultimately to the manufacturers of Europe, America, and Japan.

The government of the Republic of Indonesia consolidates the local societies into a unitary state in which control flows from the top down and from the center outward. The republic is divided into 26 provinces, each ruled by a governor who is appointed by Djakarta rather than elected by the provincial people. The pattern on Java, with slight variation elsewhere, is that the province controls regencies headed by a regent (*bupati*). The regency subsumes subdistricts, each of which is ruled by a *tjamat*, a cluster of whom are coordinated by a *wedono*.[6] The subdistrict subsumes villages, each ruled by a *lurah*. The village includes hamlets, each headed by the *kamitua*. Only at the village and hamlet level are officials elected; at higher levels they are appointed, indicating a high degree of centralization.

Complicated local histories, difficulties of travel among the islands, and inadequate systems of telephone and telegraph make the centralization and uniformity of the nation greater on paper than in practice; one sign of decentralization is the variation in terminology and function of village administration. In varying regions of Java, the lurah is called by such terms as *bekel, perbekel, demang, penatus, kuwu,* or *pelinggi,* for example. In Rarak the equivalent of the lurah is the *kepala kampung,* and he is complemented by the Islamic official, the *lebé,* in a pattern not seen on Java. In the Ma'anjan village, the kepala kampung is complemented by a *pangulu* to handle adat affairs, and in other villages, such as those of Ambon or Bali, rule is by a council. At higher levels too, variations from the Javanese pattern of province, regency, and village may be seen.

Yet, like the old Indonesian empires, the republic balances functional diversity with cultural unity. Throughout the islands, certain symbols express a strong commitment to national ideals. Among the superficial symbols are the bureaucrat's fountain pen, white shirt and trousers, notebook and briefcase, diploma, and genteel poverty. More profound is his halus deportment and commitment to *dinas,* which replaces the Dutch notion of *dienst* or "official service." As in many formerly colonial nations, the position of civil servants is remarkably prestigeful in spite of incredibly low salaries. The number of government employees has grown to over one and a half million, and many Indonesians, especially Javanese, seem to feel that one has located oneself in the cosmos only when one assumes a post in the bureaucracy. Javanese without a government position customarily list themselves as unemployed, and glorification of the bureaucracy persists even though the Suharto government actively encourages youths to enter other professions and has drastically cut its hiring.

Especially in Java, the bureaucrat is still as much a dignitary as a functionary. He is venerated for his status, but his orders are not necessarily carried out. Villagers regard him as a transcendent being whose words carry mystical rather than practical meanings; responding to him with polite ceremonies of assent, they proceed to ignore what he says. This pattern, observed by an analyst of the relation between the village headman and a subdistrict officer,[7] has impressed other observers as true of the higher levels of the bureaucracy as well.[8] Cultural and social roots of the pattern are suggested by the custom of a civil servant's subordinates addressing him as "father": the Javanese son is traditionally reared to venerate his father through halus etiquette, but the father exercises little functional control over his son. A more obvious factor underlying the bureaucratic formalism is the government's lack of material resources to implement its decrees—a lack that encourages symbolic rather than functional administration.

EDUCATION AND YOUTH CULTURE

Modern Indonesia has created a remarkably massive and unified public-school system, enrolling many times the number of pupils educated under the Dutch. An estimated 15 million children, representing 60 percent of the children of primary-school age, attend primary school in Indonesia today. Primary school lasts six years, followed by six years of secondary school and several years of college. The number of students enrolled naturally decreases with ascent to the higher levels, but even so Indonesia's 411 universities boast some 360,000 students. There are also some 3,000 private kindergartens. One might see in this great florescence of education (compared to the slight development of industry) an influence of deeply rooted traditional values. A central notion is that of the Hinduized ideal of the *guru* and *murid*, the teacher and pupil, a relationship which takes on the imagery of father and child, and is an essential building block of much Indonesian social organization, governmental as well as educational or religious. Political and military leaders, like school teachers, may be called "father," and their speeches often resemble lectures on government to children. Indonesians asked to describe the world role of their nation frequently explain that it should serve as a teacher, educating other countries in the virtues of the harmonious life. One might argue that Indonesian culture as a whole has a pedagogical emphasis, which encourages the surge in education despite low budgets and starvation wages for teachers.

Public schools are administered by the Department of Basic Education and Culture, which seeks to standardize educational practices by setting a national policy concerning curriculum, textbooks, schedules, teaching methods, school administration, and teacher training. In most provinces, early elementary school is in the regional language, but later schooling is in the national language. Candidates for high school must sit for a nationwide examination, as must candidates for a university. The schools thus work toward national homogeneity, but some diversity creeps in through lack of resources; for example, textbooks are so scarce that most pupils have none, hence must learn from the idiosyncratic dictation of their teacher.

Outside of school, the youth share a culture which has taken on a certain hedonism since the end of the revolution and Sukarno's romantic idealism. Motorcycle hoodlums roar through the streets on their Hondas, and rock music is popular, as are the Indonesian and Malay popular singers who croon, moan, and wail from the numerous phonograph records now on sale. Even the HMI, the most powerful Muslim student group, organized a rock band at the Djakarta Fair, to the chagrin and dismay of the Muhammadijah youth who protested the presence of the Fair's discotheques. Students continue to avoid technical subjects, preferring the law and social science. Only 1.4 percent of the university students specialize in biology and agriculture, even though more than half of Indonesia's gross national product comes from farms and fisheries.[9] The Indonesian youth have considerable political voice, and they are represented in parliament, but they are less politicized under the Suharto regime than in the days of Sukarno. Artistic creativity is not at the pitch today that it achieved during the revolution and guided democracy, but signs of renaissance and subtlety can be seen, notably in the brilliantly satirical dramas of the youthful troupes of the Djokdja poet and playwright, W. S. Rendra.

BASIC UNIFYING PATTERNS

Not to be neglected in a survey of unifying patterns are the tastes, attitudes, and proclivities that Indonesians share in such basic matters as food, dress, sports, pets, disease, time, and sexual roles.

Food

Rice is the staple for most Indonesians, though rice gives way to maize in the Lesser Sundas and to sago in the Moluccas and New Guinea. Hot spices are widely popular. The santri share a horror of pork and a liking for lamb.

The velvet black cap, *pitji*, formerly identified with the Malays and the santri, is officially part of the national costume. Most men wear the sarong, although the Westernized elite do so only in the home. Women also wear the sarong, and on formal occasions may don the beautiful *batik kain*, together with the tight and long-sleeved blouse, the *kebaja*, which is low-cut to emphasize the bosom. The proper hair style for such a costume is the *gelung* or chignon, constructed of the woman's own tresses, which may be allowed to grow to a length of several feet, plus quantities of false hair to produce a luxuriant and queenly effect. The dressed-up Javanese woman is certainly one of the most stunning of Asian females, and the Balinese women, of course, are well known for their beautiful figures and habit of going topless—a custom followed also by the Iban and even Javanese women in remote regions. Women wear the *slendang*, a long strip of cloth passed over the shoulder, to carry babies and packages effortlessly in workaday life but sheerly for decoration on formal occasions.

Sports

The national sport is badminton, and Indonesians (most recently, those of Chinese descent though Javanese name) frequently win the world championship, a fact about which many feel chauvinistic pride. Badminton matches are followed by radio with a fervor equal to that of American men watching a televised football or baseball game, but a difference is that the Indonesians play as well as watch; badminton requires little expenditure or space, and courts are set up even in shanty-towns or country villages. Soccer, played barefoot with great skill, is also popular, though not so much as in Malaya. Traditional games have died out except in remote areas, and modern imports acquire distorted uses as among a group of teen-age Muslim boy scouts recently observed by the author playing the children's game "London Bridge Is Falling Down."

Pets

Dogs—skinny, mangy, mongrel, and sometimes rabid—are everywhere. Chickens roam at will and live by scavenging, which renders their meat rather stringy and tough. Cocks and birds are the most cherished pets. They are used in fights and races for money, and they carry magical and sexual significance; a favorite Javanese legend is that of Sawunggaling, a peasant who became a prince with the aid of his cock, which is his alter ego and a symbol of his virility.

No one illness can be singled out as the Indonesian national disease, but among the most common are dysentery, hookworm, tapeworm, roundworm, cholera, trachoma, tuberculosis, and gonorrhea. Malaria has greatly decreased on Java, but is still rife on the outer islands. Alcoholism and drug addiction are rare.

Time

Hindu-based systems of reckoning time are restricted to such groups as the Balinese and Javanese,[10] but Islamic systems are shared by santri throughout the islands. Bureaucratic affairs are governed officially according to the Western system of a 24-hour day and a seven-day week, with Sunday the day of rest. Important too are certain informal attitudes, such as a tolerance of tardiness, reflected in the phrase *djam karet* or "rubber hour"; stretching the Western time unit beyond its expected limit, Indonesians frequently begin creremonies or performances long after the announced time, and spectators drift in gradually rather than arriving simultaneously. Certain linguistic habits would seem to encourage or reflect distinctive orientations toward time; for example, the Indonesian and Javanese languages avoid the finality of "not," saying instead "not yet" (*belum* or *dereng*) as in "our economy is not yet perfect." Implied is the idea that some predetermined pattern will definitely be filled in eventually, but not enough time has yet passed. The Indonesian language lacks tense in that verb forms do not change to express past and future, but keep the present form, as in "yesterday I go to town." The adverb clearly marks the time, however, and one should not leap to the conclusion that lack of tense implies lack of awareness of past and future.

Sexual Roles

Women enjoy high status in Indonesia. Females and males are both considered legally competent, and they are equally eligible to inherit property (except under such laws as the Muslim). Women are prominent in business and government (a woman was recently appointed a member of the Supreme Court). Even in santri circles, women are not kept secluded and under wraps as in many Muslim nations; they are active in public affairs and are required only to cover their heads with a scarf, which is often colorful and worn with the low-cut blouse and skin-tight sarong to produce a figure more seductive than restricted. One of the most dynamic Muslim women's movements in the world is the 'Aisjijah of Muhammadijah, and one of the most significant

Indonesian holidays honors Mother Kartini, the Javanese princess who initiated an early twentieth-century movement to modernize the status and image of the Indonesian woman.

The notion of the charismatic male is central in the ideologies of the majority of both Hinduized and Islamized Indonesians, and it probably stems from indigenous traditions. The Hindu-Javanese king glowed with the divine wahju and the Islamic-Malay sultan exuded a sacred magnetism that drew together his band of pirates and merchants. Messianic movements dream of the coming of a divine savior, *ratu adil*, and a line of heroes from Diponegoro to Sukarno have stepped forward to fulfill that dream. The Islamic kiai, the Hindu guru,, the *bapak* (father) who runs a bureaucratic department, and the leader of a revolutionary guerrilla band, all possess a charismatic power over their dependents which the Westerner does not easily comprehend and perhaps finds a bit reprehensible. At bottom of the phenomenon is the Indonesian's search for the meaning of existence: meaning is imported by attributing supernatural qualities to a ruler and guide with whom one enjoys a diffuse and dependent relationship like that between parent and child.

RELIGIOUS TRADITIONS

Dividing the nation in one way, uniting it in another, the three major religious streams of Indonesia—animist, Muslim, and Hindu-Buddist—cross-cut the diversity of social patterning that divides the varied ethnic groups. A contemporary sketch of these traditions is necessary to complete the historical and ethnographic accounts already presented.

The village world swarms with spirits. Spirits dwell in volcanoes, wind, rivers, trees, rocks, and graves. Daggers, gongs, and drums contain spiritual force that increases with age. Angered spirits disturb the tranquility of the heart and the community, wreaking pain, insanity, and social or cosmic disturbance. To prevent such disorder, the villager placates the spirits, feeding them offerings of rice, flower petals, and incense. To propitiate them, he celebrates collective rituals such as the slametan, which unites close neighbors, or the bersih dèsa, which harmonizes the entire village. Only through solidifying the group is the ritual effective, and as group solidarity declines, as in the urban kampung, the ritual efficacy declines too. Should a spirit enter a person, a curer or *dukun* is summoned. Possessing magical powers to command the unseen, the dukun can exorcise the spirit. He can also cause the spirit to enter an individual, resulting in his sickness and death or, in the case of love magic, his falling in love.

Throughout the islands, rituals are employed to usher the individual safely through the crises of birth, infancy, puberty, marriage, and death. An underlying premise is that if the rituals are performed properly, the individual will, regardless of his own desires and actions, safely proceed through this life and into the next. Just as the child is brought into the world in stages, each marked by a ceremony, so does the adult depart the world through gradual stages. In Java the body is buried immediately following death, after which slametans are performed at gradually increasing intervals until finally, with the 1,000th-day slametan, the soul finds its resting place. In some of the outer islands, such as Borneo, the body is not buried but is allowed to decompose, during which the soul is in limbo. A sequence of funerals occurs during this period. When the body has decomposed, the bones are taken away, a joyous celebration is held, and the soul finds its home.[11] This pattern of a series of funerals, rather than merely one, is not only widespread in Indonesia but is found in other parts of Southeast and East Asia as well. In destroying such complexes the reformist Muslims thus challenge a pan-Asian phenomenon, a reform that could have widespread and deeply rooted consequences.

The animists do not conceptualize their spirits so systematically as do the Muslim or Christian scripturalist theologians, but one mode of organization found throughout Indonesia is the dualistic. Spirits and associated elements are conceived as divided into two cosmic compartments, the left and right, female and male, inferior and superior, down and up; generally the right symbolizes the idea of sacred power, regular and beneficent, the left the feeble substance, which is also sinister and dreaded. Although dualistic cosmologies are most important among tribal peoples, they are also apparent beneath the layers of Hinduism, Islam, and Christianity that compose the civilization of the Javanese; thus the wajang kulit screen is divided into a left and a right side, and the Mataram ministers were of the left and the right.[12] "Scratch a Muslim Javanese and you find a Hindu, scratch a Hindu and you find a pagan," is an old saying which retains some truth for most Indonesians. Even highly educated Indonesians are not so convinced of the ultimate truth of either the deism or the rationalism of foreign religions and philosophies that they totally deny the animistic currents that unite them with their countrymen. Professors practice mysticism, physicians occasionally refer medically incurable patients to a dukun, and Sukarno reportedly had his own private dukun just as Suharto has his mystical guru.

Islam would seem to unite the bulk of the Indonesians since 90 percent call themselves "Muslim." Less than half voted for the Muslim parties in the 1955 election, however, and a smaller proportion than that in the 1971 election. Considering the capacity of the mosques, the proportion of Indonesians who diligently attend the Friday services must be even less.[13] But such external clues do not perfectly reflect the strength of Muslim belief. And though the majority of Indonesians are not santri, Islam serves to unite a large santri minority.

These santri feel strong allegiance to the Islamic pillars—the oath, the daily prayers, the Friday service, the fast, the pilgrimage, the payment of religious tax, the aversion to pork. A notion of individual responsibility is more apparent among them than among the animists. Rather than depending on a cycle of rites to usher him through this life and into the next, the santri tends to rely on himself and his relation to God; his own actions and choices determine his success or failure in this world and his salvation or damnation in the next. Conservative santri tend to pay more attention to ritual than do reformists, and they heed the notion of fate or *takdir*, remarking that "It's all in God's hands." Reformists retort that "God helps those groups which help themselves," expressing a Protestant-like activism, though with a collective emphasis. While praising individualism and activism in trade, the reformist claims to avoid the selfishness of the Christian capitalist. He emphasizes that Islam requires the merchant to return his profit to the community, the *umat*, through philanthropy.

Islam works toward dissolving the diverse adat customs of the ethnic groups, especially those concerning marriage and the role of women. Where adat allows child marriage, Islam forbids it. Where adat makes marriage a contract between lineages of bride and groom, Islam considers marriage a contract between the groom and a representative of the bride. Where adat permits the woman to divorce her husband, Islam gives the privilege of divorce to the husband alone. Where adat permits the woman to inherit as much property as her brothers, Islam decrees that the son of the deceased should inherit twice as much as the daughter.

Such direct conflict between the law of custom and the law of the prophet has not been without influence on local societies, as in the Padri War of the Minangkabau, but even more significant is the conflict between the underlying values of Islam and those of adat. The individualism and rationalism of Islam have strongly affected the collectivistic and ritualistic orientation of local groups. The Minangkabau are one of several cases where Islam was a powerful force encouraging commercial, social, and cultural change which worked more surely than the literal laws of the sjariah to dissolve local institutions.

Hindu-Buddhism has been of less integrative power than Islam in that it has spread only among the Javanese and Balinese. Recently, however, Buddhism has enjoyed a revival. Perhimpunan Buddha (Buddhist Association) claims to have built 90 monasteries and acquired 15 million adherents since 1965. Entire villages have formally declared their Buddhist faith and have requested the right to hold Buddhist rather than Muslim marriages. In the summer of 1970, the author witnessed many thousands of Indonesian Buddhists, perhaps half of whom were Chinese, gathered at Barabadur to celebrate the Wesak holiday. Following prayers and meditation during the day, a performance was held in the evening that involved Chinese but featured dances of the Javanese Hindu-Buddhist court tradition. One might see here a new integration of the Javanese and Chinese, achieved through their joint allegiance to Buddhism.

Growing out of Hindu-Buddhism are mystical sects, some thousand of which are estimated to exist on Java alone. The sects have flourished mightily since the banning of communism in 1966, which suggests that persons who formerly sought meaning and identity in the Communist Party now seek them in these sects. More broadly, the period since 1966 has been a decline in the influence of such abangan parties as the PNI and such abangan political symbols, slogans, and ceremonies as those propagated by Sukarno: perhaps the abangan tend now to replace political expression with the mystical.

The aim of Javanese mysticism is to mute the kasar feelings in order to perceive the underlying experience that is simultaneously God and Self. The technique is ascetic practice (abstinence from food, sleep, and sex) and theoretical analysis (philosophical speculation concerning the interconnections between qualities of the self and existence). Guidance is furnished for the initiate by his teacher, his guru, who is believed to possess charismatic and sacral qualities.

Discovery of the rasa is rewarded by an ecstasy comparable to orgasm (and signaled by the cry of "Aduh!" normally uttered during orgasm). Afterward one feels at peace and in balance. The initiate is now prepared to cope calmly with the struggles of life and, like Ardjuna, to carry out his duties with detachment. By unifying his inner being, he automatically harmonizes his social relationships as well. In fact, some of the sects believe that through meditation which orders the self, all of the Indonesian groups—indeed, the entire world—will be brought into harmony.[14]

UNITY MAINTAINED BY DIVERSITY

Any culture boasts diversities along with unities. Thus few traits that have been mentioned characterize all Indonesians. They are all under the same government, but not all eat rice or wear sarongs, and only a minority worship in mosques and live in cities. Nevertheless, the variations are arranged to produce a certain integration. Cultural and social features criss-cross so that no large group is divided from any other large group by *all* features. One may compare this pluralistic pattern with the dualistic one of Indonesia's neighbor, Malaya.

The Chinese and the Malays, each composing half the population of Malaya, are divided by virtually every sociocultural feature. Virtually all Malays are Muslim; indeed, to *masuk Melaju* means both to "become Malay" and to "enter Islam." Virtually no Chinese are Muslim; Chinese are Buddhist, Confucian, Taoist, Christian, or communist but, in Southeast Asia, rarely Muslim. Chinese eat pork, Malays do not. Malays are brownish skinned, Chinese are yellowish. Chinese are in commerce, Malays are in government, agriculture, or fishing. Chinese are patrilineal, Malays are bilateral or (in Negri Sembilan) matrilineal in their family organization.

Chinese and Indonesians do not divide so neatly. Not all Indonesians are Muslims. Indonesia contains 11 million Christians and, allegedly, 15 million Buddhists. Each of these groups contains large numbers of *both* Indonesians *and* Chinese. As in Malaya, Indonesia's Chinese dominate commerce and the indigenous peoples dominate agriculture and government, but the difference is not so absolute as in Malaya. In a Malay city such as Malacca, virtually all stores are Chinese, and even the small pasar sellers are Chinese. A stroll through an Indonesian city such as Jogjakarta reveals a strong minority of stores and a majority of small pasar traders that are Indonesian, and should one travel to such towns of the outer islands as Bima or Padang Pandjang, one will observe that both stores and markets are dominated by Indonesian merchants. Most Indonesians have darker skin than the Chinese, but some, such as the Minahasans, closely resemble the Chinese in color and physiognomy. The majority of Indonesians, including Christian, Buddhist, and abangan Muslims, eat pork just as the Chinese do. Important Indonesian groups, such as the Batak, are patrilineal in family organization.

Differences can doubtless be found between Indonesians and Chinese that are greater than the parallel ones between Malay and Chinese, but it would seem that the overall contrast is more absolute for the latter pair than for the former. Perhaps that is one reason why Chinese-Malay confrontations, such as that of May 1969, which resulted in Malaya's being placed under martial law for several months, have disturbed Malaya more seriously than has any recent Chinese-Indonesian conflict disturbed Indonesia.

Might not other groups in Indonesia contrast as totally as the Chinese and Malays, and engage in conflict as serious as they? An opposition that has been emphasized throughout this survey is that between abangan and santri, salaried workers and private entrepreneurs, Javanese and Sumatrans, and PNI-PKI and Masjumi. The first terms in the pairs tends to correlate as do the second terms, such that each set of terms defines a faction. And the most serious intra-Indonesia conflicts since World War II have occurred between these factions. The Madiun War of 1948 and the Gestapu massacre of 1965 pitted communists against Muslims and abangan against santri; the civil war of 1957 matched similar factions, except that the santri tended to be found among the Sumatran capitalists who rebelled against the abangan, anti-capitalist bureaucracy of Java. Yet these associations have always been sufficiently loose to permit shifting alliances. Santri Javanese side at times with santri Sumatrans, at times with abangan Javanese. Supporters of the PKI have been overwhelmingly Javanese, yet that party's most recent great leader, Aidit, was Sumatran. Inserting the army into the equation produces additional complexity. The army is traditionally anti-communist, yet that part of it which was loyal to the republic opposed the mid-fifties rebellion by provincial Sumatran leaders. The army sided with the santri during the Madiun rebellion, yet factions of the army have prevented the reestablishment of Masjumi and have even shown favor to the Christians. Questions of who eats pork and who doesn't would complicate the picture more, and perhaps unnecessarily. Indonesian society is clearly pluralistic but not dualistic.

The implications of this pluralism are not entirely clear. Certainly Indonesia has not escaped Malaya's communal tension. One might argue that the revolution of the forties, the civil war of the fifties, and the Gestapu massacre of the sixties reveal tensions in Indonesian society far more raw and dangerous than any plaguing moderate Malaya. Yet Indonesia has survived a quarter-century of grueling conflict and economic catastrophe to remain a republic. An optimistic explanation is that the cross-cutting divisions produce a loose integration: a unity maintained by diversity.

REFERENCES

[1] Hildred Geertz, "Indonesian Cultures and Communities," in Ruth T. McVey (ed.), *Indonesia* (New Haven, Conn.: Southeast Asia Studies, Yale University, 1963), p. 33; Geertz, pp. 33–38, has provided guidance for this chapter's formulation of urban Indonesian patterns, but I have relied primarily on my own observations of both the inner and the outer islands.

[2] James R. Brandon, *Theatre in Southeast Asia* (Cambridge, Mass.: Harvard Univ. Press, 1967), p. 173 (table 3). Concerning theater on Bali, see Beryl de Zoetre and Walter Spies, *Dance and Drama in Bali* (London: Faber and Faber, 1939). On the popular play known as *Ketoprak*, a little-known but useful source is E. Vaničkova, "A Study of the Javanese Ketoprak," *Archiv Orientálui, Ceskoslovenska Akademie ved Orientálui Ustav*, 33:3 (1965), pp. 397–450. The seminal source on folk drama is Theodore Pigeaud, *Javaanse Volksvertoningen* (Batavia: Volkslectuur, 1938).

[3] James L. Peacock, *Rites of Modernization: Symbolic and Social Aspects of Indonesian Proletarian Drama* (Chicago: Univ. of Chicago Press, 1968), p. 19.

[4] *Ibid.*, p. 178. See Mochtar Lubis, *Twilight in Djakarta* (New York: Vanguard, 1964).

[5] Clifford Geertz, *Peddlers and Princes: Social Change and Economic Modernization in Two Indonesian Towns* (Chicago: Univ. of Chicago Press, 1963).

[6] Until recently, the wedono headed the *kewedanaan* (district), which was divided into several *ketjamatan* (subdistricts). The district has now officially been abolished, though in practice it still exists.

[7] Donald R. Fagg, "Authority and Social Structure: A Study of Javanese Bureaucracy," unpublished doctoral thesis (Harvard University, 1958). See also Leslie H. Palmier, *Social Status and Power in Java* (London: Athlone, 1960).

[8] Herbert Feith, "Dynamics of Guided Democracy," in McVey (ed.), *Indonesia*, p. 377.

[9] J. W. M. Bakker, *Indonesia 1970: A General Survey of Society* (mimeographed, 1970), p. 26.

[10] See Clifford Geertz, *Person, Time, and Conduct on Bali: An Essay on Cultural Analysis* (New Haven, Conn.: Southeast Asia Studies, Yale University, 1966).

[11] Robert Hertz, *Death and the Right Hand*, trans. Rodney and Claudia Needham (New York: Free Press of Glencoe, 1960).

[12] A general survey is Justus M. van der Kroef, "Dualism and Symbolic Antithesis in Indonesia," *American Anthropologist*, 56 (1954), pp. 847–862. More depth is given by W. H. Rassers, *Panji, the Culture Hero: A Structural Study of Religion in Java* (The Hague: Nijhoff, 1959).

[13] One estimate of the number of mosques in Indonesia is 60,000, too few to house simultaneously even 6 percent of the population.

[14] On Javanese mysticism, see Hadiwijono, *Man in the Present Javanese Mysticism* (Baarn: Bosch and Kenning, 1967); Justus M. van der Kroef, "New Religious Sects in Java," *Far Eastern Survey*, Vol. 30 (1961), pp. 18–25; Clifford Geertz, *Religion of Java* (New York: Free Press of Glencoe, 1959), Chaps. 20, 21; J. A. Niels Moelder, "Aliran Kebatinan as an Expression of the Javanese Worldview," *Journal of Southeast Asia Studies*, Vol. I (1970), pp. 105–114.

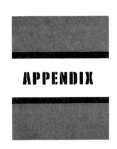

APPENDIX

ANNOTATED
BIBLIOGRAPHY

GENERAL

As is appropriate in a general work for English-speaking readers, virtually all sources listed here are in the English language. The following volumes list anthropological and historical studies in Dutch, Indonesian, and other languages:

Koentjaraningrat (ed.), *Villages in Indonesia* (Ithaca, N.Y.: Cornell Univ. Press, 1967).

Soedjatmoko (ed.), *An Introduction to Indonesian Historiography* (Ithaca, N.Y.: Cornell Univ. Press, 1965); and D. G. E. Hall, *Historians of Southeast Asia* (London: Oxford Univ. Press, 1961).

The following are detailed bibliographies listing sources in Dutch and other Western languages:

Raymond Kennedy, *Bibliography of Indonesian Peoples and Cultures*, 2nd rev. ed. (New Haven, Conn.: Human Relations Area Files Press, 1962).

W. Ph. Coolhaas, *A Critical Survey of Studies on Dutch Colonial History*, Koninklijk Instituut voor Taal-, Land-en Volkenkunde, Bibliographical Series 4 (The Hague: Nijhoff, 1960).

A selective annotated guide to sources is K. G. Tregonning, *Southeast Asia: A Critical Bibliography* (Tucson, Ariz.: Univ. of Arizona Press, 1969). A rather complete bibliography of English-language works on Indonesia published each year appears annually in the *Journal of Asian Studies*, September issue.

Essential general works on Indonesian history:

D. G. E. Hall, *History of Southeast Asia*, 2nd ed. (New York: St. Martin's Press, 1964).

J. D. Legge, *Indonesia* (Englewood Cliffs, N.J.: Prentice-Hall, 1964).

David Joel Steinberg, David K. Wyatt, John R. W. Smail, Alexander Woodside, William R. Roff, and David P. Chandler, *In Search of Southeast Asia: A Modern History* (New York: Praeger, 1971).

Bernard H. M. Vlekke, *Nusantara: A History of Indonesia*, rev. ed. (The Hague and Bandung: Van Hoeve, 1959).

W. F. Wertheim, *Indonesian Society in Transition: A Study of Social Change*, 2nd rev. ed. (The Hague and Bandung: Van Hoeve, 1959).

The foregoing volumes, especially Legge and Steinberg et al., supplied fact, orientation, and formulation that influenced numerous passages in the present work. Rather than citing all of their contributions individually, a general acknowledgment is appropriate here.

Ruth T. McVey (ed.), *Indonesia* (New Haven, Conn.: Southeast Asia Studies, Yale University, by arrangement with Human Relations Area Files, 1963), is a seminal source containing authoritative articles on Indonesian geography, history, ethnology, economics, politics, literature, and music as well as an excellent bibliography. John W. Henderson et al., *Area Handbook for Indonesia* (Washington, D.C.: U.S. Government Printing Office, 1970), is more recent than the McVey volume, though not so expert in interpretation.

Essential English-language journals include *Indonesia, Indonesië, Bijdragen tot de Taal-, Land-en Volkenkunde,* and *Ekonomi dan Keuangan Indonesia.*

On Indonesian languages, which receive only passing mention in the present work, consult:

A. A. Cense and E. M. Uhlenbeck, *Critical Survey of Studies on the Languages of Borneo*, Koninklijk Instituut voor Taal-, Land-en Volkenkunde, Bibliographical Series 2 (The Hague: Nijhoff, 1958).

E. M. Uhlenbeck, *A Critical Survey of Studies on the Languages of Java and Madura*, Koninklijk Instituut voor Taal-, Land-en Volkenkunde, Bibliographical Series 7 (The Hague: Nijhoff, 1955).

P. Voorhoeve, *Critical Survey of Studies on the Languages of Sumatra*, Koninklijk Instituut voor Taal-, Land-en Volkenkunde, Bibliographical Series (The Hague: Nijhoff, 1960).

A. Teeuw, *Critical Survey of Studies on Malay and Bahasa Indonesia*, Koninklijk Instituut voor Taal-, Land-en Volkenkunde, Bibliographical Series 5 (The Hague: Nijhoff, 1960).

CHAPTER ONE

Excellent general sources on the geography of Indonesia include E. H. G. Dobby, *Southeast Asia*, 7th ed. (London: Univ. of London Press, 1960); and Karl J. Pelzer, "Physical and Human Resource Patterns," pp. 1–23, and "The Agricultural Foundation," pp. 118–154 in McVey (ed.), *Indonesia.* The best general work on Indonesian demography is Widjojo Nitisastro, *Population Trends in Indonesia* (Ithaca, N.Y.: Cornell Univ. Press, 1970). On races of Indonesia, see Carlton Coon, *The Living Races of Man* (New York: Knopf, 1965).

CHAPTER TWO

A suggestive sketch of Indonesian prehistory is in Wilhelm G. Solheim II, "The 'New Look' of Southeast Asian Prehistory," *Journal of the Siam Society*, Vol. 60, pt. 1 (January 1972), pp. 1–20.

The most encyclopedic English language account of life in a Hindu-Javanese kingdom is Theodore Pigeaud, *Java in the Fourteenth Century: A Study in Cultural History*, 5 vols. (The Hague: Nijhoff, 1960–1963). For information on a Buddhist-Sumatran kingdom, see O. W. Wolters, *Early Indonesian Commerce: A Study in the Origins of Srivijaya* (Ithaca, N.Y.: Cornell Univ. Press, 1967). Broad principles underlying the early empires are formulated in Robert Von Heine-Geldern, *Conceptions of State and Kingship in Southeast Asia* (Ithaca, N.Y.: Southeast Asia Program, Data Paper 18, Cornell University, 1968). Art and architecture of the period are depicted in Fritz A. Wagner, *Indonesia: The Art of an Island Group* (New York: McGraw-Hill, 1959), Claire Holt, *Art in Indonesia: Continuities and Change* (Ithaca, N.Y.: Cornell Univ. Press, 1967), and A. J. Bernet Kempers, *Ancient Indonesian Art* (Amsterdam: van der Peet, 1959).

CHAPTER FOUR

General works on Indonesian Islam include P. A. Hoesin Djajadiningrat, "Islam in Indonesia" in Kenneth Morgan (ed.), *Islam: The Straight Path* (New York: Ronald Press, 1958); Clifford Geertz, *Islam Observed: Religious Development in Morocco and Indonesia* (New Haven, Conn.: Yale Univ. Press, 1968); G. W. J. Drewes, "Indonesia: Mysticism and Activism," in Gustave E. von Grunebaum (ed.), *Unity and Variety in Muslim Civilization* (Chicago: Univ. of Chicago Press, 1955); C. A. O. van Nieuwenhuijze, *Aspects of Islam in Postcolonial Indonesia* (The Hague: Van Hoeve, 1958).

Material on the general development of Indonesian Islam appears also in several excellent specialized works: Harry J. Benda, *The Crescent and the Rising Sun: Indonesian Islam under the Japanese Occupation, 1942–1945* (The Hague: Van Hoeve, 1958); Clifford Geertz, "The Javanese Kijaji: The Changing Role of a Cultural Broker," *Comparative Studies in Society and History*, Vol. II (1960), pp. 228–249; Syed Hussein Alatas, "On the Need for an Historical Study of Malaysian Islamization," *Journal of Southeast Asia History*, Vol. 4 (1963), pp. 62–74; Jacob Vredenbregt, "The Hadj: Some of its Features and Functions in Indonesia," *Bijdragen tot de Taal-, Land-en Volkenkunde*, Vol. 118 (1962), p. 91–154.

On the kingdom of Mataram, see Soemarsaid Moertono, *State and Statecraft in Old Java: A Study of the Later Mataram Period, 16th to 19th Century* (Ithaca, N.Y.: Modern Indonesia Project, Cornell University, 1963).

CHAPTER FIVE

General accounts of the European penetration include Kristoff Glamann, *Dutch-Asiatic Trade, 1620–1740* (The Hague: Nijhoff, 1958); and M. A. P. Meilink-Roelofsz, *Asian Trade and European Influence in the Indonesian Archipelago between 1500 and about 1630* (The Hague: Nijhoff, 1962). Classic is J. C. van Leur, *Indonesian Trade and Society* (The Hague: Van Hoeve, 1955). A perceptive sketch of broad changes in Java resulting from Dutch influences is provided by D. H. Burger, *Structural Changes in Java: The Supra-village Sphere* (Ithaca, N.Y.: Modern Indonesian Project, Cornell University, 1957). On the outer islanders during the eighteenth and nineteenth centuries, see G. J. Resink, *Indonesia's History between the Myths* (The Hague: Van Hoeve, 1968).

CHAPTER SIX

General accounts of forces operating in Indonesia during the period 1870–1940 include Clifford Geertz, *Agricultural Involution: The Processes of Ecological Change in Indonesia* (Berkeley: Univ. of California Press, 1963); Julius H. Boeke, *Economics and Economic Policy of Dual Societies as Exemplified by Indonesia* (New York: International Secretariat, Institute of Pacific Relations, 1953); and J. S. Furnivall, *Netherlands India* (Cambridge: Cambridge Univ. Press, 1944).

CHAPTER SEVEN

A general description of twentieth century cultural and political movements in Indonesia is provided by Robert Van Niel, *The Emergence of the Modern Indonesian Elite* (The Hague and Bandung: Van Hoeve, 1960).

CHAPTER EIGHT

An excellent anthology relevant to this chapter is Herbert Feith and Lance Castles (eds.), *Indonesian Political Thinking, 1945–65* (Ithaca, N.Y.: Cornell Univ. Press, 1970). George McTurnan Kahin, *Nationalism and Revolution in Indonesia* (Ithaca, N.Y.: Cornell Univ. Press, 1952) provides a thorough account of the revolutionary period, and a seminal source on the Sukarno era is Herbert Feith, "Dynamics of Guided Democracy," in Ruth T. McVey (ed.), *Indonesia* (New Haven, Conn.: Southeast Asia Studies, Yale University, 1963), pp. 309–410.

CHAPTERS NINE AND TEN

A survey of Indonesian societies is provided by Hildred Geertz, "Indonesian Cultures and Communities," in Ruth T. McVey (ed.), *Indonesia*, pp. 24–96. A suggestive perspective on the outer islands is F. A. E. Van Wouden, *Types of Social Structure in East Indonesia*, trans. Rodney Needham (The Hague: Nijhoff, 1968).

CHAPTER ELEVEN

A suggestive paper is Edward M. Bruner, "The Expression of Ethnicity in Indonesia," (New York: The Asia Society, 1972). A classic work on plural society in Indonesia is J. Furnivall, *Colonial Power and Practice* (Cambridge: Cambridge Univ. Press, 1948).

GLOSSARY

Abangan Javanese nominal Muslim who does not adhere strictly to the rules of Islam but follows practices and beliefs of such non-Islamic religions as Buddhism, Hinduism, and animism.

Adat Local or tribal custom.

Ahmadiyya Movement which was founded in 1889 in Qadian of the Punjab by Hazrat Mirza Ghulam Ahmad and which had the objective of modernizing Islam and declaring Ahmad the modern successor to Muhammad.

Alang-alang (*Imperata cylindrica*), a tropical grass with slender, erect stems and narrow, woolly panicles which is found in Indonesian flatlands where virgin forest has been destroyed.

Banjan An East Indian fig tree whose branches take root and become new trunks; the symbol of the coalition presently in power, Golkar, is the banjan.

Batik A dyeing method in which designs are made by covering fabric parts with removable wax; also, the cloth thus dyed.

Bilal *Muezzin*, one who summons the faithful to prayer.

Brahmin Member of the highest Hindu caste, originally composed of priests.

Dalang Puppeteer and narrator of Javanese and Sundanese shadow plays.

Dukun Shaman, seer, sorcerer, and healer.

Gamelan	Percussion orchestra found primarily on Java and Bali.
Gotong-rojong	Mutual aid, mutual cooperation.
Gusti-kawula	Lord-servant, a relationship conceived by the Javanese as sacred.
Hadith	Sayings and stories concerning the life of Muhammad which have been validated and codified by Islamic scholars.
Hadj	Pilgrimage of the Muslim to Mecca.
Hadji	One who has made the pilgrimage.
Halus	Refined, civilized, spiritual.
Imam	Leader of the Muslim congregational prayer (*salat*). Although the imam is such only so long as he is in the act of leading the prayer, and any respectable Muslim sufficiently versed in the technique of praying can lead the prayer, usually the community owning a mosque engages for remuneration a religiously educated man who acts as imam at all prayers.
Indische	Indonesian.
Kalijuga	Regarded in Hindu conceptions of history as the epoch that precedes world destruction.
Kampung	Village; cluster of buildings composing a large homestead or a small hamlet and including the surrounding gardens; administrative ward of a city; urban neighborhood, especially one inhabited by lower classes.
Kasar	Coarse, rude, material as opposed to spiritual.
Kauman	Urban quarter surrounding a mosque and inhabited by pious Muslims (*santri*).
Kaum Muda	Younger generation; in Malayan and Indonesian Islam, the modernist faction.
Kawi	Ancient Javanese language, the language of classical poetry.
Kekawin	Ancient Javanese poetry and song.
Kepala	Head or leader, as in *kepala kampung*, "head of the village or neighborhood."
Khatib	Mosque official who delivers the Friday sermon.

Kiai	Muslim teacher.
Krama	Refined type of Javanese language spoken to show courtesy, deference, and formality.
Kraton	Palace of a Javanese ruler.
Kris	Dagger, often bejeweled, carrying symbolic and religious significance.
Lebaran	Holiday celebrating the end of the Muslim fast month; also called *idul fitri* (Arabic), *hari raja* (Indonesian), and *rijaja* (Javanese).
Ludruk	Folk or working-class theater found primarily in the vicinity of Surbaja on east Java.
Lurah	Headman of a village unit (*kelurahan*).
Madrasah	Islamic school which, in Indonesia, normally offers secular as well as religious subjects.
Masjumi	(*Ma*)*djelis* (*Sju*)*ro* (*M*)*uslimin* (*I*)*ndonesia* or "Council of Indonesian Muslim Organizations," a political party composed of Muhammadijah and other groups, including N.U., until that organization left in 1952; banned by Sukarno in 1960.
Merantau	To sail or otherwise travel to a foreign country or region.
Musjawarah	Discussion, search for consensus through compromise and synehesis.
Ngoko	Low Javanese language that connotes earthiness, humor, and familiarity.
N.U.	*Nahdatul Ulama* or "Muslim Scholars" party, generally regarded as conservative by comparison with Muhammadijah.
Pantja-Sila	Philosophical framework of the Indonesian state formulated by Sukarno in 1945 and encompassing the five principles of deism, internationalism, democracy, social justice, and nationalism.
Pantun	Quatrain; a rhyming, four-line stanza that is sung.
Pemuda	Youth.
Pesantrèn	Muslim boarding school, traditionally teaching only religious subjects.
PKI	*Partai Komunis Indonesia* or "Indonesian Communist Party," banned in 1965.

PMI   *Partai Muslimin Indonesia* or "Indonesian Muslim Party," created in 1967.

PNI   *Partai Nasional Indonesia* or "Indonesian Nationalist Party," formerly considered the party of Sukarno.

Pondok   Muslim boarding school; also any cottage, hut, or cabin.

Prahu   Boat, especially an outrigger sailing vessel.

Prijaji   A social class possessing the right to bear titles supposedly indicating descent from officials in the ancient Hindu-Javanese courts; the *prijaji* maintain a tradition of refined manners, civilized culture, and official service to government, and many *prijaji* are employed by the government.

Qur'an   The Muslim holy scripture (Koran).

Ramadan   Ninth month of the Arabic calendar, the month of fast.

Ratu adil   The "just king," a messiah expected to right the wrongs of the world.

Santri   Originally referred to a pupil in a *pesantrèn* (Muslim boarding school); currently to a Muslim who piously and strictly adheres to the rules of Islam.

Sarong   A piece of cloth wrapped around the body to form a garment worn by both men and women.

Satriya   Caste of warriors and kings celebrated by Hindu tradition; in Indonesia often spelled *kesatria*.

Sawah   Irrigated rice field.

Serimpi   One of the two main types of formal Javanese dance, a group dance performed by young girls; formerly seen only in the courts of Jogjakarta and Surakarta.

S.I.   *Sarekat Islam* or "Islamic Union," mass movement of early twentieth-century Indonesia.

Siva   Hindu deity.

Sjariah   Islamic law.

Slamet   Security and tranquility.

Slametan   Javanese ritual meal and ceremony held to propitiate the spirits and assure the maintenance of *slamet*.

Stupa A dome or mound of stone, brick, or earth which has served as a focus for popular piety in lay Buddhism from the time of Ashoka.

Surakarta City in central Java which, together with Jogjakarta, is heir to the Mataram dynasty; also called Solo.

Umat The Islamic community.

Wahabite A follower of Muhammed ibn' Abdul-Wahhab (1691–1787), the Arabian Muslim reformer who founded a warlike sect of purists which objected to all innovations in Islam and preached a return to the original purity as set forth in the *Qur'an* (Koran).

Wahju A charismatic quality associated with a mission to rule for the protection of the *Tata*, which is the Javanese conception of social and cosmic order.

Wajang Puppet; Javanese puppet show; any theatrical production.

Wajang kulit Shadow play with leather puppets.

Wajang wong Javanese stage show featuring human (*wong*) dancers.

162

INDEX

Peasants, 54–58, 85
Pekadjangan, 68
Pelinggi, 141
Pemuda, 85–86
Pemuda Indonesia, 85
Pengulu, 106
Pengulu andiko, 106
Pentjak, 117
People's Council, 76–77
Perahu, 88
Peranakan, 47, 128
Perbekel, 141
Perdjuangan, 87
Perhimpunan Indonesia, 74
Persatuan Bangsa Indonesia, 77
Persatuan Islam, 67
Perserikatan Nasional Indonesia, *see* "PNI"
Personality, 17, 26
Pesantrèn, 25–26, 30, 32, 69
Peta, 86
Pilgrimages, 42, 66
Pithecanthropus, 7–8
PKI, 73, 79, 87, 88, 89, 91, 92, 150
Pluralism, 140
and Chinese, 128–129
PMI, 92
PNI, 76, 92, 150
Pondok, 24
Polo, Marco, 23
Population, Indonesia, 3–4
Java, 4–5
and urbanization, 4
Port kingdoms, 19–20, 25
Portuguese, 23, 38, 39
Prambanan, 13, 16
Prapantja, 15, 19
Prijaji, see "Regents"
Protestant Ethic, 33–34
Puasa, 110
Pudjangga Baru, 71
Pundèn, 18, 95

Race, 4–5
and social status, 44–45
Raffles, Sir Stamford, 43
Ramayana, 16
Rangda, 103
Rantau, see "Merantau"
Rarak, *see* "Western Sumbawans"
Rasa, 149
Rasul, Hadji, 84, 107
Ratu adil, 73, 146
Regents, 29–30, 43, 44, 45, 46
defeudalization of, 60–61
education, 29–30
and nationalism, 80

(Regents, *continued*)
"new" and "old" prijaji, 60, 61–62
role under Dutch, 41
Religion, and agriculture, 9; *see also* individual religions
Republic of Indonesia, administration, 141
centralization, 141
cultural unity, 141
Resources, natural, 1–2
Revolusi, 87
Rotinese, 117–118
Royal Netherlands Indies Army, 143
Rukun, 96

Salim, Hadji Agus, 73, 78
Sandjaja, 13
Santri, 24–27, 88, 131, 148–149
economic role of, 55
and Muhammadijah, 68
and ritual, 32
Sarekat Islam, *see* "SI"
Satriya, 29
Seba, 29
Sekatèn, 42
Semangat, 87
Semaun, 73
Serimpi, 42, 99
Shadow puppets, *see* "Wajang kulit"
Shaman, 117
Shiva, 11, 13, 14
SI, 71–72, 73
Sinanthropus, 7
Singhasari, 14
Sjahrir, 86
Sjailendra, 13
Sjamsuddin, 24
Sjariah, 32, 107–108, 117
Slamet, 27
Slametan, 27, 98–99, 146–147
Sneevliet, Hendrik, 73
Sorcery, 127
Sports, 144
Srividjaja, 13–14, 19
Status, Indonesia general, 130–131
Stratification, Indonesia general, 130
Subsistence, Indonesia general, 130
Sufism, 23, 27, 30, 33, 34, 48
among Minangkabau, 107–108
Suharto, 91–92
Sukarno, 74, 75, 76, 85–93, 146, 147
childhood, 80
apparent cooperation with Japanese, 83
in exile, 76
fall of, 91–92
and *wajang*, 76